THE

WORLD

OF

CHARMIAN CLIFT

Charmian Clift

Angus&Robertson
An imprint of HarperCollins*Publishers*

MW00912253

ACKNOWLEDGMENTS

Acknowledgments and thanks are due to the *Sydney Morning Herald*, the *Melbourne Herald*, and *Pol*, in which the essays reprinted here were first published.

Angus & Robertson
An imprint of HarperCollins*Publishers*, Australia

First published in 1970 by Ure Smith, Sydney.
Published in 1983 and 1989 by William Collins, Sydney.
This Classic edition first published in 1995.

Copyright © Jason Johnston, Roseanne Bonney and Rebecca O'Connor, 1970, 1983

HarperCollins*Publishers*
25 Ryde Road, Pymble, Sydney NSW 2073, Australia
31 View Road, Auckland 10, New Zealand
77–85 Fulham Palace Road, London W6 8JB, United Kingdom
Hazelton Lanes, 55 Avenue Road, Suite 2900, Toronto, Ontario M5R 3L2
and 1995 Markham Road, Scarborough, Ontario M1B 5M8, Canada
10 East 53rd Street, New York NY 10032, USA

National Library of Australia Cataloguing-in-Publication data:

Clift, Charmian, 1923–69.
    The world of Charmian Clift.
    ISBN 0 207 18812 2.
    I. Title.
A824.3

Printed in Australia by McPherson's Printing Group, Victoria

9 8 7 6 5 4 3 2 1   95 96 97 98 99

CONTENTS

Introduction *by Martin Johnston*

MY MOTHER, THE WRITER CHARMIAN CLIFT, died well over a decade ago. For most writers with only a couple of novels — by no means bestsellers — a couple of travel books, and miscellaneous essays to their credit, that would have been that. And yet it hasn't been. I couldn't begin to count the number of people who've asked me, ever since my mother's death, when they could expect a re-issue of one or all of the books, so I can hardly be alone in welcoming this one.

Charmian Clift thought herself primarily a novelist. But I doubt that she'd be unduly distressed at being remembered, as she undoubtedly is, far more for her non-fiction: the subtly, romantically, acerbically beautiful books about Greece, *Mermaid Singing* and *Peel Me a Lotus*, and in particular her essays. The essay was a form as new to her, when she undertook to produce one weekly for the *Sydney Morning Herald*'s Women's Page in the mid sixties, as it was at least the level she immediately achieved — to the Australian newspaper reading public. Indeed, it was a form that had never been particularly cultivated here, except perhaps by Walter Murdoch.

As it turned out, it suited her particular combination of gifts uniquely well. She had a mind — I make no qualitative comparisons — not unlike Montaigne's. She was ready to look at everything and listen to anyone (indeed, she couldn't help doing either) and also to listen to herself. She had a vast range of what used to be called 'curious learning', especially of the sort she most loved: that of Shakespeare, Donne, Burton, Aubrey, Browne and Sterne. She wrote an English that in its love of the long, complicated yet ringing sentence went straight back to those favourite antecedents; brought a new kind of literacy to the Australian press; and, if it occasionally 'went over the top' did so in the manner of Hokusai's *Wave,* with strength and grace.

She loved people, sometimes hated them: no fault, I reckon; at least, no Laodicean shilly-shallying. She replied to a massive mail bag (not all fan mail) despite a huge and increasing workload; she never missed a deadline. Her faults, I think, in writing as in person,

7

were those of generosity: she was never mean with her time, her empathy, or her subordinate clauses. And she never once let her own principles down, in any of these respects.

As recent years' efforts in the field of essays demonstrate, any owl can be learned as least at night, and any pin-head can sparkle. All too demonstrably, Charmian Clift founded no school. Too bad: but at least it's good to have this selection of her own essays again, to show—no, she'd think that too strong—to suggest how it might be done. We need another of her.

1983

Introduction by George Johnston

THE WORLD OF CHARMIAN CLIFT, and a very large part of my own world, ended quite suddenly on a night in July of 1969, and with the death of this remarkable woman who had been my wife for almost twenty-four years there was also abruptly terminated a phenomenal aspect of highly personal communicative writing in Australia.

I say 'communicative' advisedly, because if one thing was revealed by the unprecedented public tributes and the months-long spate of private and deeply felt testimonies of sadness and loss which followed my wife's death, it was that in her weekly newspaper writings Charmian Clift had come to mean something important and personal to a very great number of Australian people.

By this I mean more than the mere fact that the audience for her weekly newspaper essays probably numbered a million or more readers; what was significant was that to an extraordinarily large number of these readers she had become almost a magical personality in a kind of talismanic way. One of these readers, after her death, wrote: 'She had a quality in her writing that left her readers feeling that they had not so much read an article, as spent a few minutes with a valued friend.'

The distinguished writer-critic Allan Ashbolt, in a moving obituary memoir published in the *Sydney Morning Herald*, obviously felt this also. 'Although she was a disciplined journalist-novelist, with a fine command of her craft,' he wrote, 'one tends to remember Charmian Clift less as a writer than as a person—or rather as a person for whom writing was merely a way of expressing her own conscience, her own sense of moral values, her own passion for social justice, and above all her own lyrical delight in being alive and belonging to the human race. . . . she did retain a sort of pagan vitality or inner glow of mischief which illumined her whole personality. . . .

'As a columnist she found, I think, a role eminently suited to her witty and humane outlook.

'She was never a literary lady in any snobbish or even academic sense; she was always closely bound to the life of the normal suburban

9

citizen, and in these weekly essays she displayed an extraordinary capacity for widening the intellectual and emotional horizons of ordinary men and women. . . . She went straight to the human essence of any problem, straight to what a situation would mean in human happiness or human suffering. . . .'

I think it is in that last sentence that we find the secret of Charmian Clift's writing magic—her instinctive and total commitment to humanity. She was an extremely urbane and in some ways a highly sophisticated woman, deeply read, well informed, widely travelled, but she was, above all else, an implacable humanist. Her great gift was her ability to reach people of all types and on all levels, young as well as old, rich and poor, men as well as women (that there were thousands of devoted male readers of her columns was something of a phenomenon in itself in this land of masculine-dominated mores), with her undeviating insistence on the simple and ancient verities and values of being. She wrote with honesty, compassion, wit, and love—and often with startling moral courage—about both the things she believed in and the things she hated, like hypocrisy, apathy, injustice and cruelty. Primarily she believed in life and the role that all human beings had in living, as individuals, and not merely as numb components of a mass society. She believed, as I say, in humanity, with its problems and dilemmas, its hopes and aspirations, its inextinguishable will and courage. Through everyday evocations she was able to make these complex abstracts articulate and understandable. During the four and a half years she was writing for newspapers the most common expression used in the thousands of letters she received from her readers was to the effect that 'this is exactly what I have always *felt*, but I've never been able to quite put it into words, and now you've summed it all up for me so beautifully. . . .'

Her effect on Australian journalism, I feel, was considerable, and not merely because she glitteringly returned to us the long-tarnished currency of the popular essay as a journalistic form, although this in itself was a splendid effort. (Parenthetically one might point out that she invariably referred to her writings as her 'pieces', never by a term so high-falutin as 'essays'.) She also put guts and sinew into what had been the bland formularies of the women's pages. She wrote with a graceful and highly personal style, but she wrote to no formula. One never knew from week to week what she would come up with, yet she always had something to say that was different and original and fresh. Sometimes she was very funny, sometimes very angry, sometimes very truculent—for she took up causes, often unpopular causes, if she deeply and sincerely believed in them, although she was never a professional 'crusader'. But whatever she had to say she said it with great panache.

Her style was quite inimitable. Limpid and evocative prose, or long stately passages like the beat of summer surf, fitted in perfect harmony with sudden surprising slap-in-the-guts colloquialisms or abrasive wry passages of wit or memorably haunting images: in the one sentence Wagner and a currently favoured pop group jostled shoulders or the metaphysical poets shared the wall with some bawdy graffiti. There were very few of her pieces that did not leave you with a sting at the end, or something to ponder over for a long time. She was very much an original. Nobody else could adopt the exact stance of her viewpoint any more than they could imitate her style. (I tried to once when she was very sick with pneumonia and I thought I could 'ghost' her column for her. I struggled for half a day with the first paragraph before abandoning the task as hopeless. She sat up in bed with her typewriter on a tray and feverishly wrote her piece. A very good piece, too. It was one of her great professional prides that she never missed a deadline, even though she was often sick and desperately worried; indeed in the last few months of her life nobody was allowed to know how very sick she was—she went on being cheerful, helping others, and meeting her deadlines. . . .

This selection of my wife's essays is culled from the last two years of her writings for the Melbourne *Herald* and the *Sydney Morning Herald;* a few of the essays come from the monthly magazine *Pol,* for which she was also a columnist at the time of her death. Some of her best pieces I have had reluctantly to discard on the grounds of topicality, and I have not duplicated any of the essays printed in a previous collection called *Images In Aspic,* although that earlier volume contained several classic pieces which, like quite a few in the present collection, many Australians to my knowledge still carry around as treasured clippings, folded and much-thumbed, in wallets and handbags. Other essays, I know, are still preserved even after several years as texts for English studies in a number of secondary schools throughout the land. Any selection, therefore, is a personal matter. Most of Charmian Clift's readers seemed to have had their treasured favourite pieces; all I can hope is that if some, for one reason or another, have had to be omitted, others will be found in these pages. Two editorial matters should be mentioned here. First, the essays

11

have been broadly grouped according to subject, not arranged in their order or writing; the reader will therefore occasionally find himself jumping back and forth in time if he reads the essays consecutively. Second, in the few places where the facts of a situation commented on have changed since an essay was written, no updating or correction has been done: the point of view expressed is the important thing.

In conclusion I must express my delight at the publication of this posthumous commemorative collection. Both as a woman and as a writer Charmian Clift is worth remembering.

1970

NOSTALGIAS

The Magic of Mornings

By breakfast time the complexion of the day had turned sallow and rather muddy-looking. 'You'd never believe,' I said, 'how gorgeous it was at dawn.' And they all groaned and accused me of being smug as well as masochistic.

I don't care. It *was* gorgeous at that. Crisp as a stalk of fresh celery, and as the earth rolled over to the sun the night unpeeled along the horizon behind sleeping silhouettes of houses and church spires. All the yellow studs of municipal lights snapped out, and for a moment there was a wonderful giddying roller-coaster feeling of hurtling towards the narrow chink of revealed day. Between darkness and darkness it was the coolest, palest green, a sea-colour rather than a sky-colour, and as if to prove that fair exchange is always possible, the inlet of the harbour down below blushed suddenly and quite modestly pink.

I like this mysterious still time before reality is quite declared. Before shapes really emerge, when everything floats nebulously in that queer drowned light that makes one think, atavistically, of the beginnings of things. Before the milkman clatters furiously up the steps and the daily quota of world folly comes sailing over front fences and the garbage men try out fiendish variations on a theme of tins and bottles (shunning all cardboard cartons) and neighbours' alarm clocks begin shrilling dementedly and the rolla-doors of garages go groaning and thunking and the efficiency of the plumbing throughout this building is put noisily to the test and the world reveals itself to be, after all, pretty much what it was yesterday.

Over-indulgence in sunrises leads, I know, to some fairly grandiose and unrealistic thinking, especially if one has a taste for the gaudy and spectacular.

Sunrises, like sunsets, are pretty pompous affairs on the whole. I have even heard people dismiss them as vulgar, and carp about the inexpertness of the stage machinery that jerks that huge glittering bauble up over the hill or out of the sea: it isn't a smooth performance at all. I expect that it is sour grapes on the part of the critics, because all that splendour makes one feel rather seedy by comparison. I suppose that's what the Druids were really doing prowling and chanting among the sarsen stones convincing themselves that they were an integral part of the whole extravagant ritual: such elaborate capers, like the blowing beards, made them feel a bit more significant.

I am becoming addicted to sunrises. I suspect I always was, only these days I get up for them instead of staying up for them. Staying up needs stamina I don't have any more, although I remember with pleasure those more romantic and reckless days when it was usual for revelries to end at dawn in early morning markets, all-night cafés or railway refreshment rooms, with breakfasts of meat pies and hot dogs and big thick mugs of tea, or—in other countries—croissants and *cafes au lait,* bowls of tripe-and-onion soup, skewered bits of lamb wrapped in a pancake with herbs and yoghourt, in the company of truckers and gipsies and sailors and street-sweepers and wharf-labourers and crumpled ladies with smeary mascara: it is amazing how many people and of what a rich variety belong to that indeterminate dawn time. Real enjoyment of this sort of thing depends, probably, on a sense of drama, the resilience of youth, and whether you can get in a decent kip after.

In the military period of my life dawn was always the time that the battery major—an eager and conscientious man—staged sneak raids on the gun-emplacements. To keep the guards, he said, on their toes. As if one could keep on one's toes in those great clumping boots, besides being weighed down with the full panoply of war, including tin hat and rifle. Thus ludicrously arrayed we sleepy Amazons patrolled the perimeter of barbed wire that fenced off our guns and igloos from the rest of the peaceful and pretty golf course, peering into the paling light for the cunning major and his crew, who were out there somewhere crawling on all fours through the frost-spiked grass. These exercises proved to be invigorating and mirth-provoking as far as the girls were concerned, and, I regret to say, brought out some pretty sadistic instincts in otherwise well-behaved young women before the battery major, discomfited and dishevelled, gave up. Dawn is traditionally a time for the hunter and the hunted—for going around the traps, as it were—and no man in his right senses should involve women in such an atavistic business . . . not if he wants to get out of it whole, that is.

I don't know whether it is true that dawn is also the time that the majority of people choose to enter the world or to leave it, but it does seem to be a suitable hour either to slip out with the last of the night or make an entrance as the day breaks. In the Cotswolds we used to help out with the lambing, and there were many many dawns when we felt exultant and good and fulfilled, walking home from the fields through lingering crunchy snow, and often carrying one of those absurd trembling creatures to the warmth and benison of the kitchen fire. It's good to be present at birth. Even the sardonic farmhands, inured to wonder, you would think, blazed with flickering excitements during lambing time, and would rather sit in the kitchen, sipping at a rum and ginger wine and telling tales in the dawn, than go home to their beds after the long night's vigil in the freezing fields. I think I'm lucky to have had that.

And I'm lucky to have seen dawns from fishing boats and shepherds' huts and mountain slopes, and I shall never forget waking in the dawn at Delphi, with the goat bells tinkling on Parnassus and the olive groves a shining river of silver all the way down to the Corinthian sea: it was possible to believe anything, anything beyond the world then.

And there was that first May Day in the Dodecanese Islands, which was not marked by labour processions, but by the whole town rising before dawn to fetch fresh water from the wells, and then to clamber up the dark mountainside to watch the sun shoot up all jazzy orange out of Turkey over a sea as white and thick and still as milk. And that must have been as weird a sight as the Druids among the heathen stones . . . all those hundreds of twentieth-century people rising up among the mist-wreathed mountain rocks, with their faces turned to the sun.

Afterwards we all gathered mountain flowers and made them into wreaths to hang on our doors, and that is a charming thing to do and I have kept it up as part of family ritual, although the month is wrong here and the flowers more civilized around town and you don't have to climb a mountain to pick them, or watch the sun come up either.

Nobody could ever tell me why it was necessary to watch the sun come up on May Day. It was. It had always been so. Perhaps it was a collective affirmation of life and warmth and continuity, like examining one's safe deposit on a certain day every year.

I only know that I go on doing it, and watching dawns. Immoderately. And that, my family tell me sententiously, is why I am so hopeless in the afternoons.

Taking the Wrong Road

It used to be said, by Victorian novelists, that the black sheep of the family, the young man who had ignored (or disdained, or rejected) the dignities, the duties, the responsibilities, and the good name of the family, and had whooped it up in undesirable company and high living, or hooked off to sea, or joined the French Foreign Legion, or taken to wife a chorus girl or an opera singer, had 'taken the wrong road'. (Vicars were always terribly good at pronouncing this, mournfully, over tea and very thin cucumber sandwiches.)

Young women were also prone to taking the wrong road, which led them to carriages, boxes at the opera, furs and velvets, bouquets of camellias, suave gentlemen in cloaks and top hats, champagne suppers at midnight, boudoirs hung (I love that word in reference to interior decoration) with satin, muslin, or lace (or Eastern shawls, which is even better). All of which was the prelude to maternity, disgrace, and stumbling around in the snow with a pitiable bundle wrapped up in a shawl (cashmere). From this condition they usually went to a watery grave (Thames, Seine, Danube, or Volga). Or humble penitence and good works. Or even positive saintliness in plain black rep, by which time the poor offender had become wan and pale and glided rather than walked.

It is interesting, I think, that the young men who took the wrong road were always from the most aristocratic families, while the young women who took the wrong road were always from the most humble. Now East might be East and West might be West, but it is nothing short of marvellous that the poor little Nells and the wicked Rodneys always managed to meet up somewhere on the wrong road and have a ball, which perhaps consoled them a little in the time of retribution, which followed as inevitably as the Hound of Heaven.

Personally, I have always been attracted by wrong roads (I mean literally rather than morally) and have wandered off down one whenever I could, on the principle that you never know where it might lead, and while, quite often, it has led to some nasty shocks, on the other hand it has sometimes led to the most pleasurable and delightful experiences. (I was going to write 'surprises' there, but then, of course, one is never surprised by the unprecedented. That's what ought to happen. Every day of the week.)

Once, driving into Freiburg, in torrential rain and with the windscreen wipers out of action (one of our children used to call them 'skweepers' and I'm sure it is a very good name for them, but whatever they were called they didn't work), we went through our Michelin Guide from one-star hotels to (desperately) three-star ones, and there was no room for us anywhere. Freiburg was having a festival. So we drove out again, and because of the rain and our skweepers we took a wrong road. This wrong road led us (crawling and cursing) to a railway track and a small, melancholy sort of inn, dripping with rain and budding vines, and it turned out to be an inn where Goethe had lived for many years, so we stayed there and ate the most delicious food and drank the most delicious wine and slept on feather mattresses about six feet deep, and all night long trains hooted and wailed like Woody Guthrie (as a matter of fact I don't think that there is all that much difference between Goethe and Woody Guthrie; they would have got along famously: I remember thinking that in my bed of feathers). As another matter of fact I don't quite know why I think that story is romantic, but I do—experience is so unique, and nothing, nothing in the world can be imagined beforehand. Everything is made up of particulars.

Once too, when I was young, and out with my rifle on a Saturday (my brother's rifle actually, which he used to lend me sometimes, our father having some queer notion that girls ought not to own guns although they should be able to use them; he was the same about fishing rods and pocket knives: it used to make me spit), I didn't take the same old quarry track through the lantana and the blackberries, but a different one—a wrong one. And this led me up a hill to a group of Moreton Bay figs, where I was attacked by a whole gaggle of enraged crows, who must have been nesting. They darted and swooped and dive-bombed, trying, I thought, for my eyes. It was a purple, growly sort of day, the way you get them sometimes on the South Coast of New South Wales—thunder and lightning and blasts of wind and rain (rather like the beginning of the film version of *Oliver Twist*)— and I didn't even try to shoot the crows, but I ran and ran and ran, screaming. So that wrong road led me to the first real fear I had ever felt in all my life. I have been afraid of birds ever since.

There was another wrong road that led me to six cypress trees and some shards and blocks of marble that are all that is left of the oldest temple in Greece, and some prickly pear fruit offered on a fresh-cut vine leaf, and the most profound statement I have ever heard, from an old man, villainously moustached and dressed in faded blue, patched and pieced and darned in a way that Mondrian could never invent. And he said: 'Nothing worth knowing ever happens beyond the distance of a mule ride.' I have often thought of that since, and if we could all get back to mules, and town-criers instead of newspapers, we might settle ourselves in our various states a little more comfortably than we do at present. I don't think that this idea is blinkering oneself: it is Confucian rather: cultivate your own garden and let the others cultivate theirs. I am certain that we all agitate ourselves much too much about what is happening beyond the distance of a mule ride, which we can't do anything about anyway. Confucius said, 'The good man makes the good family. The good family makes the good neighbour. The good neighbour makes the good village. The good village makes the good community. The good community makes the good state. The good state makes the good country.' I suppose the good country makes the good world.

It is an interesting thought, anyway.

When I was sixteen I took a wrong road (a track rather, fern and bracken and scrubby sort of trees) that led me to an armful of wild peach blossom, which I will never forget: no flowers have ever been so beautiful since.

When I was seventeen I took a wrong road (asphalt) that led me to a couple of crazy painters and an introduction to poetry (I mean I knew *The Lady of the Lake* before and 'Roll on thou deep and dark blue ocean' and 'Pippa Passes' and all that, but I had never really met Carl Sandburg or Mr Eliot or John Donne or Robert Frost or lots of others I have been in love with ever since—Marvell and Suckling and those gents).

When I was eighteen I took a wrong road through great Norfolk pines, that led me to disaster.

When I was twenty-one I took a wrong road (only a stairway, actually, and deeply carpeted) that led me to love, and poverty, and three children, and great times.

I think all I mean is that the straight and narrow is terribly straight and narrow, and that there are so many interesting tracks branching off, and winding away, and we don't have to be poor little Nells or

20

even wicked Rodneys to be brave enough, or curious enough, or devious enough, to go exploring every now and again.

You never know what might happen.

The Time of Your Life

'It was the best of times, it was the worst of times, it was the season of Light, it was the season of Darkness, it was the spring of hope, it was the winter of despair. . . .' So Dickens began a tale, ostensibly about two cities, but really all about people, as all good tales are.

Ecclesiastes, that unknown preacher, had used the theme a good deal earlier, of course, and to even better effect: Mr Pete Seeger's contemporary paraphrasing adds nothing to the original message (and fortunately detracts nothing from it either). Clearly, the time of your life is all of your life, and infinitely varied.

Still, in current coinage, when somebody says he had the time of his life, we understand him to mean pleasure or happiness.

I can remember being asked once, in an interview, if I considered myself to be a happy person. I found this a curly sort of question, because one of the things that experience teaches is that happiness is not a permanent human condition, nor is the single-minded pursuit of it ultimately rewarding. It occurs, but occasionally, and often quite incidentally to some other purpose or endeavour. But if I am not a consistently happy person I think I am an optimistic one, in that I believe in the possibility of happiness and my own ability to recognize it.

Perhaps I am wrong about this, but it seems to me that a great many people are only really happy retrospectively. Others, vicariously. And others guiltily, with a kind of built-in remorse, poor things, as if they had no right to be it and had better start paying for it now rather than later.

Ask of anyone: 'What has been the best time of your life?' And who (apart from lovers) will answer: 'Here. Now.'?

The young in their leaping time, restless with dreams and ambitions, are more likely to see the time of their lives in the future, beyond some particular goal or achievement: it is only when they have reached it that they will be able to look back and find that the happiness was in the striving.

On the other hand, in spite of all the pious platitudes to the contrary, I have never heard anybody say with any degree of sincerity that the best time of his life was his schooldays. I know that elders are always exhorting the succeeding generation to appreciation and gratitude and warning them that they'll never have it so good again. This seems to be a formal drone stylized for speech nights: conviction is lacking and therefore nobody is convinced, least of all the young to whom it is directed.

Neither, at the further end of the time scale, have I ever met anyone who looked forward with actual relish to retirement and the muted pleasures of inactivity. The 'best' that is 'yet to be' appears, alas, to be consolatory rather than inviting as a prospect. If one is to regard the reminiscences of the aged it seems more likely that the best has been already, and will never come again. No such moons will ever shine for us lot, no such suns will gild our days, and if they did we would not appreciate them: the pot-pourri of memory is spiced with resentment as well as regret.

Time has a particular trick, and a very clever one, of threshing and winnowing experience. As years pass the inconclusiveness of events in actual formulation is husked off and blown away like chaff on the wind. All that memory retains is a hoard of separate grain. Oh, I was happy then, one says. Or, that was the greatest time. Forgetting that the happiness was inextricably mixed with all sorts of vexatious problems and irritations and interruptions. Jobs still had to be done. People knocked on doors at the wrong moment. One waited and waited interminably. And the greatest time ever was probably husked in boredom, doubt, and even fear.

Memory sifts out the facts according to individual requirements. It is fascinating to hear, years afterwards, the recounting of an experience by several people to whom it was common. Each one of them will remember it differently, and each of them will have retained only what he needs. Family reunions are a wonderful example of this, explosive as they are with: 'But no, dear, it wasn't like that at all!' and 'For heaven's sake, you were in the bathroom vomiting up the trifle anyway!'

My mother used to say that the best time of her life was the period that followed her arrival in Sydney as a young runaway from the country, with two pounds in her pocket and not the slightest previous acquaintance with the city. She used to tell of it with a wicked glee and an overweening pride in her own audacity. But the facts, the indisputable facts, are that for a year at least she scrubbed floors, emptied slop buckets, waited on tables in a boarding house, was snubbed and derided and neglected, and lay down to sleep at night in a bed where bugs lurked.

Surely even the brave glow of audacity must sometimes have been dimmed by sheer sordidness, loneliness, doubt, terror? Panic in the night? She was only seventeen, and motherless.

And this brings me back to Dickens, with whom I began, because it does appear that for most people the worst of times are transmuted, retrospectively, into the best of times, and the times of peace and plenty and success and material security seem dull in comparison.

I know a great many successful people, recognized, established, respected, some of them even famous (for what that's worth), living in gorgeous houses with style, who look back with the deepest nostalgia to foggy days when they starved in London lodging houses, pawned their overcoats to buy paints and brushes or paper and ink, pooled coppers with friends for bread and beer, and, young, poor, unrecognized, had the time of their lives.

I also know a pair of grandparents, who married against parental opposition and all good sense in the worst of the Depression. Oh, they're fine now. They own their house and their furniture and their car, and they have nineteen grandchildren who adore them. But the time they talk of most, the time of their lives, was that unspeakably terrifying time when even a job was luxury and home was any sleazy room, and to stay alive themselves, let alone to create new lives (which they did quite recklessly), seemed to be defiantly flying in the face of a very stern providence.

And how many men of middle-age does everybody know who speak of World War II as though it had been a great big wonderful rort? The other night, in the Oaks Hotel at Neutral Bay, one of them approached me. 'Are you Captain Clift?' he said. (He had up-ranked me but I liked it.) And we talked about generals and brigadiers of our common acquaintance and Old Times (one has to use caps for this) and when he left he said, wistfully: 'It was a great time.'

So the time of your life is for ever enshrined in an army uniform, or a mushroom hat and ankle-strap shoes, and hazard is attendant on it, and danger and difficulty and a high wild heart. All this is fortifying

23

for the years of peace and plenty, which one strives for, achieves, and finds dull in comparison.

But I wonder if the best times in our lives were given back to us, intact, if we would even recognize them.

Horseless Carriages

Emily called for me at half-past eleven as promised. Emily is older than I am, but much better preserved—so well preserved, in fact, that she is still the embodiment of Flaming Youth and all the insouciance and rakishness and come-hell-or-high-waterishness of the Jazz Age. A pampered, purring creature, Emily, with a sort of flip cheekiness bred out of absolute confidence in her own ageless, unstaled charm. Emily is a red Rolls-Royce.

I had asked hopefully about motoring veils and been told 'No', which was ever so slightly disappointing, particularly as Emily's owner thought it fitting, himself, to wear a desperately dashing cap that Bertie Wooster would have envied. But it was enough, really, that I should ride high on Emily's blue leather upholstery, purring through the Sunday suburbs where householders ran to their front gates to watch us pass in glory and drivers of the ordinary plastic-lined sardine tins that serve, these days, as motor-cars, goggled and stalled their engines and missed the traffic lights, and whole groups of bored teen-agers were sent, man. It would not be true to say that everybody stood up and cheered our progress, but it felt like that. One was tempted almost to try a regal bow, or at least to wave a graceful glove. No wonder Mr Toad fell in love with motoring.

Our rendezvous was in the grounds of one of the stateliest of stately homes. Very properly, I thought. Nothing could be too good, or possibly good enough, for the glittering beauties already assembled, older than Emily and younger than Emily, and ranging in temperament from pertness to languor, but all stamped indubitably and absolutely with the family likeness. Those long, aristocratic noses. Haughty. One has known, once or twice, a marvellous old woman who has retained until her death the dazzling authority of real beauty. A Rolls-Royce of the classic period is a little like that.

24

Homer, in the Iliad, relates how one day on Olympus Hephaestus (or Vulcan if you prefer him Roman: I don't) constructed twenty tricycles for the pleasure of his fellow gods and goddesses, and '. . . wondrous to tell instinct with spirit roll'd from place to place around the blest abodes, *self-moved,* obedient to the beck of gods.' So very old is the dream of the self-propelled vehicle.

It is a dream that has changed hideously in our time out of fulfilment into a shrieking nightmare of death and destruction. It is a dream that has laid waste to countrysides, polluted cities, filled casualty wards and psychiatric clinics and cemeteries, fostered bad tempers and bullying natures, demoralized timid or gentle ones, made week-end excursions into grim endurance tests, befouled pleasant places with mountains of junk and rust, debased craft in favour of shoddiness, and bred, incidentally, a race of economic sharks. I could go on. But as Emily, self-moved, roll'd obedient to the beck of David in his Bertie Wooster cap to take her place among her peers, I saw what the dream had been in the height of its fulfilment. It was a dream of leisure and grace and beauty and luxury. It was craft brought to a pinnacle of perfection to serve man's restless need to widen his physical boundaries, to overcome the tyrannies of space and time, to control speed and power—and to satisfy, of course, his love of status and display.

Under the trees the distinctive radiators glittered proudly in a long row with their winged emblems poised for flight and their bonnets open for inspection. The gleaming boots were all open too, on wicker hampers stuffed with cold chicken and champagne and claret and tossed salad and asparagus and leg ham sliced fine and thin bread and butter (with *The Wind in the Willows* on my mind I thought of Ratty and Moly and their picnic and this one seemed just as good). The annual Concourse d'Elegance of the Rolls-Royce Owners' Club might indeed be a serious affair, but it was evidently good fun too. There was an air of high excitement and irrepressible gaiety, as there should have been with all those corks popping, and everybody wandered about munching on chicken legs and squaffing wine and speculating on the probable chances of Emily and Maude and Annabelle and Milly and gauging the amount of restoration or cosmetic surgery that had taken place since the last meeting, and there were eddies and flurries of furious last-minute activity with dusters and whisk-brooms and polishing cloths, and much possessive banter and jealous back-chat, good-humoured but fierce with loving pride.

25

Because these exquisite pieces of machinery are no longer owned by the very rich for whom they were custom-built, but by the people who love them. A clerk, a boat-builder, an airline pilot. A tinker, a tailor, for all I know. Bought as bombs and painstakingly restored over years and years to their original flawless beauty and purring efficiency.

I felt my responsibility as judge of the elegance of these beauties to weigh rather heavy. So did my co-judge, a tall quiet expert on antiques who describes himself, modestly, as a junk man. He confessed to having left his own plebeian car parked out of sight behind some bushes. 'With the engine running,' he said, 'for a quick get-away.' I admired his prudence and foresight.

We agreed that elegance is refinement, grace and symmetry, as of action, form or structure (obviously have the same dictionary). But, oh dear, every one of those haughty creatures qualified. We stood off and discussed lines and sweeps. We peered in and examined interiors. We agreed on a classic period that was purely personal taste. We took out notebooks and allotted points. We went into a frenzy trying to decide whether grey brocade is more elegant than beige leather, brass fittings more elegant than silver. We turned down cunning tables, ran our hands over rosewood dashboards, drooled about cut crystal decanters, silver flower vases, thick silk braid hand-cords, fitted vanity cupboards. We became infatuated with an impertinent piece vintage 1912, flaunting brass bugles and a huge wicker basket where the balloon used to be kept in case the day was suitable for ballooning. We squabbled over the elegance of a rake-hellish Twenty and, thin-lipped, hurried to a landau for reference. We sternly refused glasses of champagne pressed upon us by owners with a view to corrupting our judgment. We fell for a silver Phantom (at least I think it was a Phantom) but it belonged to a committee member and wasn't in the judging. We went back to the beginning and started again and found that we had narrowed our choices to six and that they were the same six and we felt terribly expert and pleased with ourselves and each other.

Fortunately a wise committee had divided the judging into sections, so no one judge could be held responsible for the total score. Maude won by a half-point, in all her elegance of maroon and black and silver, and discreetly luxurious grey brocade upholstery and silver-grey carpets. She was a popular choice, because actually everybody is terribly fond of her, in spite of the fact that she carries the elegance bit just a little too far perhaps. Jazz-age Emily twinkled understandingly as we toasted the more reticently beautiful Maude, and took off in a cheeky blare of red and brass.

I roll'd out of the blest abodes in the Phantom (at least I think it is a Phantom), feeling incredibly knowledgeable, pampered, and superior. I won't say that people stood up and cheered, but it felt like that. And I'll tell you something about classic Rolls-Royces. I want one.

Is There a Hypochondriac in the House?

Far be it from me to go touting for the *Encyclopaedia Britannica* (unless they make it worth my while, that is), but I really must mention that with our latest Year Book they have delivered some come-on enticements for a new fourteen-volume Medical Encyclopaedia that should make every hypochondriac drool with anticipation.

Quite apart from hypochondriacs I think that most people are probably just as interested in medical subjects as they are in sex, say, or the supernatural, and this is rightly so, because the whole ingenious contraption of working parts that makes up a human being is indeed very mysterious and awesome.

Consider that the noblest of human concepts, the most inspiring of paintings and sublime of harmonies, all the poetry and all the dreams, all the whispered lovers' vows have depended upon the functioning of slippery lumps of offal, horribly coloured, horribly shaped and horribly named. Uggh! No wonder we fear our insides and placate them with pills and potions and daily rituals. Medical men, even these days, inspire the same sort of awe and respect as when they wore magic symbols, muttered incantations, and diagnosed with the help of Outside Powers.

A little knowledge, they say, is a dangerous thing, but even a little knowledge is more comforting (and probably more useful) than black ignorance.

When I was growing up in the country, doctors' visits were beyond the means of most ordinary families, and community health relied very largely upon Epsom salts, soap-and-sugar poultices, Saturday doses of sulphur-and-treacle, the bluebag for bites and stings, red-flannel bands for arthritic complaints and pads of lily leaves against

27

rheumatism, senna tea for adolescent disorders, and a good dose of castor oil for just about everything else.

But many households, as well, owned a medical dictionary of some sort—'The Doctor's Book'—kept locked away from children's inquisitive eyes and consulted by adults only with deliberation and gravity. Our Doctor's Book, I remember, was red-bound and weighty, and during our childhood our mother trusted its authoritative pages to bring us through such hazards as mumps, measles, whooping cough, worms, black boils, sprains, strains, scalds, ear infections, embedded ticks, spider bites, festering wounds from sea-urchin spines, and other homely afflictions.

Many many years later in time but backward in medical sophistication I found myself in much the same situation as my mother. On the Greek island of Hydra reliable medical guidance was not readily available (in fact it was a steamer journey away), although, paradoxically, the one chemist's shop on the island was packed out with every miracle drug known, labelled in French or German or Italian and available in any quantity without prescription—you just grubbed around on the shelves until you found something you recognized from previous use or had read about somewhere, or you took a punt on a bottle or package whose instructions you thought you could half understand. This cornucopia of pharmaceutical wonders was an odd sort of Aladdin's Cave in a community where people believed firmly in the power of the Evil Eye, babies were swaddled as tightly as Egyptian mummies at birth and hung with blue beads and charms, old crones mixed love potions (and more sinister potions, too, it was said), and home remedies might include pounded cuttlefish mixed with honey, yoghourt-and-methylated-spirits, infusions of camomile daisies, sage, and other spicy mountain herbs. Sleep was induced by swallowing a clove of garlic whole, bleeding could be staunched by an application of shredded tobacco, and the infallible cure for jaundice was a garlic poultice applied to the forehead freshly cross-hatched with razor cuts like a tribal marking.

There was one splendid old island matriarch who prided herself on her skill with a hypodermic, and every Tuesday between nine and ten in the morning injected a steady stream of ailing ladies with the waters of the River Jordan, which she had brought back from Palestine in a barrel and decanted as required into ouzo bottles. No one appeared to take any obvious hurt from these curious religiopathic ministrations, and spiritually it may have done them good for all I know.

28

However, like my mother before me, I relied on a medicine cupboard well stocked with remedies that had proved efficacious in the past, plus the medical section contained in *Pears Cyclopaedia,* which also had a lovely recipe for chocolate cake in the cooking section, and many household hints as well as flags of all nations, pet care, home carpentry, sporting compendium, and all sorts of odd and appealing information. When in doubt of my own powers as a diagnostician I trundled the sufferer on to the first boat to Athens and hung the expense.

I don't want to seem ungrateful to *Pears,* but poring over the *Britannica's* brochures I think quite wistfully that if I had had such a wealth of medical information to hand in those days I might have been saved many hours of anxiety and much steamer travel. The combined knowledge of sixty distinguished specialists on tap, as it were, and the answers to 'many questions you hesitate asking your physician'. What absorbing and instructive hours I could have spent riffling through 'Illustrations never before revealed' on living colour transparencies, *MEDI-GRAPHS,* or clinical photographs!

Moreover, volume 1, *ABAS-ARTH,* is free, and the thirteen succeeding volumes will be sent on a seven-day trial period—one each month—as they become available. The brochure says you can stop any time, with no obligation whatever, and still keep your original gift volume, *ABAS* to *ARTH.*

Now all this is pretty enticing, but what does one do if one is faced with cholera, catarrh, colitis, or concealed warts (the last three afflictions having been unreliably predicted for me, years ago, by a famous European palmist) before the C volume is off the presses?

Scant solace in being on expert diagnostic and healing terms with arthritis or arteriosclerosis or aberrations (sexual) or astigmatism; and come to think of it astigmatism isn't *in* the first vol. anyway.

And while it would be reassuring to know exactly what to do 'in those agonising moments before help arrives . . . often crucial, life-saving moments', vital first-aid information might be months and months away—imagine the thirteen months of lingering suspense, for instance, waiting on the good news concerning yaws (tropical)—and even comparatively commonplace things like hysteria and nausea could easily turn into something much more complicated if kept waiting for seven to ten months.

I mean can you really *afford* to wait, even for a free trial at no obligation? Wouldn't it be better, in fact, to get a doctor? Fast?

Babylon Versus the Corner Store

Every Friday afternoon Mr Mannall delivers the groceries. He, like his brother and partner, is a gentle, elderly man, short on hustle and long on courtesy. Their store is small, rather old-fashioned, and very quiet and cool. The scales are polished brass and the dockets are handwritten and itemized in pounds shillings and pence as well as dollars and cents and there is always time for enquiries about health and families, and unhurried, speculative social philosophy. One suspects that for children there would also be a couple of cream biscuits or a handful of jelly babies in a twist of white paper.

The two Mr Mannalls are, of course, anachronisms. Strictly they and their store have no right to exist. After all, isn't there a supermarket just up the street? With a parking lot and wire trolleys and bins of specials and a staggering range of merchandise all on display and starred with bargain prices and a ceaseless busy chatter of computation from ranks and ranks of machines where people and goods are ejected efficiently and impersonally and if you've forgotten the lemons or the butter you just join the incoming queue and go the rounds again.

When I was young there was a corner store, and the corner store was patronized by all the families at our end of town, as it had to be because there was nowhere else where you could just run up and buy a pound of flour and sixpenn'orth of Pork Fritz and a bag of washing blue and a dollop of yeast for the bread baking on Wednesdays and Saturdays and a tin of melon and lemon jam and a needle for the sewing machine, and every family had a grocery book in which all purchases were entered, to be paid for once a fortnight when the men were paid at the quarry.

But the corner store was much more than the place where the children ran messages after school. It was also the corner parliament, where the men sat on the step after work in their grey flannel three-button undershirts discussing Jack Lang and the dole system and the country's economy and the Tombstone Flat cricket team and whether the bream were biting around the rocks under Jacob's Ladder. And the owner of the store, in a black baize apron, always took part in these discussions while he patted bulk butter into half-pounds with a wooden paddle and bagged sugar: there were great sacks and bags piled up everywhere and wonderful scoops and ladles that were always highly polished and big glass jars filled with aniseed balls and liquorice twists and striped satin lollies and for a penny any child could buy a whole bag of broken biscuits.

When tobacco rationing was strict and my father was dying the owner of the corner store always managed to crib a bit or sneak a bit or juggle a bit from other customers so that my father was never without his plug of chewing tobacco or my mother without her ready-rubbed for the dreadful cigarettes she rolled with lamentable inexpertise. That man must have been owed thousands of pounds during the Depression but nobody ever heard him carry on about it and as far as I know he never cut off supplies from any family in our neighbourhood and through all that terrible time there were sweets for the children and biscuits and the telephone was available for emergencies and the step for political and philosophical discussions and he always made a special order for the particular ripely rotten cheese my father perversely favoured.

I understand that this sort of attitude is probably completely uneconomic and it would have served that man right if he had gone broke, but in fact he didn't go broke even if he didn't make a fortune either and I think on the whole his customers honoured their debts —or at least paid what they could when they could—and the corner store was as much a part of our lives as the quarry whistle or the Daylight Express or the men coming home at five o'clock all plastery with metal dust.

There was another corner store I knew later, in Greece, and this store was owned and operated by the brothers Katsikas and their wives and children and nieces and nephews who were brought over from tomato and tobacco patches on the Peloponnesus to be given educations or married off. The Katsikas store was so much a part of our lives for years that it would have been just about impossible to have got along without it.

You bought everything there, from olives to earthenware water jars, and if they didn't have it they sent to Athens to get it for you—like instant coffee and breakfast cereals and such unlikely exotica—and you met your friends there at one of the six scrubbed deal tables at the back of the store among the sacks of beans and festoons of onions and the tin baths and coffee roasters hanging around the walls and the

31

piles of cotton waste and brooms and whitewash brushes and birdcages and mousetraps and drums of kerosene and the blue-ringed wine barrels. And that's where you hired masons and plumbers and consulted the caique captain about transporting goods from Athens and talked to the donkey men and bought water from the freighter and read your mail and arranged your social activities and entertained visitors and finally (when modernity hit) even took telephone calls from London or Australia.

Katsikas' store was your club and your pub and your community centre and if you were a bit down on your luck you could keep your book going for six months or a year and the brothers Katsikas would force folding money into your hand so you could pay cash at the market stalls and keep face in the community. I am glad to say that no foreigner ever ran out on his Katsikas bill and eventually the brothers became very rich indeed and all the nephews were educated and all the nieces properly dowered and the store became quite famous and sported a scalloped blue awning in summer to shade the great and notorious who made pilgrimage there to sit at the same six scrubbed deal tables and drink wine with one-eyed Barba Yanni the muleteer and Tzimmy the pedlar and Master Lefteri the mason.

I know that I am being idiotically romantic to pine for the intensely personal in commercial transactions. The supermarket is probably cheaper really and the range is wider and what does it matter anyway if the lady behind the cash register keeps her eyes and her hands on the keys and doesn't waste time with idle gossip? She's got her job to do and nobody's going to pay her extra to learn the names of your children.

Last week I had occasion to visit Babylon. I met my party at the Raindrop Fountain, between Household and High Fashion, I think, but it could have been between two other departments because I was lost for about half an hour and there were a number of other fountains of equal magnificence as well as a profusion of statuary and a bewildering number of escalators ascending and descending tirelessly between an assortment of heavens—food heavens and fashion heavens and beauty heavens and book heavens and kitchen heavens and Heaven knows what else, but I am certain a particular heaven for every particular taste.

It all tired me rather, and it seemed to take hours to get home after and I was stupidly depressed by such overwhelming scale and thinking that perhaps I am unfitted basically for life in this society when there was a discreet knock on the door and it was Mr Mannall carrying a cardboard box of groceries and we had a pleasant chat while he unpacked them on to the kitchen table and the docket was handwritten and itemized in pounds shillings and pence as well as dollars and I was so cheered that I sat right down and wrote to my friends the Katsikas brothers in Greece. I hope they are both Lord Mayors at least.

Other People's Houses

The first other person's house which really impressed me profoundly —indelibly as it turned out—was a weatherboard cottage just up the hill from our own similar one. Three bedrooms, living-dining room, kitchen, tin shed tacked on the back for ablutions and laundry, sentry-box style lavatory at the end of the yard, and all painted that grim colour called, I think, 'builders' stone', and topped by a roof of sun-faded red corrugated iron.

So everything about this cottage was familiar to me, as the home base of any of the kids who played around with us would have been, but it happened that I called when the family was preparing for the evening meal, and unlike us, who ate in the main room, they were eating in the kitchen. The father, a small meek anonymous man, was sitting in shirt-sleeves at a table covered with lino. The children were putting away their homework. The mother, a large woman without upper teeth and shapeless from the recent birth of a baby, was serving food on to plates at the iron range; she had a towel tucked into the bodice of her print dress and held the baby against one hip.

The kitchen smelled of cabbage steam, damp baby, and boiled corned beef. It was crowded with unnecessary furniture, cheap and ugly, and family photographs, and simpering religious prints, and inexplicably I wanted to cry, wanted to be part of it, wanted to eat corned beef off lino and live in that steamy kitchen for ever and ever.

I have been hooked on other people's houses ever since, or perhaps hooked on other people's lives, because people live inside their houses in a way they do not publicly. The very arrangement of a chair and a table is intimate, almost shockingly personal. All objects in daily use are revealing. And I have felt this sharp, stinging sense of recognition that I felt in the cottage kitchen as a child in other houses too—in a little French château on the Loire once, in a shepherd's hut on the high Greek mountains, and in a lovely old house in Tite Street in London that was owned, when I knew it, by a painter who had plundered Europe to fill it with treasures. But it doesn't matter whether the house is great or small; a set of blue saucepans on a whitewashed wall can be as poignant as the four-poster bed hung with tapestries where generations have been born and died or a child's high-chair drawn up to a table.

A very curious thing happens, though, if you actually live in another person's house, no matter how desirable that house may be. And of course I am not talking about renting a furnished holiday house or flat, but taking over a habitation that has been lived in for a long time by people with intensely personal tastes and quirks and idiosyncrasies.

It happened to us once that we exchanged houses with an English family for a period of six months. They took over our island house, and we took over their Tudor farmhouse in the Cotswolds. Each of us had children. We had the same tastes in reading and music and living generally. We were simple or sophisticated to about the same degree. It should have been ideal.

But what actually happened was that we found, by living in their house, that we began living their lives. We began playing at landed gentry and hob-nobbing around with other landed gentry and our conversation became knowledgeable about sheep and lambing and crops and point-to-point meetings and field labour and their friends became our friends and their retainers became our retainers and their problems became our problems. While on the island they became islanders to the manner born and took on our role as completely as we were taking on theirs.

It all ended badly, as these things are bound to do. In both cases personal possessions were damaged, things were lost or mislaid, books were missing, and some sadly querulous correspondence ensued in which a very real friendship suffered traumatically never really to recover.

Because of course you can't turn into somebody else by living in somebody else's house and using somebody else's personal things and following somebody else's life pattern. It is all make-believe. Because you didn't choose the things, nor will you use them in precisely the same way. I know, for instance, that my bent wood table with the slate top is rickety and mustn't be leaned on, and that the lamp with the porcelain hood must always be taken off the ledge before the shutter is closed because the iron bar swings. What I didn't know, in the Tudor farmhouse in the Cotswolds, was that the writing desk that was always shedding its handles was sacred and not meant to be actually used, or that the dog, if locked in, had a habit of chewing the curtains, or that the pretty little carved chair in the corner was spavined and was there for ornamental purposes only.

I've known other people since who have also lived in other people's houses and their experiences have been much the same. Never once has it turned out successfully. Other people's houses obviously are entrancing only if you don't try to live in them.

Still, I will, I suppose, go on peering into windows, and being emotionally moved by glimpses seen through open doors and hankering after lace balconies and half-seen courtyards where vines hang and rooms that are exciting, probably, only because they are different to my own rooms, and seem, momentarily, more desirable.

My newspapers are absolutely crammed these days with drawings and photographs of brick veneers and textures and fibros and timbers called Winston and Pamela and Madeira and Tudor which you can buy in so many squares already packaged and ready to set down on one of the new housing estates itself bulldozed flat and cleared of anything growing. None of these habitations looks to be permanent nor can one imagine being moved in any way at all by anything that could possibly take place in them once they are occupied. I could be wrong about this. Perhaps people will make them interesting.

Anyway, there are still a lot of other people's houses to be curious about, and I would rather write about them than about state visits or invasions of bluebottles, and go on being rather excited at living in my own house.

Where My Caravan Has Rested

The card, which is salmon pink bordered in green and blotched with age and liquor rings, is made out in my husband's name as a vice-president and director of the Rio Grande Steamship and Navigation Company (Whaling and Blubber) and entitles him to transportation, life-preserver, and boots and spurs when needed, on 'all vessels operated by the company over the entire system'.

It is only one of a number of similar wartime whimsies, like the Burma Road Jeeping and Marching Association, and the Short Snorter Club, and I came across it in the portable attic, which is a rusted tin trunk that has accompanied us on our perpetual odyssey and which I turn out every time we make another move in the vain hope that some of the accumulation of all the years can be discarded. None of the accumulation can. Never. Not ever. Not a bit of memorabilia, not the discarded beginnings of a manuscript, not a faded photograph, not a creased and tattered document, not a yellowed newspaper clipping. Not even though the portable attic is only opened at moving times. Perhaps we've really been hoarding all this stuff to form the nucleus of a permanent attic for the amusement, edification—and possibly the mystification—of our grandchildren and great-grandchildren, who might reasonably be expected to have some small interest in their forbears. Romantic fiction is filled with verbena-scented ghosts flushed out from attic cobwebs at the first crackle of an old love-letter or the discovery of a pressed dog-rose between the pages of *Sesame and Lilies* or something similar. I would quite like to be a verbena-scented ghost, although I think 'Ma Griffe' is actually more me and would be racier and more intriguing generally.

Apart from the egotistical calculation of this posthumous attention-seeking, my household moves have always been characterized by an incurable and quite unwarranted optimism. I go on believing in Fresh Starts. This time, I say to myself, it is going to be different. I am not quite sure what I mean by 'it', but the places we have occupied in these nomadic shiftings of abode have always seemed to me to be like a series of staging posts on a fairly rugged journey. One is always galloping madly and at breakneck pace to get to the next one, convinced that the prospect beyond will open up pleasant and fair. And by the time one realizes that the prospect is pretty much what it was before one is, of necessity, galloping on again.

This particular staging post is pretty close ahead now, and pretty inviting, and this time, this time for certain, surely the reaching of it will mean that life will become gracious and orderly, that everybody will be struck—as with a blinding revelation—with the unutterable beauty of tidiness. There will be a place for everything and everything will be returned to its place after use. Towels will be hung on rails instead of dropped on the bathroom floor, socks will stay in pairs and books on shelves and records in sleeves and clothes on hangers and cups on saucers, caps will be screwed back on to shampoo bottles and toothpaste tubes, papers will be filed in appropriate folders, letters will be answered, appointments entered into the book provided for them, and the kitchen reminder pad will be used for kitchen remindering and not for chess scores, mysterious and unidentifiable telephone numbers, illegible messages, or plain and fancy doodling. Dressmaking scissors will be used for dressmaking, hair-cutting scissors for hair-cutting, and kitchen scissors for the kitchen, and from now on wire will be cut with wire-cutters instead—which reminds me that I had better try to find all those scissors and have them sharpened in anticipation of this happy state of affairs. Also the screwdriver, which I feel answers its function better than the best knives or my nail file, although I've not yet been able to persuade anybody else of this.

In the meantime, in preparation for the placidity and harmony that will undoubtedly surround me after the move is made, I am vigorously and determinedly tidying up this camping place where my caravan has rested for the last year or so. Of course I was confident of achieving grace and order when we came to rest here too. I admit that events proved such confidence to have been misplaced, but then there were certain unforeseen circumstances.

As a matter of fact it does seem to be a little extraordinary now that we moved in here such a short time ago with only a bed apiece and a desk and four chairs and not enough personal possessions to even half-fill the cupboard space. How did we manage to acquire so many things? And what on earth is one to do with them all? How did so many things, once acquired, wear out so quickly? For certainly all our possessions have a terribly used look. There is a heap of garments that I had earmarked for the collection bags which are left on our doormat several times a week, but which, on examination, might more decently be shoved into the incinerator. Is it worth while packing sheets that look as if they might shred in the next wash anyway? And the blankets that the dog chewed up the move before last? Will the handleless cups come in handy as receptacles for something or other or is it better to pitch them out now? Cupless saucers also. Will it be possible this time to find a sponge that fits the squeegee or should one leave it with the other squeegee handles that proved to be the wrong shape or size or brand for any sponges I could find? If a new broom is to sweep clean I would like the broom to really be new and not moulting. And there is something terribly disheartening about packing old dusters, even though one knows one will need dusters. Not to mention old teatowels. What does one do with bent safety pins, odd ear-rings, elastic bands, spare suspenders, assorted buttons, saucers filled with one-cent pieces, ends of string, torn packets of paper clips, old birthday cards, and all the other miscellaneous small items that have collected on shelves?

The furniture, I think, might just fit in the new house, but what a pity that a bottle of nailpolish should have been spilled on the coffee table and the filing cabinet scratched so badly and the sofa arms looking so greasy where people have been sitting on them and the gilt screws lost from one leather chair strap and the refectory table scored with so many rings and spillings and burns and general crud and the metal bed frames out of alignment and the mattresses gone rather lumpy and the bathroom towels, while still in good order, quite unsuitable in colour for the new bathrooms.

I mean, it would be nice to start all fresh and new. There's one thing, though, and I think of this as I sort out papers and documents and newspaper clippings and pages of unfinished manuscript and photographs that have no conceivable use but that I cannot bear to throw away. There's still some room in the portable attic, and I have every chance of fooling my grandchildren and my great-grandchildren yet.

Return to the Orgy?

An integral part of the Australian legend (which I admit is looking a little threadbare these days) was always the Homeric or epic Australian 'rort'.

'Rort' is a curious word, and might conceivably derive from the statelier 'rout' of Regency days, when the bucks and macaronis often indulged in waggish pranks. Anyway, the classic Australian rort, which probably had its origin in shearing shed or gold-diggings, is (or was, rather, because it is fast disappearing, along with many other cherished customs, like mateship, and two-up, and rolling your own) an all male gathering—females of an unfastidious kind might be included but would be unlikely to stay the distance—and had as its totem the Keg, with supplementary totems of Prawn and Cray.

A good rort lasted all night or until the Keg ran dry, and properly included fisticuffs, wagers, prodigies of strength, vocal choruses, harmonica solos, practical jokes, tall stories, and some isolated incident bizarre or startling enough to make an impact even through the stupefying effects of the Keg and so impress that particular rort for ever on the memories of everybody who took part in it. No minutes were kept at a rort, but the participants remembered a good one twenty or thirty years afterwards, with relish and nostalgia and a wealth of detail. I know. I've listened to a hundred reminiscences that began, deprecatingly enough, with: 'Well, we had this bit of a rort, see. . . .'

I was set to thinking of the old-fashioned rort by the social pages of this week's newspapers, which are agog with the glad tidings that this week is Party Week.

I have a confused and rather kaleidoscopic impression of thousands and thousands of indefatigable hostesses determinedly Transforming their tasteful residences into Parisian bistros, Spanish hacienda, English tithe barns, Venetian palazzia, circus tents, desert islands, American cattle ranches, petrified forests, Prospero type cells, and all sorts of similarly unlikely settings.

I think too, with awe, of the acres of gladioli reaped to grace these scenes, of frenetic hairdressers demented with the touching up of wigs and wiglets, of distraught dressmakers gulping pins over last-minute fittings, of wild-eyed caterers running out of pastry cases, of television celebrities and social editresses importuned, battered and swamped by invitations, of heart-burnings and passions and envies as to who is asked where and who isn't and who accepts and who doesn't (any or all of which can depend, maddeningly, on garbled and incomprehensible telephone messages recorded by temporary foreign 'help').

A party these days to be successful must be more than enjoyable. It must be newsworthy. Even if you have to bring it out into the street so that nobody can ignore it. Art-openings are apt to spill into the public highways, perhaps because galleries are rather small, or perhaps because it is good publicity. Even a recent Adelaide Festival included a champagne party where guests were served seated in the street gutter on a Sunday morning, while agitated curtains twitched in all the houses opposite and the bells of St Peter's solemnly summoned the pious in the city of churches. My husband, who attended this gathering, assures me that the function, though surprising, was not in any sense a rort.

The contemporary, or go-go, rort not only comes right out into the street, but right into public transport. Trams have been hired for rorting in Victoria, and also trains, in both Victoria and New South Wales. And ill-fated vehicles they seem to have been too. Reports of the rorts are horrendous. And now, of course, we have had a Bacchanal in the public precincts of the Sydney Opera House, or at least an attempt at a Bacchanal, because obviously it fizzled rather badly.

But all of this makes one wonder if the current trend in rorts is not tending towards the orgy. I am using the word orgy in its modern connotation of 'drunken carousal', 'lewd revelry', or 'the unrestrained practice of debauchery'. These are dictionary definitions and I believe them to be a philological blunder, for the Greek *orgia*, which the Romans adopted, referred to religious or sacred rites.

Still, none of us are in any doubt about what an orgy means these days. And I think we Australians, as a particularly self-conscious people and awkwardly suited by temperament to public and spontaneous exuberance (even when organized and the Press informed well beforehand), have a long way to go to come anywhere near real orgy standard. The rorts of antiquity are still way ahead of anything we can even attempt. Think of Nero and Tiberius and Caligula. Or the Sybarites, who made pleasure such an art that men whose work was noisy, such as carpenters and smiths, were forbidden to practise their crafts within the confines of the city. (As a matter of fact, there's a lot to be said for that law: there is a block of flats in the building on the lot next door and I could wish myself sometimes to be a Sybarite.)

In any case, whether rort, orgy, or suburban transformation scene, a party, I have always believed, is for enjoyment. And in this connection the best party I have ever heard about (and I will regret to my dying day that I was not present for at least a taste of it) was arranged, compered, conducted, and hosted by a diminutive Greek whom I knew as Tzimmy the pedlar, selling dead men's clothes and seamen's contraband out of an old Benghazi basket, making impassioned speeches about Cyprus, or raucously contending with the foolish cockerels of Hydra who didn't know night from day anyhow.

Tzimmy lived in America for ten years, and in that ten years he worked in a restaurant, slept on the floor, saved every nickel and dime, until he had amassed (the word is proper for what Tzimmy did) a sum of several thousands of dollars, with which he returned to his native island, a glad man, and, by Greek standards, a rich man.

The first thing that Tzimmy thought of (and who wouldn't?) was a welcome-home party. So, being glad and rich, he set 'em up for everybody and anybody in the taverna he had used to frequent before his foreign travels.

The welcome-home party proved to be so successful (I mean successful in enjoyment and not press publicity) that it went on all night and all the next day and all the night after. In fact it went on for six whole months. Tzimmy, who was glad and rich, hired bands of musicians from Athens, took over tavernas, coffee shops, bakehouses for the roasting of sheep, showered golden sovereigns on orphan girls in need of dowries, and laughed and sang and danced (and cried too, with too much happiness) for six delirious months, surrounded by all the friends and all the simple pleasures he had missed so terribly for ten years.

At the end of six months Tzimmy was broke and the party was over. There has never been anything like it since. Tzimmy is an itinerant pedlar now, but if business is bad he need never worry about where the next meal is coming from. The meal, the carafe of wine, is always supplied by somebody who attended the greatest party ever, or even by somebody who heard about the greatest party ever.

Ah well. It's probably going to be a long time before we are capable of such superb simplicity in the way of parties. Actually, I do believe that Tzimmy's party was a classic rort.

Living in the Kitchen

The valleys and hills that surround our place are densely grown over with cottages that are middle-aged now. Some of them are even getting on towards being elderly. They are dowdy rather than quaint, and have a definitely old-fashioned look among the new blocks of home units, where space has been manipulated so that the maximum number of people can be squeezed into the minimum of it.

One imagines the cottages to have odd spare rooms, and broom cupboards, and crannies where wet mop and bucket can be stowed away, and possibly even pantries. They also have chimneys, three or four or five apiece, suggesting open fireplaces and kitchens that were designed for big black iron ranges and family living.

Of course no smoke plumes up from the chimneys these days, not even on an autumn evening turning crisp and sharp at just about the time that the men should be coming home from work and the children abandoning their play in anticipation of supper. Queer that. All those hundreds and hundreds of quite useless chimneys, as obsolete as the open fireplaces and the black iron ranges for which they were built.

I am not advocating a return to the kitchen kindling box and the cinders and the soot and the recalcitrant flue and the filthy pot-scouring and the weekly task of black-leading and polishing the stove. But it is strange to think of a whole way of living passing so unobtrusively that the transition from chimney to television aerial as an essential roof-cropping is scarcely remarked.

Kitchens used to smell so good once. Stockpot on the back of the stove, vegetables simmering, steak-and-kidney pie browning in the oven and potatoes roasting in their jackets. All the fragrant steamy odours that scented every winter evening settling down just like T. S. Eliot's and drew families down the passageways to the hearth and centre of home and the fulfilment of the day. Funny, I don't suppose it would ever have occurred to anybody then that those mouth-watering smells (and suddenly I think of brown onion soup, chopped herbs, and the sharpness of cored apples) would one day be transformed by advertising into 'unpleasant kitchen odours', and that all self-respecting housewives would be exhorted, admonished, and morally bullied into spraying them away with artificial scents of spruce woods or lavender gardens, for fear that sensitive guests might be offended by such homeliness.

The homeliness of kitchens was the essence of their powerful, deep-rooted appeal. They were rather more than cooking places. They were the assurance of continuities. 'Certain certainties.' They were family gathering places, places for conference, discussion, anecdote and reminiscence. Places for pipes and shirt-sleeves and evening news-papers and playing cards and children doing homework and ironing boards and baskets and treadle machines and paper patterns laid out on scrubbed pine tables.

Places, too, for confidences and confessions. Shelling peas or stringing beans is a thoughtful sort of occupation: many a daughter has been led to spill all to her mother (I know this one well) by forces of which she was not consciously aware—the movement of hands, formal and subdued, and the fresh green scent of spring in her nostrils.

Once, a woman in her kitchen was a high priestess, presiding over rituals and ceremonies, repository of hoarded culinary lore. The mysterious and temperamental nature of yeast worked to her wishes, eggs and oil blended without rebellion, she knew to the precise half-turn of a wooden spoon when the sauce in the double-boiler was about to curdle, the marmalade boil past its setting point, or the chutney spoil. She was an expert at judging textures and consistencies and how the alchemy of heat would transform them, knew the differing merits of earthenware and copper and iron and aluminium as containers and cooking utensils, was intuitive with cakes and scones and pastry and proud of her intuition: a light hand in the mixing is as unaccountable but demonstrable as a green thumb in the garden. There was wisdom and knowledge in this, and power too. She transmuted substance into food and food into life. She dealt in essentials.

There are still country kitchens with that sort of atmosphere, and of course there are still good cooks everywhere: neither gas nor electricity has ever spoiled a fine meal, but only made its production quicker and less complicated. And, anyway, what woman in her senses would spend half her day peeling vegetables and chopping up bits of this and that and rolling out stale bread for crumbs or laboriously and messily crumbling butter and flour in her fingers for pastry when she can buy all these things, pre-peeled, pre-chopped, pre-beaten, pre-crumbled, pre-mixed, and probably pre-digested too, and everything at peak nutrition and with the flavour put back in (however did it get out; one wonders)?

What I find curious, and entertaining too, is that as women gratefully take advantage of packaged liberation the real sorcery, the abracadabra, the mystique of the kitchen is being taken over by men, who are more finical and fine and perfectionist and fussy than we ever dreamed how to be. Nobody who has ever been asked to a meal by a reputedly fabulous male cook can be unaware of this. Every dish is a miracle of skill and originality and patience, so exactly timed that a late guest or a single moment's lingering over pre-dinner drinks or conversation or another cigarette can ruin hours of preparation. The food is such a conversation piece that one is inclined to wonder whether the meal was made for the guests or the guests for the meal.

But whenever I am shamed or humbled by so much artistry in comparison with my own methods of short-cuts and slapdashery I reflect that they, after all, are doing it for pleasure and from choice, not out of a tradition of enslavement to the fire and the cooking pot.

And it would be mad to mourn such enslavement. I don't. But just as I regret the passing of the open fireplace as the focal point of a cosy winter living-room (roast chestnuts and toasted marshmallows or just dreaming while you poke the coals with the toe of your shoe) so I regret the passing of the kitchen as the centre of family life.

Kitchens are so small and compact these days that there is scarcely room for a stool, let alone a table and chairs and a comfortable sofa for conversation while the meal is in the making. Instead of being the warmest and most hospitable room in the house the kitchen has been metamorphosed into a little shining efficient factory for the turning out of meals, which are then eaten in a different room entirely. Meals out of context. I suppose my real grudge is that while I am cooking I am left out of interesting conversations in which I would rather take part.

Oh well. The freezer is jam-full of pre-peeled and pre-mixed packets, and if I want to go to the lengths of breading the frozen veal steaks there is a packet of Krisp, Krunchy, Krumbly Krummies to hand.

Who says I'm a romantic.

A Rembrandt in the Kitchen

The oriental merchant, a man past middle-age and grown gross with good living, stands confidently in his brocade tunic and fur-lined cloak. His breeches are tied with ribands beneath his strong knees, his fur cap is decorated with a plume, and there is a jewel riding high on the hugely complacent curve of his stomach. The tall cane that rests lightly against his stubby but balletic foot is a fashionable accessory to his costume, not a necessity; there is no suggestion in his posture that he is leaning on it.

His face is furrowed with thought as well as years as he considers something observed across his right shoulder, something outside the tiny rectangle of paper—$3\frac{1}{2}$ inches by $4\frac{1}{2}$ inches—that contains him.

He has been considering now for 310 years. I suppose in all that time his surroundings have changed so much and frequently that there has always been something over his right shoulder worthy of his deliberations. In the thirteen or fourteen years that he has been my house guest I have sometimes tried with glittering objects that might be of interest to a merchant to tempt him to turn his head and look out at the world directly, but although occasionally I have detected a definite change in his expression his attitude has remained consistently oblique: besides, someone caught me at this prank once and I felt so silly that I gave it up.

I owe the permanent presence of the oriental gentleman to a fortunate conjunction of circumstances—an imminent birthday, a transient period of affluence, the discovery, one day in black Bloomsbury, of the print shop of Barnard and Crouch, and the fact that this particular pull of the Rembrandt drypoint, although in a good state, had been nicked on the plate-mark at some stage and was therefore worthless to a collector.

Since I am just as prone to snobbishness as anybody else it has given me pleasure and satisfaction to keep my Rembrandt in the kitchen. I can't here, on account of all the built-ins, but for many years my opulent and exotic guest occupied a space on a whitewashed wall mid-way between a plaited rope of garlic and an old copper ladle. So

45

contrary is human nature that I was perversely gratified by the fact that of all the people who ate and drank and talked and laughed in that kitchen not more than half a dozen recognized my oriental gentleman for what he was, or indeed even noticed him at all.

One of these half-dozen, at the time preparing prickly pear leaves (or plates?) for a culinary speciality of his own which proved to be inedible, remarked that he thought it was pretty high camp to keep a Rembrandt in the kitchen (considering, he did not add but only inferred, the tat displayed on the living-room walls: he had a poor opinion of modern art, and now I come to think of it a great many of our paintings were hung for sentimental or cowardly reasons or merely to camouflage bad plastering).

Well, perhaps it was high camp at that, and I have admitted my snobbishness, but actually the kitchen atmosphere of whitewash and oiled beams and flagstones, bunches of herbs and garlands of onions, wooden benches, earthenware bowls, brass lamps, ribbed water jars, red cushions and copper pots suited the little etching very well. Hanging there so unobtrusively it was a private luxury—a very personal talisman against the plausibility of present poverty and future apprehension and uncertainty.

At this same time on Hydra—which was where we were living then—a rich Californian friend of ours, with the whole Aegean on his front doorstep, was building a Hollywood-style swimming pool in his backyard. He planted a lawn too when all vegetation was seared with heat and the wells had run dry and every drop of household water had to be pumped up from intermittent water-tankers at great cost. The pool and the lawn were his talismans. Luxury is only a question of degree. Some sort of personal compensation for residence in the Kingdom of Lack. Like dressing for dinner on a desert island, or retiring to a cave with a steady supply of Fortnum and Mason hampers packed with truffles and caviare and *pâté* and hothouse grapes.

I've never yet been forced to live in a cave, so I have never actually craved Fortnum and Mason hampers, and that might be just as well because truffles make me sick. However, the Kingdom of Lack is familiar old territory.

Come to think of it I have never owned more than two pairs of stockings (one snagged) at a time in my whole life, or more than a couple of changes of underwear. I've never had furs or diamonds either (although it's true I've never wanted them) or a handbag that

46

wasn't all-purpose, and for years I carried what money I had in air-mail envelopes because I didn't have a purse and couldn't bring myself to buy one.

I've never had a room of my own, or a personal bathroom heated and carpeted and fitted with shelves freighted with exclusive soaps and creams and glittering bottles of costly fragrances (I mention this only because I would like it very much, also a bath with a sort of lectern thing for a book and a built-in table for oranges and cigarettes and ashtrays). I've never had a comb or a pen that hasn't been annexed by somebody in more immediate need, or a favourite sweater that didn't end up being communal to whoever could get into it, or enough cups and glasses and plates to be able to ignore the washing up, or beautiful thick writing paper with envelopes to match, or a proper linen cupboard stacked with fine sheets edged with hand-made lace, or a working corner free of family invasion, or indeed any corner completely free of some sort of makeshift.

On the other hand I have six hats, a silver pill box, a Byzantine medallion, and an amphora more than 2,500 years old. If I have slept very often on broken springs they have been covered with a goatskin rug that is splendidly baronial.

At this stage in my life I doubt very much if I will ever have a swimming pool, or a silver-grey Jag, or a Givenchy gown, or a luxury holiday, or even a complete set of anything practical.

I don't think I care all that much. Not really. One of the wheels has fallen off this overworked typewriter, my pen has been purloined again, the cheap beds I bought to make do have collapsed under their occupants and sheets and blankets have been ripped in the debacle. But a huge parcel of books has just arrived, and the Nolans have finally been reframed quite gorgeously and hung above the sofa (which is rather grand and the reason for my economizing—falsely as it turned out—on the beds).

The oriental merchant averts his eyes, oblique and considering, as he has been considering for the last 310 years. And feeling very high camp indeed today I do believe—built-ins or no built-ins—I shall hang my Rembrandt where he properly belongs. In the kitchen.

On Turning Slightly Sepia

The photograph isn't sepia really—more a sort of reproduction gruel colour in the commemorative booklet to mark the fiftieth anniversary of the school's founding—but you feel that in its place in the family album the edges are probably curling.

The group is of ten fifth-year students in the year 1937, five boys and five girls, formally posed with the boys lined up behind the girls and their hands resting on the girls' shoulders. The girls are wearing clumsy tunics practically down to their black-stockinged ankles and assorted white blouses that look crumpled. One girl wears a skirt and white blouse instead of a tunic. Their hair is short and frizzy at the ends in the fashion of that time when permanent waving was still a crude business and curling tongs were often used instead. The boys are all clipped short-back-and-sides. Their necks are stalky and their protruding ears poignant. They wear various wide-lapelled suitings, not uniforms.

Every one of those young faces, frowning, smiling, staring sternly front, squinting into the sun—caught that long ago summer day all unwittingly 'in period'—is a face still hauntingly familiar to me, because they were seniors while I was still a junior and as seniors they were august, individualistic, and for ever memorable. So I can still see one of those girls arched in a perfect swallow dive, and remember precisely a collar of little pearl buttons on a blue crepe dress that another of them wore to an end-of-term dance that year. They are associated with prefects' badges and house colours, cheering, strange war-cries, trophies, speeches, prize-givings, and all the high-hearted accomplishment and hopefulness of eager youth about to attack the world.

The faces are only vulnerable in retrospect, now that 1937 is period in fact, and it is already twenty years and more since the name of that serious boy second from the left was inscribed on the school's honour roll under the draped flags among all the other names of students who never came back from the war.

It is probably only hindsight that makes me see Depression stamped

48

all over that grey group photograph—hindsight and a formal visit to the city of Wollongong, where for some years, and before it was a city, I went to school.

There are high schools all up and down the Illawarra coast now, but in those days Wollongong High School was the only one for fifty miles. From the sweetly pastoral dairy country to the south and the harsh grandeur of the coal cliffs to the north, where the mountains slide straight down into the sea, boys and girls travelled each day to Wollongong in ancient uncomfortable railway carriages that were hitched behind the normal passenger coaches: waterless, toiletless, segregated strictly as to sexes, we clattered and hooted to school, and there were many who walked or cycled miles to a country station before the journey even began.

It seemed ordinary enough then, just as it seemed ordinary that many fathers were out of work, and ordinary that senior students might repeat their leaving year once or twice because there were no jobs for them to go to, and ordinary that other students dropped out at fourteen if there was the least chance of a job or a trade apprenticeship offering.

That was the climate of our time and because we knew no other we accepted it blithely and even felt privileged, I think, to be able to go to a high school at all. And well we might have done. Most of us were familiar with the official forms our parents filled out to state that the family income was less than £250 a year and therefore claiming exemption from examination fees and other school dues. But without that high school—for us in the country towns and hamlets, anyway—there was no future beyond working behind a counter for the girls, and for the boys an alternative of helping out on a farm, delivering groceries, getting acquainted with a pick and shovel, or joining the queues of shabby desperate men who turned up each day at Port Kembla for the chance of a day's work on the coke ovens or in the steel mills. All along the coast, in colliery, quarry, smelting works, and mill, men were taking wage cuts or being laid off altogether. To a man in a dole line-up, or a man in a gang uselessly shifting sand from one end of a beach to the other, it must at times have seemed unimportant that his son or daughter was penetrating the mysteries of French and Latin, of physics and chemistry, of algebra and geometry, all unaware then that even their teachers were sometimes uncertain of the next salary cheque.

It's an old story now, the bitterness and the humiliation, but I

49

thought of it facing the massed ladies of the club which had asked me to luncheon—ladies of Depression vintage most of them, my vintage, pressed in the pages of a photograph album. And I thought of it clutching my safety helmet and gasping and gaping in proper awe at the Dante's Inferno of blast furnaces, slag heaps, flickering blue fire, rivers of molten prosperity rushing to the moulding: all the vast industrial complex of the Port Kembla Steelworks that has now eaten up the old Tom Thumb lagoon and the miles of wild sandhills and the swamps and the marshes. Thousands of degrees, millions of tons, miles of metal, production figures, employment figures, expansion figures, safety figures, consumption figures, so many full-time training scholarships, so many part-time training scholarships.

My brother's first job, at sixteen and with an honours pass, was turning men away there every morning.

And I thought of it driving with one of my hostesses up into the newest residential areas terraced into the mountains, where the houses are architect-designed and the views are stupendous, and where still, anachronistically, there remain a few little ramshackle weatherboard cottages as a reminder, and all the weatherboard cottages are curling at the edges like the photographs in the albums. The coast below, farmlands and wastelands alike, has disappeared under a solid crust of houses. The town has become a city indeed, and over it the great chimneys of Port Kembla dominate, pluming further prosperity. Nothing there to mourn. The mountains are still noble, and I expect that men still hunt there, but for sport now and not to eke out the dole ration. The immensity of the sea—so blue, so vast, so hugely glittering—is untainted, and the beaches curl in dazzling scallops of clean sand still, free to executive, steelworker, shopkeeper, migrant, academic, farm labourer, housewife, student. For an industrial city it is singularly fortunate in its setting.

Between the ocean and the mountains there is a complex of modern, well-designed buildings set in acres of green space that I heard many residents refer to as 'Education Valley'. The University College is there, the Teachers' Training College, the Technical College, and the new-look Wollongong High School, which ten years ago grew out of the old jumble of buildings and temporary classrooms that I once knew.

It was a queer business to face the whole assembly of those boys and girls, so smartly, neatly, and precisely uniformed now, so confident of well-appointed classrooms, splendid playing fields, up-to-date sporting

50

equipment, music rooms, libraries, so confident in their right to secondary education and tertiary education beyond it, and beyond that careers of their own choosing, so amused by stories of educational makeshifts and student misdemeanours and absurd travellers' tales dating from that impossible-to-imagine time before they were born.

And I wonder if they realized that standing up there before them I knew myself to be curling at the edges and turning slightly sepia.

An Old Address Book

One of my gifts this Christmas was a new address book, and I have lately been occupying myself with the enthralling (if somewhat saddening) task of copying out names and addresses from the old.

Who were all those people crammed into the pages of the battered old red leather book? Such a busy book, jam-packed with names and numbers, scored and underlined and darted through with imperative arrows, and 'See page so-and-so', and hurried messages scrawled in blank corners, times and dates and crude maps of streets with X's marking spots that no longer have the slightest significance. Polygotou 2, for instance. Whatever was I doing *there?* And at 8 p.m.?

I think the book dates from the winter we spent in the Cotswolds (although Polygotou 2 is obviously Athens) under an exchange of houses plan that didn't work out quite the way we had intended, or the way it sounded when we all talked about it in the back of Katsikas' grocery store. Good in theory, but quite frightening in practice, since —quite apart from the ordinary problems of living in other people's houses—the essential ingredient (that is to say, money) was missing, we having counted on a batch of royalties which proved to be non-existent.

Still, we did have that lovely old Tudor farmhouse to be marooned in, and the staff of retainers that went with it, and their names are all there and we did keep in touch with them for quite a long time after we had ransomed our way back to Greece.

There are also names with addresses like Chipping Camden and Bourton on the Water and Cheltenham and Broadway and Winchcombe—Manors and Granges and Lodges and Rectories and Old Farms and Chestnut Farms (ours was Charity Farm, which was thought-provoking at times)—and these were the people who were kind to us socially even when we must have been a terrible nuisance to them, having neither car nor telephone, and needing to be picked up for every social outing to which they were kind enough to invite us, and delivered home again afterwards.

One or two, or even three, became our friends, but, sadly enough, of the others I have only collective images—of men wearing either tweeds and caps and driving farm utilities or dinner jackets and driving Bentleys, mucking in with the pigs or serving champagne by candlelight, and ladies who alternated between maintaining an Amazonian posture on perfectly frightening horses (and that horn so plangent over the Cotswold hills) and rising with that twitch of the trailing skirt that summoned all females at the table to retire and leave the gentlemen to their port.

But they were very kind to us (or bewildered by us; I'm never sure which) and I will always have a happy memory of our farewell party, when we invited them all, and the retainers too, and the lady of the Manor danced with the gardener and our daily char with the Squire, and at one point everybody sang, all together, marvellous Cotswolds' songs until I was bursting with tears and didn't want to leave ever.

Then there are all the names that must belong to boat voyages, or trains, or hotel encounters. All those people who seem to be so charming and *sympatico*—one promises so eagerly to 'keep in touch', and presses them, fervently, to 'look in and see us if you are passing through'. It happened sometimes that some of them did—absolute strangers with whom we had nothing in common except a voyage once, some talk in deck chairs or bars or dining cars or rooms. What is it, I wonder? Everybody does this sort of thing. Is it a longing for human communication when one is rushing from point to point across the world? A wish for continuity? Or does one know in the back of one's head that this particular contact doesn't really mean anything except the momentary social pleasure it provides and that the writing down of names and addresses is hypocrisy?

Well then, some of them did look in when 'passing through', as we had begged them to do. More often they sent their friends, or friends of their friends, with letters of introduction, and their names too are written into my old red book—tongue in cheek, doubtless, but going through the forms. How many luncheons and dinners they must represent, how many picnics to that jewelled bay called Bisti, where the turquoise and sapphire and emerald of the water and the rocks and the scrub of pines all drowsy with cicadas would make you weep just as poignantly as the Cotswolds' songs, how many visits to tavernas that mere tourists never found, how many times we must have related the history of our long island sojourn, explained again about the children's education, conducted tours of our house, walked people through tourist shops to protect them from being cheated, found hotel rooms, farewelled steamers at afternoon or dawn, and written into the old red book the names and addresses and telephone numbers, promising to look them up if ever we passed their way. Surely we must have needed those strange people in some way or we would never have gone to such trouble . . . needed them momentarily, I mean, perhaps to convince ourselves that our lives were as meaningful as we hoped they were, or, perhaps, selfishly, to preserve a reputation for hospitality of which we were proud. (But weren't the squires of the Cotswolds just as kind to us?)

And there are other names. French, Italian, Swedish, Norwegian, Italian. Poets and painters and potters and novelists. I remember these better, because I connote them with long early-morning sessions over the kitchen table, cups of coffee, making up spare beds, the lonely, the lost, the desperate, the raging dreamers, the sick and the desolate, the stifled, the suffocating. Did we give *them* anything, I wonder, except momentary comfort? I remember one Swedish poet we used to call 'the Baboon' because of the leather patches on the seat of his jeans, and he stole a black felt shepherd's cape and used to leap the high Hydra walls at dead of night, like Dracula, and throw up on the carpets if he felt like it (he didn't throw up on ours, and I am grateful to him for his restraint: he was removed, later, by his Embassy). But there were some of them who went on and wrote novels, and painted paintings, and wrote poetry, and there are some of them with whom we still keep in contact, and their names I am transcribing into my brand new book.

And, of course, the old red book does contain more than social hypocrisies (if that is what they were, and I am still not sure about that, knowing loneliness, and need, and desperation). There are some names and addresses that I am transcribing into my new book that belong to people who were once just passers-through or briefly encountered somewhere and came to mean the word 'friend' and have gone on meaning that through years and absence. Many names are

53

transcribed from the book before the old red one, and some of them from the book before that; some of them have been transcribed from book to book for twenty years.

And of these there are a few that I will not transcribe, like the name that leapt out at us from an American magazine the other day among a spread of beautiful photographs of the Himalayas. And the story said that he had fallen to his death while balancing on a ledge to focus his camera, and it seems a good death for a man to die, doing what he loves best in the part of the world that moves him most. He used to wear thick bifocals and a baseball cap and hideous flowered shirts, and he was a brave and simple and good man and one of the finest photographers in the world.

I suppose in five years time, or six, this new book of mine will look exactly like the old. There is little enough in it at the moment, but I suppose it will fill up with hurried scrawls and maps and scribbled memoranda. And in five or six years time I wonder what I will transcribe.

News of Earls Court—Fifteen Years Ago

The fog didn't come on little cat's feet exactly. It hung around like bits of dirty drapery, looped up in places, tattered in others, and around the thick ugly pillars that supported the porticoes of soot-stained residentials it trailed streamers sometimes. It smelled something acrid, something lean; not anything one had ever smelled before, but right, just right, just what a London fog ought to smell like. The streets were soggy with a mulch of leaves, old newspapers, and the evidence of many dogs having been walked. In the Fulham Road there was a shop that sold clowns' masks and joke kits and all the appurtenances of magic.

It was the Festival of Britain that year, and the Australian designer Gordon Andrews was living in Earls Court, and being very involved in the (then) futuristic complex over on the South Bank. His wife, Mary, and I used to roster ourselves for duty chores with our assorted children, like picking them up from school and walking them in parks

(Holland Park and Kensington Gardens for preference) and riding them around on those buses so vehemently red in all the grey, or traipsing them through museums. London buildings, the Portland stone ones, looked like bleached bones behind the tracery of bare black branches, and every spring stall was noisily yellow with massed daffodils.

That year, too, I was sitting for a portrait to an Australian painter, Colin Colahan, who lived in Whistler's old house in Tite Street. He had been an expatriate then for more than twenty years and one knew, with certainty, that he would never be going back. His studio windows looked out on the Chelsea Hospital for old military pensioners and he often played Mozart's Requiem Mass while he painted me because he couldn't quite believe that I would always cry at exactly the same point, but I always did. I was filled to bursting with excitement, and I felt very young and very muddled and very choked with being excited and young and muddled, not to mention Mozart and Whistler's house and Nell Gwyn and London London London.

There were a lot of other Australians being excited in London that year. Paul Brickhill had finished *The Great Escape* and was waiting for publication, knowing already, I think, that he was going to crack the best-seller lists. Peter Finch was over in Dolphin Square, not quite yet daring to believe what everybody was saying about his talent, and sometimes needing reassurance. His brother, a test pilot, was obsessed with something called the Sound Barrier, and at dinners or parties would always be found in a corner, drawing diagrams of leading edges and air-flows. Loudon Sainthill hadn't then designed those magical sets and costumes for *The Tempest* that would take us down to Stratford later, in a blizzard, behind a snow-plough, the car waltzing on the iced roads (but worth it to cheer Loudon for a success so spectacular), but he was there, and Cedric Flower was there, doing the rounds of the theatres and painting buses and bridges and guardsmen and the Round Pond and posters for the London Underground, and Pat Flower was there, writing her first thriller, and Albert Arlen was there, talking about the music for *The Sentimental Bloke,* and Sidney Nolan's drought paintings were receiving attention although the buyers weren't stampeding in those days, and more fools they.

I used to think that the most desirable state of being that could be imagined was to be a young and talented Australian in London. Weren't we healthier, more vital, more buoyant? And didn't we have so much enthusiasm, so much talent that it was frustrating to the point of actual discomfort to keep ourselves within decent British bounds? We kept bursting out all over the place. I thought we were like a lot of healthy Antipodean sponges, sopping up everything that touched us, good and bad and smelly and all. The musty smell of the tube stations was in it, and the marvellously comic sight of gentlemen in yachting rig sailing toy boats on the Round Pond, and the prophet with the streaming white beard who held a placard that read 'God Is Going to Get You', and the chars who actually (and unbelievably) called one 'madam', and ration cards and bus queues and Homburg hats and nannies wheeling titled babies in extravagant carriages, as well as theatres and galleries and concerts and all the other intellectual food we were gorging ourselves on. We talked immoderately and played records from clumsy albums of twelve (of which one would invariably be chipped or broken), and collected bits of Victoriana in Church Street and the Portobello Road, as well as funny stories about the English. We were enchanted, amused, excited, indignant, frustrated, discouraged, and sometimes contemptuous.

Australia, which we had left in the Jubilee year of Federation, seemed very far away. 'A cultural desert', we said (but only to other Australians), remembering it as being a distinctly unpleasant place in the immediate post-war years, more prosperous than it had ever been but paralysed by strikes (bathing the babies by candlelight night after night, and never knowing whether there would be a milk delivery or not), cynical with the disillusionment of peace, and the taxi-drivers rapacious and the shop assistants rude and the licensing laws barbarous and creative nourishment scanty.

These memories have been teasing me lately, what with all the passions and vituperations that have been seething and boiling and even exploding (nastily, and with a stench of sulphur) in the cauldron where everybody in the world, it seems, is trying to cook up a brew that will turn out to be an authentic Australian Image.

The Japanese have had a stir in the pot, and the A.B.C. and the Sydney Civic Fathers, and the B.B.C. have added a few toads, and lately the present batch of Australian expatriates—the Australian Londoners—have been articulate in defence of their expatriation.

Australia, they still say, is a cultural desert. They feel themselves to be less expatriates than 'cultural refugees' from the chase after the quid and the G.N.P. They feel in Australia a sterility, a barrenness, a paucity of ideas, and they make the point that if every creative Australian in London came back it still wouldn't make any difference to Australia's cultural development because Australian society as it is presently constituted couldn't find room for them, and wouldn't even want to anyway.

All this is so hauntingly familiar, echoing fifteen-year-old conversations that must still be palpitating faintly in the fog draped around Earls Court and the Bayswater Road and Notting Hill Gate and Chelsea and innumerable film-set pubs all over London.

Only, what strikes me as curious, in a particularly distressing sort of way, is that fifteen years ago, when we were saying the same things (only not so publicly), radio in Australia was flourishing, writers and actors were as busy as could be, people went to theatres for entertainment as a matter of course, we had a film industry, and a best-selling book—in hard covers too—might sell sixty to eighty thousand copies. There was no T.V.

In the fifteen years since we went away the Government hasn't changed and neither has much on the cultural scene, except to wither slowly, even to atrophy completely. Most radio is only glorified juke-box, the theatre is struggling more desperately than ever before, the film industry is moribund, and if a hard-cover book sells ten thousand it is a fantastic success. There is T.V., which ought to be absorbing all sorts of talents, but—alas—isn't.

A queer business. It is distressing, really, to remember Earls Court fifteen years ago. These days, they tell me, it is known as Kangaroo Valley.

Winter Solstice

Sometimes when we were young it was winter. Not very often, because when you're young it's mostly summer. Endless. Golden. Not the 'unimaginable zero summer' you dream about now, but the real thing.

But, yes, there were a few winters too. Dramatic winters, with great turbulent aubergine skies rolling and crashing about, and moments of prescience so still you reeled in the darkening silence and held your breath and waited for signs and wonders and portents.

Lightning, maybe, stabbing and forking and ripping that purple arras, or pall, that so ceremoniously looped itself over our winter world. Thunder, peremptory, barking some challenge to us. To us? God to god, more likely—in immortal combat. We believed in gods then. That much was easy.

And then the rain. Sheets and gallons and oceans of it scratching the world over with a million diagonals, or sometimes verticals, sogging up the tussocked paddocks, gurgling down the gutters, springing freshets where the cannas grew by the creek, sounding a din on the tin roof like all the kettle-drums that ever summoned Marlborough, and drawing up and out of the earth such a smell as I have never smelled since—not through all my winters—of the pungency of life. Soil, growing things, paspalum grass, seaweed, creek mud, cow dung, and bruised white flowers.

When it rained like that we didn't go to school because school was a mile away over the hills and we'd only get soaked and be sent home anyway. What we did was to kneel in a row on the cracked brown leather couch under the weeping window—long-haired Margaret, skinny Barre, and I, Charmian, the youngest—rubbing it clear, or writing our names on it, or drawing mandalas. We didn't know we were drawing mandalas then, of course, excepting in so far as children know some things instinctively, and do some things instinctively.

The window faced the creek, and in the rain, chewing on some sticky mess of confection we had just made on the kitchen range —toffee, maybe, or coconut ice—we waited and watched for its rising. Never-failing drama as the water crept up the furred rushes wading now plume-deep in the boiling brown and began to seep over the mud-flats, carrying on its errant surface bits of swirling driftwood and bobbing pumpkins washed down from the high farms.

And then: 'She's out!' we would shriek, watching the bits of flotsam twirl tentatively and begin to rush towards the beach, gathering speed as the momentum of the current caught them and flung them from side to side in the wild desperation of water about to lose its identity in the sea.

Our sluggish little creek seemed a mighty river then, and the banks of sand gouged out by its impetuous dash across the beach were wet gamboge ramparts, splitting and plopping heavy slides of sand that fanned out darkly for an instant and then were lost in the churning water.

Then we ran. Bare-legged and bare-headed, hauling on slickers as we went. Down to the wild wet beach and the squeaking sand and the enormous winter sea, dark to purple almost and frilled and frothed with the coldest white, lashing and pounding at the rocks and the cliffs but pulled back and out at the creek's mouth, and stained with the reception of that muddy flood-tide. Rippling now at the beach's edge, fast and shallow. To be waded in until the ripples rushed up your legs and made fountainy high-boots. And the wet gulls belching up like a cloud of scummy steam and hanging there, beating, with their red legs stiff and talons spread, wanting the pumpkins.

And sometimes there was hail. The sky was black-green then, a marvellous colour like the beginning and end of things, or what children might imagine the beginning and end of things to be. The sea, black-green too, exploding into millions of little jumping gushers. Silver cake-lozenges bouncing and scattering and rolling. Piles of them. Cars stopped on the roads. And the noise on the roofs to wake the dead. Ice pebbles leapt and bounded like golf balls. You rushed out and grabbed hands full and crammed them into your mouth, scrunching and scrunching. And the black world roared and your hair was hung with diamonds.

Afterwards there was always a rainbow hanging gauzy in a sky the colour of an old green bottle, blown unevenly, with flaws and whorls of thickness and darkness and one crackled patch where the sun was breaking through. Out winter world lay in a marvellous silence then. Only the brilliance of the paddocks singing, and the raw sienna sand, and every house and every wall frosted—piles of ice pebbles banked up, blue-white, green-white, polished and glittering like crystal beads.

In the winter our mother made fires. Out of wet billets of box and scoops of coal. She had a way of coaxing fires. And at night we three would sit around the dining table, covered decently with brown bobble-fringed cloth, colouring in the Virgil drawings in *Smith's Weekly*, sticking shells on to cigar boxes for birthday or Christmas presents, cutting out things, pasting things, while our mother, curled up on a cushion by the scaly grey and leaping blue-and-orange of the fire—and prodding it into a frenzy—read to us.

> Blow, winds, and crack your cheeks! rage! blow! . . .
> I tax not you, you elements, with unkindness . . .
> You owe me no subscription: then, let fall
> Your horrible pleasure. . . .

We shuddered with delicious terror at such wonderful words and pleasure in our warm young selves, safe and protected from the elements' horrible pleasure. We wondered if there would be a shipwreck, and hoped there might. Sometimes there was seaweed draped and rotting on the picket fence in the mornings: that's how close the sea was. Our father had been shipwrecked once, and had had to swim five miles to shore. We thought we might quite like to be shipwrecked ourselves. Under certain circumstances, and with an audience. We would save somebody.

Winter tasted of hot soup and toffee and cocoa, smelled of wet earth and burning box billets, sounded of the elements' horrible pleasure shrieking and whining and howling and drumming, and felt of comfort. We dressed up sometimes and played at kings and queens: the Shakespearian influence was strong in our house.

There have been winter solstices since. Many and many of them. Too many perhaps. I saw snow for the first time. London fog. Blizzard. Picked mistletoe from a Druid's oak-tree. Walked Cornish moors in the mist and watched a ship pounded to death beneath a lighthouse. I huddled in the Black Forest once, in dark and primitive terror. And once I shouted in to the rumbled guts of the worst storm I have ever known. A yellow storm. Yellow's always the worst. It's more angry somehow. I've always shouted in to yellow storms, being defiant by nature, I suppose. And once in a yellow storm there was a yellow balloon too, skittering madly over the yellow sea, and a cheque in the mail that day, signifying something. The gods' favour, I thought then, being a bit exalted with the weather.

Isn't it strange how your childhood dogs you and tracks you and will not let you be?

Because of mine I have always loved weather. All sorts of weather. In a way, the worse the better. I vibrate in a storm like a tuning fork, and long for beaches, long, wave-lashed beaches, gulls, splinters, spars, dripping weed, squeaking sand, the fury of the sea roaring up the cliffs and sobbing down in impotence, and a creek breaking its banks to make a playground for wild wet children.

Eliot says:

> There are other places
> Which also are the world's end, some at the sea jaws. . . .

> Where is the summer [he asks], the unimaginable
> Zero summer?

But I ask where is the unimaginable winter? Sometimes when we were young it was winter. But not very often, of course. Perhaps children aren't allowed too much of a good thing. They might become addicted to the elements, believe in the old gods, turn hieratic and identify themselves with old cults, old sacrifices, and neglect their civilized destinies in the most patriotic Australian wool, turning on the central heating and drying out their smart umbrellas. Wool's in this season. Lovely colours, too. Toffee and caramel and raw sienna and kelp green.

It's a long way back to the sea's jaws. The world's end.

Christmas

The harbour view from my study window, so cool and magical until now, offers nothing at the moment but intimidation. The sea is dull and battered flat by the burning wind, and in the foreground my favourite eucalypts are streaming sorry parched banners. My daughter, wilting, reports that the sea is unpleasant to swim in, like bathing in sticky soup (if one can wiggle through the half-naked crowds milling there in the hope of relief and get to the water at all), and the sand is too hot to walk on barefoot.

The city is ringed by bushfire smoke—one gets the sharp, dangerous acrid smell every now and again, and the sirens of the fire-engines have been wailing hysterically all the morning. In this house we flounder about gasping, like landed fish.

It is really rather strange to be having a hot Christmas again.

Not that it *is* actually Christmas at the time I write this, but the parties started weeks and weeks ago, and the advertisements are now so urgent as to make one fearful of forgetting or missing, or being late with the suitable emotions as well as the expensive gifts. Shop assistants are looking really harried, young mothers exhausted, children fretful, fathers worried (for their bank accounts undoubtedly). It is difficult to imagine cheer and goodwill eventuating from it all, although one knows from experience that it often does, like those wobbly stage productions where everything comes right on the night. I suppose Christmas is about miracles anyway.

I will never forget our first Christmas in Greece. We had arrived only a few weeks before, filled with our own audacity but bewildered nevertheless. Rain storms went raging and fuming on every day, our temporary accommodation—unfurnished—leaked, our children were punch-drunk with unfamiliarity and discomfort to the point of near imbecility. No more dismal or disillusioned little band ever stumbled into its Promised Land.

The approaching feast and the indisputable fact of Christmas was to the children the one familiar safe beacon beckoning in a world that must have seemed then to be on the point of disintegration.

But the imminence of Christmas was for us parents a nightmare. For as the days passed and the rain storms gave way to that deceptive December sun of Greece and we scouted around the little island desperately for a single sign of festive preparation, it was gradually made apparent that the Christmas celebration, as we mindlessly knew it, did not exist.

Easter is the great feast of the Greek year, New Year is the time for gift-giving. Christmas is a religious day, honouring the birth of Christ, but definitely not a spree. Nobody, alas for the children, had ever heard of one S. Claus.

There were no gewgaws, bells or decorations for sale in the few island shops, no children's toys, no greeting cards, no bon-bons, coloured lights, tinsel, holly wreaths or imitation snow. And —Mother of God!—what could we possibly want with a *tree?*

Nevertheless we found one, or, rather, our new and completely mystified Greek friends found one for us. Not exactly a tree, but the branch of a tree—a salt tree branch still encrusted with hen droppings and with a couple of tentacles of dried octopus hanging from it. And on this precious bit of greenery we hung poison-coloured sweets, hundreds of sweets, kilos and kilos of sweets on poison-coloured ribbons. Both sweets and ribbons seemed to be in plentiful supply.

And we found (miracle of miracles) five tiny and rather dented celluloid dolls forgotten in a dusty box marked 1921 below the counter in a coffee house (bought for what child, when, and why never given, we wondered), and we dressed them, Mary, Joseph, the Kings and the Baby, in scraps of material cut from underneath the hems of my dresses and more poison-coloured ribbons, and we carefully undid the links of all my brummy bracelets and ear-rings and necklaces for jewels to deck them with.

We made haloes from chocolate wrappings, silver and gold, and a flock of sheep from scraps of sponges and matchsticks for legs, and a manger from bamboo and straw, and frost from a packet of coarse salt, and we painted—from the children's watercolours still surviving —a backdrop of kneeling shepherds, Hark Herald Angels (with trumpets) and a marvellous wobbly five-pointed star.

The children didn't have any Christmas presents that year, but they gave a wonderful party for the swarms of island young who had tagged them since their arrival. All the tree decorations were eaten as well as the peculiar assortment of food I had been able to assemble, and the party stood in front of the crib with its bank of church candles and sang the one Greek Christmas carol over and over and over again.

I don't think Christmas was ever quite as basic for us after that, but the crib survived year after year, re-furbished, re-decked, and the backdrop re-painted by artists famous now, but not then. And it became custom for the carol-singers to sing their one carol in front of it, at four o'clock in the morning usually, which could be distressing —snotty-nosed tots, bands of high-school girls sweetly conducted by one of their mistresses, village drunks, wharf-labourers carrying a gramophone with an ancient horn to do their carol-singing for them. It was part of Christmas ceremonial.

So was the tree. On Christmas Eve Barba Yanni the muleteer brought two donkeys and left them at the gate of our house and our neighbour lady graciously gave the children permission to climb to the top of the mountain and cut two small fir-trees from her grove. One for us and one for her. We used to make an all-day picnic of it, experienced children, bewitched guests, loaded with food and straw-covered wine flasks, climbing for miles in the crisp and sun-dazzled weather to the thicket high above the highest monastery. Not many Christmases passed before it was common to meet other tree parties out on private or communal foray. A tree had become a status symbol.

Fortunately the gradual seeping through of the true commercial spirit of our Western Christmas saved the little fir thickets of the island from total destruction.

Last time Barba Yanni brought his donkeys the neighbour lady said wonderingly: 'Of course you may have a tree, but why put yourselves to so much trouble? Look, I have such a pretty plastic one. See? It goes up and down like this. Put it away after. Use it next year just the same. You can buy one from Mitso.'

Indeed one could buy a plastic tree from Mitso. A miniature

plastic tree or a little plastic tree or a middling plastic tree or a plastic tree so tall it wouldn't fit inside the shop. And from Yanni also. And from Sotero. And from every tobacconist, grocer, fruit-shop on the island. And one could buy gewgaws and bells and coloured lights both plain and flower-shaped and bon-bons and tin toys and imitation snow and holly wreaths and Christmas stockings and celluloid figures of that recent saint added to the Greek calendar—S. Claus. Caique-loads of turkeys were being unloaded onto the waterfront, where they paraded before prospective buyers with ludicrous elegance, gobbling. And one could, if one wished, buy greeting cards depicting a map of Cyprus with S. Claus himself shaking hands across tinselled barbed wire with a gallant evzone in a frilly skirt on guard.

And one could buy plastic cribs anywhere.

Before we left Greece we gave our crib to the little girls next door who had loved it for so long. Every year they had helped with the re-dressing and decking of the dolls, and suggested further additions and fancifications to the manger, and saved silver paper for haloes and stars and angels and cherubs. Every year they had been the first of the pre-dawn carol-singers.

And the last we saw of it—as we dropped in next door to say good-bye to their parents—was a ruin of cardboard and bamboo and bits of sponge, and Mary, Joseph, the Kings and the Baby, haloes skew-whiff, robes definitely awry, sitting down to a nice meal of bread and oil served on bougainvillea petals and drinking retsina out of yellow bell-flowers.

Presenting Moonshine

He wrote, that traveller Frank Borman—I know because I read it: 'The moon was so desolate, so uninviting, so completely devoid of life or anything to indicate that there had ever been life. Nothing but this great pock-marked lump of grey pumice.'

This great pock-marked lump of grey pumice.

Oh Hecate, Astarte, Isis, Phoebe, Selene, Artemis of the silver bow, chaste Diana, is that all you were all the time—for all those thousands of years? A great pock-marked lump of grey pumice.

I don't know that I can bear it. Not this final disillusion. It couldn't have been just grey pumice that I dreamed on, sighed under, turned a sixpence over in my pocket for, never looked at through glass, or, in the full of it and in the spring, was snared by, running through its tangling silver net to meet a waiting lover.

It used to pave the paddocks with coins, turn sand silver, and the swishing frills of the sea's hem, tugged by it, so luminous that the light seemed to pour upward and you could feel yourself falling off the turning earth, falling slowly, slowly, with outstretched arms and trailing hair, falling away into glory.

Dogs howled to it and cats stealthily stalked the rooftops, black bats and young witches flew, graves gaped, milk curdled, the dusty track grew white as chalk or cherry-blossom, flowers opened to it petal by petal, releasing such scent as would bowl you over, and lovers, lying in it, turned to each other faces as strange and smooth and innocent as the kernels of nuts or the faces of madmen: we read poetry by it one summer, not having enough words.

There was still a man in the moon then. Endymion, perhaps, lured there in sleep by sly Selene. Or Cain? With a bush of thorns, the briars of the fall, and a dog, the foul fiend himself. 'This man, with lantern, dog, and bush of thorns, presenteth Moonshine.' Or was it a man leaning on a fork with a bundle of sticks picked up on a Sunday? Sometimes he was a smiling man, and sometimes he was a sorry man, sometimes he winked and sometimes he frowned, but he was always there in the full . . . 'yesternight the moon was round' . . . and worth endless speculation. Children have been known to cry for him to play with, not knowing, poor innocents, what they were asking for.

But the moon itself was female. The triple goddess herself who waxed and waned enigmatically through her three phases, pulling the tides of the sea and women and driving men mad. You could hang your dreams on her horns once, or wish, or yearn, or, if you were game enough, bathe naked in her radiance and be transfigured. Or lose your wits.

Once we worshipped her. From first thin paring of silver rind to last lovely sickle she had her rites and sacrifices, and when she was gone we called her Hecate and gave her dogs and honey and new black lambs, always at crossroads, and begged her back from the darkness of the underworld with spells and sorcery.

We called her Artemis, we called her Selene, we called her Astarte, we called her Isis, we called her Phoebe, sister of the sun. We called

65

her Invincible Queen. And every queen, once, was also a moon-priestess, a triad in herself, so powerful that even when she was conquered and forcibly married by a rain-making sky-king he too had to become a complimentary triad. Three-bodied Geryon of Spain, three-headed Cernunnos, the Gallic god, and the Irish triad, Brian, Iuchar, and Iucharba, who married the three queenly owners of Ireland. And then those invading Greek brothers, Zeus, Poseidon, and Hades, who married the pre-Greek moon goddess in all her three aspects, Queen of Heaven, Queen of the Sea, and Queen of the Underworld.

You great pock-marked lump of grey pumice.

What will the poets do now? And Tin Pan Alley, without the moon to play with? And such virgin huntresses as there might, perhaps, still be?

We used to wonder once upon the aspect of her far unfathomable face, for ever hidden from us and veiled in mystery. What was there?

The wasted things of earth, some said. Time misspent and squandered wealth, broken vows and trysts and promises and appointments, unanswered prayers, desires not fulfilled, good intentions, fruitless tears, wishes never gratified, nor dreams. Unconsummated loves. Unfinished business.

Ariosto's Astolpho found there when he went that bribes were kept on gold and silver hooks, and princes' favours in bellows. Wasted talent lodged in vases, each labelled with its own sad name. But Pope, in 'The Rape of the Lock', said the vases were for heroes' lost wits, although the lost wits of beaux were consigned to snuff-boxes and tweezer cases.

> There broken vows, and death-bed alms are found,
> And lovers' hearts with ends of ribbon bound,
> The courtier's promises, and sick man's prayers,
> The smiles of harlots, and the tears of heirs,
> Cages for gnats, and chains to yoke a flea,
> Dried butterflies, and tomes of casuistry.

Edward Lear, as he described in a private letter, travelled there in imagination, by way of moonbeams, which, he said, 'far from being mere portions of light, are in reality living creatures, endowed with considerable sogassity, & a long nose like the trunk of Nelliphant, tho' this is quite imperceptible to the naked eye.'

And what didn't he find there! Jizzdoddle Rocks, and planets orange-coloured and pea green, the Rumbytumby Ravine, with the crimson planet Buzz and its five Satanites on the horizon, the Blompopp tree, so called from the Blompopp, 'a gigantic and gorgeous bird which builds on its summit'. Also the tall Vizzikilly trees, which grow to an immense height and bloom only once in fifteen years, 'when they produce a large crop of immemorial soapbubbles, submarine sucking pigs, songs of sunrise and silver sixpences'. Which last, he said, were ground into powder by the lunar population, and drunk in warm water without any sugar.

And then, one day, after all our lovely and exciting speculation, after we had stretched our imaginations to the limits of fantasy, soared and spun in wonder and terror and the wildest dreaming, we knew. On the far face of the moon there was a piece of hardware, dourly labelled CCCP.

And that was the beginning of the end. The end of thousands of years of mythology, legend, worship, cult, fearful rite and magic ceremony, the end of wonder and the end of terror, the end of dream and wish and moon-mad lovers slowly turning silver.

It is, after all, only a great pock-marked lump of grey pumice.

. . . the odds is gone,

—oh sweet enchantress of the night, did Shakespeare guess?—

And there is nothing left remarkable
Beneath the visiting moon.

PEOPLE

Out From the Centre

Being addicted as I am to works of reference, particularly those with all sorts of odd gobbets of information on unlikely subjects, I often have a pleasurable browse in the encyclopaedia.

This is not with any set plan of self-improvement. I know all too well I could do with it, but am always reminded of the unfortunate man who educated himself diligently as far as H before he had the inevitable nervous breakdown, and spent the rest of his life in a state of acute schizophrenia—a suave, amiable, and positively scintillating fellow in the conversational channels between A and H, but a morose and surly lunk outside them. Humorous with Harpsichord, but hopelessly ignorant of Islam.

He would have been on home ground this morning, because the word I hit on was 'eccentric', and there was a lot of stuff about the use of the word in ancient astronomy, and what it means in engineering presently, and it was all very interesting. But its literal meaning, the encyclopaedia says, is 'out from the centre' and it is used generally to connote any deviation from normal.

There's nothing terribly illuminating in that, of course. Most of us have known some real way-out cats long before the term became popular, and people who were definitely off-centre, if not completely dotty. Usually these sort of people are infinitely more interesting and stimulating as human beings than the solid mass of conventional citizenry (I was going to say 'normal' citizenry, but then I'm not quite sure what normal is, although I might look it up in a minute if it teases me too much).

Just the other night we went to the twenty-second birthday of a young man whose mother lets out rooms to students in a house furnished entirely with loot from the tips, which she haunts with the dedication of Schliemann rooting up Priam's treasure. To her own intense satisfaction, and the surprise of her friends, she had just produced a baby daughter, and so might have been excused from attending a predominantly student party. Instead she serenely hostessed the occasion in a go-go dress that was rather reminiscent of a green plush lampshade, of which the base was the long black lace legs of a pair of old-fashioned drawers. Above this extravagance she glowed with a gentle radiance that quite outshone any of the young girls. She didn't look matronly enough to have a twenty-two-year-old son. In fact she didn't look matronly enough to have a brand new baby. She didn't look matronly at all, but only—and most beautifully— herself. She is mildly astonished that anyone should think her eccentric.

There used to be a lot of them about once. Eccentrics, I mean. England has always had the lien on them, of course—bearded prophets, dedicated bird-watchers and ghost-watchers, spiritualists, hunting parsons, amateur criminologists, village characters, decayed gentlewomen with odd tastes in clothing and even odder personal habits. Quirky people, original people, idiosyncratic people, immoderate people, people following their highly individualistic tastes and habits and convictions with sublime unselfconsciousness.

English life as well as English literature is stuffed with them as liberally as a rich Christmas pudding with raisins. Margaret Rutherfords abounding. Gully Jimsons in fact as well as fiction. Latter-day Lawrences and Burtons and aspiring Hester Stanhopes. Uncle Tobys and Mr Shandys. I don't know whether it is breeding, education, or that climate that produces such a crop. One meets them all over the world, usually pottering after improbabilities, like the English canon I met once on a wild hillside in Greece. He was dressed in his black clericals and he was digging valiantly among the asphodel for a long-lost porphyry mine. I recognized him immediately as Rose Macaulay's invention, and looked for Aunt Dot and the camel: perhaps they were loping up Olympus to convert the gods. Actually it is only outside England such people seem odd, because in England itself there are so many of them that they are scarcely remarked.

Still, we used to produce a fair old crop ourselves once. There was a whole generation of journalists before the war who created legends that are still good in the telling and perhaps even better for the burnishings and embellishments of the years. Like the journalist who set out to go around the world with the express intention of recording his opinion of his erstwhile overlord in every men's convenience he found on the way. The said opinion, succinct and pithy, has been reported by travellers as far afield as Omsk, Rio, Peking, Paris France and Omaha Nebraska. I think it sad that he never came back.

And there was another with the singular habit of flinging himself on the wrought-iron gates of the metropolitan rich, shouting as he hung spread-eagled there: 'Master! Master! The peasants are starving! The peasants need bread!' As a protest, he said. When it became evident that his protest was quite ineffectual he went to Mexico, where he became one of Trotsky's bodyguards. (One wonders now whether Trotsky was assassinated in spite of his bodyguard's peculiarities, or because of them.) He was last heard of in New York, which is another fine breeding-ground for eccentrics, as Damon Runyon knew. Most travellers with a nodding acquaintanceship of the drugstores and steak joints around 2nd and 3rd Avenues have met at least one man who knows where Captain Kidd's treasure is buried.

But all that lot of excessive scribes are dead or fled, and they don't seem to grow that way any more. I don't know why.

I am told that there are still real characters in the country, but have no knowledge of them from my own experience. Bill Harney was certainly one, but then Bill Harney is dead too, and I haven't heard of anybody inheriting his colourful mantle: I would feel reassured if I did.

There is a photographer of my acquaintance working out here on a major project for an American magazine, and he thinks that the breed must be extinct. He's been searching hard enough for survivors all over the country. It's terribly strange, he says, that wherever he goes he meets the same fourteen people, and wonders whether they were type-cast by his masters when the project was being 'structured' with proper American efficiency and given instructions to take faster planes and trains and automobiles than the photographer himself so that they would arrive just ahead of him at every place on his list and take up their 'character' poses for his camera.

'I always thought,' he said mournfully, 'that this was the land of the individual.'

Maybe it is at that, and both he and I have been unlucky or unobservant or haven't looked in the right places. I do hope so, because, as Bishop Berkeley said, 'Excesses, defects and contrary qualities conspire to the beauty and harmony of the world.' Besides, they're fun.

Eccentrics, my encyclopaedia informs me, are also used to work the jaws of powerful crushers and to close quick-acting clamps and safety mechanisms. So it must be useful as well as entertaining to be out from the centre. I always suspected it.

Uncrating Mr Nolan

Mr Nolan looked thinner than when I had last seen him. I thought he looked smaller too. But that might have been only in contrast with Hal Missingham, the Director of the Art Gallery of New South Wales, who is sizeable. Or, more likely, the fact that the packing crates were so large.

The vaults of the Gallery were stacked with crates, opened and unopened. The uncrated paintings leaned against still-crated ones and walls and posts and pillars, backs outward, revealing nothing but masonite, nails, fluff, brass hooks, numbers, gallery stickers (Redfern, Marlborough, Tate, Museum of Modern Art) and chalk-scrawled identifications—Collection of So-and-So. I thought if I had been So-and-So I would have been a bit leary of relinquishing a piece of my collection, even temporarily, by lending it out to the other side of the world, even to the painter himself, even for a great retrospective exhibition, as this was to be. Too many things could happen between here and there.

Hal Missingham said that once a whole exhibition of French paintings had run aground on the Tasmanian coast. But it had turned out all right, he said, because that particular hold hadn't been waterlogged. He'd been able to mount the exhibition, complete and undamaged. And, thankful to the Fates, he'd be able to mount this one too, although he confessed his great relief at having it all assembled finally. He had had a bad scare with the closing of the Suez Canal. Mr Nolan said he had had a bit of a scare too. He had thought of Burke and Wills on the Bitter Lakes, but this time they had been paddling the painting.

They had a great thick swatch of numbered slips between them on the deal table. Hal Missingham said it had been hell trying to get the paintings into chronological order. The exhibition covered a span of thirty years, and Mr Nolan's memory, although better than good, was not absolutely reliable on actual dates. When you paint as prolifically as he does I suppose some confusion is inevitable. It seemed that he had dated two paintings, ten days apart, the wrong way round. There were letters he had written twenty years ago, referring to the paintings in the right order.

I thought it must be a queer thing to be fifty years old and sitting there at a deal table in the cold vaults surrounded by thirty years of yourself, crated and uncrated, bits of yourself gathered from all over the world, cut up into uncompromising oblongs and stacked enigmatically, backs outward, like random packs of playing cards waiting for the magician's trick.

You could cut the stacks anywhere and come up with anything—the pier at St Kilda, Mrs Fraser in a tropical forest, an African monkey, Leda and the Swan, a drought carcass. Hal Missingham cut a stack and came up with a painting still in wraps. The fact that it was still in wraps was mysterious and exciting, and I had one of those strange flash-backs that everyone has some time, to a hot, dusty workaday street in the Piraeus in 1959. There was a big trench dug in the street, and shovels leaning everywhere, and out of the trench, reverently raised by a team of men and with his beautiful green-bronze flesh still wrapped in Piraeus clay, came an archaic Apollo, lost for two thousand years.

It wasn't Apollo who came out of these wraps, though, but Sergeant Kennedy, dead at Stringybark Creek. Mr Nolan looked surprised, as though that wasn't what he had expected. He said the pink hill had got a lot pinker in the twenty-one years since he'd seen the painting last. He ran his fingers exploratively over Sergeant Kennedy's spilt blood and suddenly grinned and said: 'Still fresh.' There was a clump of what looked like snowdrops growing in the blood. He said yes, yes, Adonis and the flowers springing up eternally.

After a while of looking he nodded a couple of times—acceptance? confirmation?—and Hal Missingham staggered out of the stacks with a huge Wimmera landscape, which Mr Nolan had painted only last year, so that shouldn't have surprised him at all, particularly as it belongs in his own collection anyway. But he looked at that one for as long as he had looked at the other, and touched it, and he said what was interesting was that he had painted two paintings of this same landscape, from exactly the same viewpoint, but the paintings were twenty-five years apart.

So the early one was brought out from another stack and placed alongside, and it was just as if the magician had brought off his card trick, because the effect was startling. You could see that there was twenty-five years between them, and in that twenty-five years nothing

75

had happened to the landscape but a great deal had happened to Mr Nolan. He looked as pleased as if he had won a bet. You knew that those two paintings were terribly important to him, spiritually important, I mean. A sort of touchstone. Hal Missingham said that they were both very very good paintings. Mr Nolan said that the Australian landscape became beautiful when you couldn't farm it. He said the key to Australian landscape was the light—it had an incandescence, he said—he said the sky was more important than the landscape itself. He said that the earlier Wimmera painting was the first time he had managed to tilt the landscape, but he couldn't make the lakes stay flat. Hal Missingham said he still couldn't—all the water was still running out, twenty-five years later.

After that he asked to see the Trojan Women, or what had begun as the Trojan Women, stacked like firewood in the sacked city of Troy, but had turned into the Inferno, where their dead white flesh, blooming with wounds like flowers, spiralled and floated as a flock of white birds might, loosed into eternity. There were three panels of this major work uncrated, six still in crates. When it is assembled and hung it will measure forty feet. I thought that Hippocrates had stated categorically that art is long, and wondered if he could possibly have had Mr Nolan in mind.

But art was pretty long in Hippocrates' day too, and I thought, shivering a bit there in the cold vaults among the crates and the protective wraps and the enigmatic stacks of thirty years of a man's life assembled piecemeal from all over the world, that the longest thing about art is that it goes on working through time. Hippocrates could say with confidence: 'Life is short but art is long'. Pericles could say with confidence: 'Future ages will wonder at us, as the present age wonders at us now.' And Mr Nolan could say, running his fingers exploratively over Sergeant Kennedy's spilt blood: 'Still fresh.'

I kept on thinking of the archaic bronze Apollo, smiling his archaic smile through the protective wrapping of two thousand years of Piraeus clay.

Betrothing a Daughter

I realize that there are all sorts of very important and meaningful things going on in the wide world at the moment, but the most important and meaningful thing that is going on in my more constricted one is that my daughter, as a prelude to marriage, is being formally betrothed.

'Engaged' they call it now, but I like 'betrothed' better, and if there's some formal plighting to be done let us by all means have it of troth, and with proper ceremony.

It's all right. I promise I'm not going to be sentimental—although I've no doubt I'll weep buckets on the night—but I find myself walking around her warily and looking at her sideways and blinking suddenly to try to surprise the image of this young woman who is my only daughter. And sometimes she looks about fourteen and sometimes she looks about ten and I find myself thinking wildly that this contract is quite impossible—child-brides are out in this family—but then I realize I am getting her mixed up with that incorrigible little barefooted mahogany-brown island kid who sat on the rafters in slaughter-houses, chased funerals, jumped from the masts of sponge boats, played five-stones, disappeared down trapdoors, I think, whenever she knew there was a possibility of being carpeted for misdemeanours.

And when I blink back into focus again she looks so adult that I feel like asking her for advice on some of my own problems, and wonder why on earth somebody didn't nab her years ago. Then of course I remember that various somebodies did try just that and what my reactions were—ranging from consternation and dismay to absolute outrage.

It's a very mysterious business. I've never had a daughter betrothed before—at least not with parental consent: what contracts she contracted privately herself, on sunburnt rocks overlooking the jewelled Aegean, in damp misty-green English villages, or on the moonlit decks of various liners, I wouldn't know: I've never dreamed of asking. Girls have to practise a bit for the real thing. I know I did.

77

And then again I've never been betrothed myself but for once, and that was in wartime, and not formal in any way at all and no parents involved, and the restaurant was sleazy and he fumbled the ring. In any case the betrothal proved to have been an error, although I did like flashing that half-hoop of family diamonds around the barracks for a while, and was quite reluctant, really, to have to give it back.

No, when I finally married it was only as formal as nipping around the corner to the registry office and signing up for life. I sat on a beach in the morning and darned the seat of my husband elect's pants (he having but one pair) and then we waited for a man getting a dog licence.

Asking around among the friends of my generation I find that most of them did much the same thing, and I am wondering now, with all this formality facing me, whether this generation of our children are not perhaps rebelling against their non-conformist parents as their parents rebelled against their own conformist ones.

I even know a couple of mixed brace of students who did everything that was wild and outrageous and designed to shock and turn their mothers grey and wear their fathers out of weary patience. And then, quite suddenly, they walked with perfect composure up conventional aisles in conventional mists of tulle and flowers and conventional dinner jackets to the conventional manner born, not only forsaking all others but apparently their former wild ways.

I don't mean I disapprove of all this at all. But it puzzles me. Perhaps the wheel has turned full circle and the conventional has now become the unconventional. The need for ritual and ceremony might be manifesting itself. Or maybe girls just love to wear all that white gear, like the bride-dolls they played with when they were little.

Anyway, being involved willy-nilly in this betrothal, I begin to realize what I spared my own mother by just nipping around that corner to that registry office.

It's not that I haven't turned on parties before. Indeed I have. I love giving parties when the mood and the time and the people are in harmonious conjunction and I know I can sit on the floor before the night's over. But I am entirely unpractised and unlettered in even the ABC of formal ones. Australian style, that it. I think I could mock up a fair imitation of a Greek one fairly well, having danced the soles off my shoes at so many village betrothals, but then I lack the requisites, such as the gallery of the bedshelf for the old people and the very young children who are there as spectators, and the wicker flasks of retsina, and the musicians—with violin, bazouki and tsabuna to play and play and play the whole night through. And, alas, I lack the innumerable black-garbed ladies of close or distant kin who bog in and do the actual serving and cooking and the cleaning up after.

I even turned to the encyclopaedia for guidance, and found there many interesting betrothal customs that kept me interested for hours.

In ancient times I could have had all this over and done with when she was between the ages of seven and twelve. That made me thoughtful. The party would have been jelly and custard and hundreds and thousands, and I think that would have been simpler.

'If you lived in rural France,' I said, 'all I would have to do would be break a coin and give you a piece each in front of witnesses. And your betrothal gift would be a crooked sixpence.'

And she said—quite sternly I thought: 'Come on, mum. Smoke-oh's over. Back on your head!'

So here I am back on my head (that's the tag line to a rather ribald joke that my children enjoy) surrounded by lists, and I am quite certain I am doing everything quite wrongly and it might have been more practical to look up a book of etiquette instead of a fascinating encyclopaedia.

'Wouldn't a crooked sixpence do?' I wheedled. And she said warningly: 'Mum. . . .'

'But look,' I said, 'if you've turned all conventional why do you have to bulldoze me into being conventional too? Why should I turn into a conventional mum now when I've spent all my life sheering and dodging and even bolting upon occasion?'

She said: 'Catering Equipment for Hire in the Pink Pages.'

I suppose every other mother in Australia is conversant with what one can hire when one's daughter is being formally betrothed, but to me it was a revelation. I lost myself in it as I had done a little earlier in the encyclopaedia. I lost myself in urns and pot plants and marquees and portable dance floors and festoon lighting and folding tables and trestle tables and tablecloths and red carpets, and even slippery dips (that would be fun, I thought). I grew ambitious. In imagination I transformed my house into a sort of glittering gala night-club.

'Smoke-oh's over,' she said again.

And I thought, still reeling with revelations, but coming out of it fast, there's the wedding after this. Oh Lord.

'Look,' I said, 'why don't you two elope? It's terribly romantic. Your brothers will hold the foot of the ladder so he won't fall off getting up to your window, and I promise I'll pack your suitcase beautifully and hold the curtains back so you don't get hitched up.'

I think I might give the crazy little biddy a crooked sixpence anyway. As well, I mean. One day she'll know what I meant.

A Portrait of My Mother

My mother creeps into my writings quite often, as she should indeed, with one small swollen blotched ragged-nail over her mouth. It was a gesture that was characteristic of her, but whether it was because her teeth were in shocking condition, or in case we should interpret correctly the wickedness in that loving tobacco-stained smile, I don't know. I suspect the latter. And the honey-coloured eyes all melting with mischief and delight at our misdoings. She had misdone them all.

Somebody said, the other night, looking at old photographs, that I should write a portrait of my mother. As if I needed to, she being so indelibly etched upon my heart and my memory that sometimes I don't know where she leaves off and I begin.

I don't know when she was born, because she was the most endearing liar about her age, but I think it was in the middle or late eighteen-eighties, at Inverell in New South Wales, of a Scottish father with a dash of French in his blood, and a mother who was a beautiful Irish Jewess. She won waltzing competitions, my mother said, with egg-shells on her heels and a glass of water on her head, and her hand was so small she could put it inside a lamp chimney. She had six children, of whom my mother was the only girl (what a pity, they said, she'll never be as pretty as her mother), and died of the sixth of them, not putting aside until the last moment of agony the lace she was making to trim my mother's petticoat for market day. Her name was Sara.

When Sara died my mother, with all the others, was farmed out on various relations, and it was my mother's misfortune to be allotted to her Jewish grandparents, who kept a store. They immediately took my mother from school, sacked the maid and put my mother to work. This grieved and angered a young girl mad about learning but she bided her time, read books at night by a candle, and saved every penny she could. (The first photograph was taken at the beginning of this period: looking at it I always think of Beth in *Little Women*.)

Four years after this, or it could have been five (as I said, you could never pin her down on precise dates or years), she judged she had enough money to get to Sydney and have two pounds over. And after hasty and secretive conversation with her favourite brother one night she let a sheet down from her window in approved fashion and slid right into the buggy which her brother had standing there, and in a mad midnight dash across the countryside held up the train for Sydney at a siding and set out for adventure. Besides her two pounds she had, I think, the most terribly innocent faith in her own future. She believed in a personal star. She had, as it were, exchanged a wink of conspiracy with God. She skivvied again in a boarding house in King's Cross, graduated to selling lingerie, and all the time worked at night at shorthand typing until she was accomplished enough to apply for a job. She became a Gallery Girl, she went to concerts and theatres, she wrote romantic verse in secret notebooks and locked them up in her tin trunk. She must have blossomed in those years. Anyway they must have affected her deeply because she never made a visit to Sydney without making a pilgrimage to the old boarding house. Until, one day, it was gone.

The second photograph was taken on her wedding day, maybe ten years after. I don't know about the time, but she was married sensibly in a coat and skirt and chiffon blouse to a young English engineer she had landed in the boarding house at King's Cross, where he, just being down from the Newnes Valley, was staying while he decided what to do next. My mother, against the competition of the daughters of the house—blondes all and fine figures of women—won my father by pretending to let him teach her chess (she spending her savings on private lessons from a chess-master), and my father said he had never met a more intelligent pupil in his life. Oh Lord, she was immoral! I can never remember her playing a single game of chess in all the time I knew her. Certainly not, she said, it was the most boring game on earth.

They moved romantically from the city to the coastal town where they lived until my father's death, and for years it must have been a golden idyll. My father had a fine set of machines to tinker with at his place of employment, and there was a great sweep of ocean at their doorstep for swimming and fishing, and the lovely hills for strolling and Saturday shooting, and my father bought for her pleasure as well

81

as his own a second-hand schooner which they refurbished at the week-ends. And she planted vines and shrubs to hide the little cottage, which was only temporary of course. Next year, if they could sell the schooner for a decent profit they would have a good scout around for something roomier, where she could display her pretty linen and lace and china, and scrap the old deal furniture they had only bought to Make Do.

I wonder how long it took her to realize that she was stuck. She didn't have children for six years, and in the meantime life was pleasant enough, although she couldn't go on fishing expeditions any more, and found herself spending her week-ends entertaining the wives of my father's fishermen friends. And then my father heard of a better schooner and sailed his up to Port Jackson to get it, and was in such a hurry to get home to show it off that he forgot to insure it, and they were caught in a terrible storm and the schooner sank. And now there was no money any more for houses. I wonder whether she upbraided him, of threatened to leave him with storms of indignant tears, or was she just so thankful that he had made it to shore safely that she held back—at least until another day.

I only remember her really from the time of the last photograph, although I have little glimmerings before and beautiful sharp little pictures of picnics on the beach. That last photograph has been retouched, but it doesn't matter, to anyone excepting me, and I remember that her face was crumpled and sagging with neglect, seamed with worry lines, and her fine silver hair floated in wild wisps, like a hobgoblin, which indeed she was.

By this time she had transferred all her dreams and ambitions to her children, and spent most of her time, while scurrying out to the clotheslines, wrestling with the copper-stick, weeding the back vegetable rows (to save on the greengrocer), or treadling away at the old sewing machine, on elaborating our glorious futures. We understood quite clearly that we would never have to shin down sheets to make a getaway. If we didn't go we'd be pushed.

But when she was watching the sea her face was different, calm and ardent, and sometimes at night, very late, I could hear her scribbling away with a scratching pen, writing more poetry to be crumpled up and shoved into the fire, and once I saw her (having heard a commotion in the kitchen and poked my head around the door) stamping on a dress she had been making until three in the morning and kicking it around and around the kitchen.

82

I wonder, all in all, if she had a happy life. Whether the Yang and the Yin balanced out finally. She was a little bit of a selfconscious martyr sometimes, but never in an accusing way. Oblique, rather, and flurried and flustered, as if she really didn't want us to worry about it.

But she was never less than ardent (which is such a good word for her), and loving and kind. And I think these three photographs merge into one eventually. She was the same person all the time.

A Taxi Journey

The taxi-driver was foreign, which is usual, and disposed to chat, which is usual too, but what was unusual was a sort of warm credulous happiness he seemed to radiate. He talked like laughing instead of talking like yawning or whining, which is the way most people talk these days, and he drove his taxi with confidence and style, as if he enjoyed that too.

Gemütlich, I thought, and I was right because he was Austrian, and he laughed when I said gemütlich and explained that gemütlich was something you carried in the heart, not the head. It seemed like a useful sort of thing to carry in a taxi, anyway, especially if you were heading for an appointment that promised nothing but unease. He said he had been in Australia for nine years and he liked the country very well and he liked driving a taxi very well and he had married an Australian girl and he liked her very well too and this was very refreshing after the complaints and disgruntlements of so many foreign drivers and home-grown drivers too.

'But surely you miss something?' I asked, and he thought about this while we nosed out experimentally into the next lane and took advantage of ten clear yards to inch in behind a Chrysler where we wedged again bumper to bumper in a stink of fumes. 'The music. I miss the music,' he said. 'And the wine. And the mountains a little. The ski-ing is good here,' he added quickly, as if in reassurance. 'Very good. But there are not real mountains.'

We crawled along in the beating hot metal caterpillar that is city traffic, and he hummed away happily to himself something that was tuneful and gay and tugged some thread of memory in me, something to do with music and wine and mountains, so that I asked him specifically where in Austria he came from.

'*Not* Vienna,' he said, and laughed again. 'Vienna is old men drinking coffee and pretending gemütlich. Too many old men. Too much coffee. No. You will not have heard of my little town. Very small. Nothing much. Feldkirch it is called.' So I grinned then and said, 'Feldkirch in the Vorarlberg?' and at that the gemütlich fizzed so effervescently that if the cab had popped its roof or even taken off vertically, like a balloon, I wouldn't have been at all surprised.

'And St Florian?' I asked. 'How was St Florian when you saw him last?' I hadn't remembered St Florian in years, but suddenly, there in the peak-hour traffic, inching along laboriously towards an appointment I didn't want to keep, I could see the dark eaves with the rows of red and yellow maize cobs glowing under them, and smell the smell of wood and dung pungent from cavernous doorways, and see the women in their kerchiefs and aproned skirts gathered about the water-trough, filling their pails beneath the gaudy statue of St Florian, and St Florian holding his own water-pail high under the overhanging branch of a cherry-tree, old and blossom-heavy. I liked St Florian very well.

'*Grüss Gott,*' the women had called, very courteous, and '*Grüss Gott,*' we had replied awkwardly and had felt embarrassed to be hung about with cameras but took some photographs anyway because it had seemed a pity not to when we might never be in Austria again. And indeed we never were in Austria again, but I don't know why because we loved it that spring even though it was not a good time so soon after the war with seasons bad and prices soaring and the tourists kept away by money restrictions. And the young men then were restless, unsure, sighing for cinemas and motor-cycles and far-off cities, or perhaps just for the lost carelessness of days when the old ways had seemed good enough, and satisfying. The gemütlich cab-driver would have been a schoolboy that spring we were in Austria, and he must have been restless and sighing for far-off cities too, because here he was in Australia, driving a taxi happily and happy to be married to an Australian girl, but missing a little the music and the wine and the mountains.

I remembered the mountains. The Arlberg Pass was open but only just, and all the peaks were pure and dazzling above the dark smudges of spruce and larch and fir, above the huddling wooden villages and the needle-spired churches, and the air was so crisp that words tinkled in it: there were carved wooden shrines on tall posts in the snow, with little offerings of maize cobs and buttercups and drifts of blue forget-me-nots, quite improbable.

There was a mountain called Wildekaiser—Wild Emperor—which we looked out on from the best room in the Gasthof zum Engel. The room had a carved bed and a carved chest and embroidered sheets and a billowing white feather eiderdown, and the window framed the orchard and the spindly hay-huts poking up in the home meadow and Wild Emperor soaring above them. There are more impressive mountains, I know, but that one was mysteriously mine and I thought I would come back one day and climb it: the innkeeper said it was not a difficult climb.

Queer, but in the taxi I remembered the innkeeper too, although there was no reason why I should, because he was a remote sort of man for all his gross Roman head and comfortable paunch. Locked behind a wall of pride. Or sorrow, perhaps, since he had lost all four sons in the war. It was the daughters who looked after the guests and served the meals in the low white eating-room with the round stove of green majolica tiles. Big girls they were, with the miraculous clear skins of the mountain women and heavy sculptural bodies laced into embroidered bodices and full swinging skirts and flowing white lawn sleeves. They had a sort of large calm beauty that was so much a part of the eternal beauty of hill and stream, mountain and meadow, that it did not compel particular attention.

They came to see us in London the next year, and we did not recognize them in their fur coats and fashionable hats and tight shoes; they looked ugly and thick and lumpish and alien, dispossessed somehow. They belonged with St Florian and the cold pure glitter of Wild Emperor rising above the larch forests and the wooden eaves of the village houses and the slow soiled oxen with their soft stupid eyes and their panniers of bright pale wood. And they belonged to the Saturday night dances at the Rathaus, when all the girls wore their best embroideries and all the young men wore their lederhosen which should have looked silly but didn't, and even if they were restless young men sighing for far-off cities you would never have known it on Saturday night, when there was enough music and singing and dancing to make you reel without any wine at all, and at four o'clock in the morning you ate a great meal of sausage or steak and went on talking until the valley brimmed with light and Wild Emperor emerged all rose and gold in the dawn.

'But how could you leave all that?' I asked incredulously, remembering. The city was crowded, and smelling the way cities do at peak hour, and the faces were all looking harassed or irritable. Only the driver's face was warm as he turned to give me my change, and he looked about as happy as a young man can be. 'It's like gemütlich,' he said, as if he was letting me into a secret. 'It belongs in the heart, not the head.'

The Household Treasure

Mrs Dapp always wore a navy-blue felt hat with two rabbit-ear arrangements sticking up in front. It was not, in fact, a dowdy hat, because it gave an air of alertness, even perkiness, to her large, soft bulk. An ample woman, Mrs Dapp. Her given name was Mildred, and her name suited her too, like the rabbit-ear hat and the navy-blue coat with the fur tippet for outdoor wear, the sensible shoes, the lisle stockings carefully darned, the seemly dresses with long sleeves, three-button bodices, and matching belts with a little oblong buckle always riding high on her stomach.

Her aprons were of the large, plain, old-fashioned sort with crossed straps at the back and a square bib top, and she carried them—always freshly starched and ironed—in an imitation crocodile bag with two handles.

She was at least thirty years older than I was, and I appreciated that her twice-weekly ministrations—which she performed, as she said, only 'to oblige'—conferred upon me a totally unearned status.

This was in London sixteen years ago, and I was still too newly arrived, and too Australian also I expect, to accept unquestioningly the menial services of another human being or the title of 'madam', which made me giggle. I think most Australian women have this (perhaps) overweening pride in their own capability. They can cope with every domestic and social demand faster and more efficiently than any women in the world. That's true too, and their pride is justified on the whole. What is difficult is to accept that so much coping isn't always necessary, and that one needn't lose one's self-respect by relinquishing a few chores to somebody else willing to undertake them.

This is reasoning in retrospect. At the time I found it not entirely easy to adjust to such a novel situation. Actually an *un*easy situation. Because before Mrs Dapp there was May, who had a permanent sniffle in spite of layers of dropping woollens, fur-lined boots, gruel-coloured headscarves, and responded to my overtures of friendship with a profound suspicion that alternated with inquisitiveness and over-familiarity. I don't know whether she envied me or despised me. Certainly she resented me, and this made me so unhappy that I spoiled her outrageously, and guiltily too, because no matter how often I reminded myself that poor May had never had a chance I really believed that she hadn't ever deserved one.

May lived on the Fulham Road in lodgings with an unfortunate spouse who had never had a chance either apparently, and seemed unable to grasp one when it was offered him: he could never find employment 'to suit'. But they both made a weekly pilgrimage to the public baths for a ritual cleansing (and the water never hot enough, and the soap inadequate—'But you mustn't grumble, must you?') and May hung her curtains so that the lining faced inside the room and the pattern to the street, I presume for the sake of the neighbours.

When this dismal girl left me—of her own accord and with a disproportionately large guilt-offering: I was much too painfully involved with her to have nerved myself to a dismissal—I swore roundly that I would never be encumbered by a treasure again.

Yet there I was a month later, waiting on Mrs Dapp hand and foot, and wondering what I had done to deserve such luck. She said it was the flat that had decided her. She did like a nice parquet floor and french windows. She liked a fire in the basket grate too, a real one, not one of those nasty gas things, and I used to scuttle down to the basement before she arrived to lug up enough coal to keep her warm while she sipped her first pot of tea comfortably and sighed and smiled and let herself be coaxed into telling stories of her early days 'in service'.

'I'm sure these old stories don't interest you, madam. . . .'

But the stories interested madam so much—the Unas and Bessies and Alices and Herberts and Henrys below stairs, the mistresses and masters, the vicars and colonels and curates and younger sons, the larks on Thursday half-days, the constraint of evening prayers—that it was usually time for elevenses before we had fairly disentangled the delicate strands of relationship that had existed once (and to Mrs Dapp would exist for ever) between the 'higher orders' and the 'lower orders' and the indeterminate orders in between who slithered up and down the social scale at the whim of chance or opportunity as if it was a game of Snakes and Ladders. Mrs Dapp wasn't comfortable about indeterminate orders. She liked people to 'know their place'. She also liked two oatmeal biscuits with her elevenses, and two poached eggs for her lunch, which she insisted on eating in the kitchen, perhaps because she 'knew her place', or possibly because she liked to go through the morning papers undisturbed, with many little murmurs of distress, dismay, and disbelief at the state things had come to now that nobody seemed to know his proper place any more.

It didn't occur to me for a long time that my own place was equivocal. I waited on Mrs Dapp, I wooed Mrs Dapp, I fussed over Mrs Dapp, and I paid Mrs Dapp liberally for a little light dusting and arranging two days a week and a stream of reminiscence that was downright snobbish when you examined it, and should rightly have been anathema to my Australian spirit.

I suppose really she charmed me, and there is great value in that. What she had was authenticity. She was hallmarked. She was the genuine article. What I was to her I will never know. An ear, perhaps. A little appreciation. Perhaps she was stimulated by the fact that I was 'a colonial' and therefore unplaceable. Did she refer to me as 'my colonial lady', as a couple of years later Sevasti, authentic in her way as Mrs Dapp, would refer to me as 'my foreign lady', and shrug and roll her eyes up and spread her hands as though the phrase explained all of our family eccentricities.

Sevasti was indeed a treasure, and taught me many interesting things. I think we loved each other in our separate ways and wept at parting and kept 'in touch' for many years, long long after her successor, Zoe, had established herself as part of our lives and thoughts. But Zoe is a whole story, and I shall write it one day when it is far enough away in time to acquire perspective.

There is no moral in this tale of treasures, or if there is I haven't winkled it out yet. But I was thinking of them gratefully this morning, and thinking that I no longer feel ashamed at not being able to cope with everything myself. I no longer even want to cope with everything myself, so a bit of false pride in capability has been sloughed off somewhere.

Or perhaps I am just purring a little because lately, and for the first time since Zoe and I parted, I have again found a treasure. An Australian treasure. A gentle treasure. A responsible treasure who can do everything better than I can do. And if you think I am going to write any stories about her you are mistaken. Quite honestly, I wouldn't dare.

Requiem for a Spinster

Terry the postman gave us the news that Miss Young across the street had died. Peacefully, Terry said, in her sleep, with no warning illness beforehand. She was eighty-two. Terry said he would miss her very much.

In a special sort of way we will miss her too. Not that we ever knew her very well or intimately. Or perhaps we were intimate after all, in that Miss Young lived in this house for fifty years before we bought it, and when she moved from it at last, not being able to manage such a big place any more, she moved into rooms in the house immediately opposite. So she was always about, one way and another, a tall, thin, slightly stooped maiden lady, rather bird-like as to feature. Sharp, that is, and bright of eye. She was very neat in her dress, and she wore a going-out hat with a tall crown and a drooping brim, curiously chic, although this may have been accidental. Usually she carried a rolled music score, for she was a music teacher by profession.

The week before she died she was still giving music lessons. We were out in the front gardening one evening and from across the street a baritone voice boomed and faltered through one of those difficult sturdy songs that are required in every respectable baritone's repertoire. And we said, 'Miss Young's still at it,' and felt warmed and pleased that she was.

She used to give her music lessons in our bedroom, which was not a bedroom then, of course, but the front parlour. She was not a woman of what my grandmother always called 'means', at least I don't think she was, because as well as the music lessons she also rented some of the rooms in this old pile. Although that may have been for company. This would be a very big house to be alone in. Anyway, somebody told me one day that an Indonesian student used to sleep in what is now my study. That seems right, because she appeared to me to be the sort of woman who would take in students and spoil them a little and worry about them when they were out late: she liked young people. She herself told me that my study used to be the maid's room, but that, I suppose, was a very long time ago, when this house was a family house, as it is again now, and she lived here with her parents and brothers and sisters.

At least she said it was a family house, but I am guessing about the sexes and plurals of her family, and their precise relationships. Terry said that when she died she had no living relative. But I do know that one day, soon after we moved in here, I met her on the bus stop, with her usual music score rolled in her shopping bag, and her oddly chic hat drooping over her bright bird face, and she said so very kindly that she was glad the house was a family house again. It was always such a happy house then, she said, and she was sure it would be so again now.

I was very grateful for this, for indeed she might well have resented us bitterly, and been hurt and angry at the radical alterations we had made and were still making to the tall house that had been her home for so long.

Far from being hurt and angry she seemed to be delighted at the restoration, and interested in each and every alteration we had made. Before we moved in, while the workmen were still knocking down walls and changing doors and turning the pantry into a bathroom and the old laundry into part of a new living area, they said she used to stand by the old front fence every day for a while, watching, and then one day she ventured to come in, very quietly and politely, to see the work at closer quarters. After that she came in often, as if to supervise progress. She seemed to approve everything, they said, even the Japanese wallpapers, which might well have seemed extreme or odd, and she was quietly rapturous about the new bathrooms and the cooking bench and wall oven and louvred kitchen cupboards.

After we took up residence she didn't come in any more, and it is a sin of omission on my part that it was only very recently, meeting her again at the bus stop, that I asked her to tea and an inspection tour of the house, because it occurred to me that she never had seen the completed job or how we had arranged our living or what sort of things we lived with and I thought she had a perfect right to know. She couldn't accept the invitation just then because she was going away for a couple of weeks. When she came back, she said, she would be delighted, and she smiled and said wistfully that it was difficult to believe now that she had ever lived there.

But when she came back the weeks slipped past in busyness, and we must have taken different buses to the shopping centre because I didn't meet her, so the invitation languished for the want of my taking the trouble to walk across the street to extend it again, and it's too late now, and I'm sorry. Not sorry for Miss Young, but sorry for myself, because her approval would have given me pleasure, and I was pretty certain she would have approved.

I suppose she was buried from a discreet and impersonal funeral parlour, as people are now. It is silly and sentimental of me to wish there had been horses and plumes and a solemn coachman trailing black crepe ribands from his tall hat, and that her thin quiet body had been carried with grave ceremonial and many sweet-smelling flowers, if not from the house she lived in for so long, at least from the one directly opposite. Within sight of it anyway. But of course that sort of funeral belonged to the time of her youth, when thoughts of death in connection with herself would have been absurd.

What did she look like, the young Miss Young? Tall and slim and bright of eye, that much I know. Did she wear a blue sash? A sailor collar? A locket with a strand of hair and somebody's likeness? Whose? And why did she remain Miss Young? Did she love somebody once, and was disappointed in her affections? Somebody musical, somebody she met at a concert or a musical evening—here even, in this house, because there would have been many musical evenings. Or did her lover march away to war and never come back? Did she ever stand in the garden in the evenings, sodden with the scent of roses, and dream? Did she play over and over again on her piano in the front parlour one particular melody? When she taught little children were they substitutes for the children she didn't have?

How little I know about her. I work in the maid's room, shower in the pantry, sleep in the front parlour, eat in the laundry, and she's about somewhere, young Miss Young singing, old Miss Young rolling her music score and putting on her gloves. She's a bright ghost, and gentle. And of course we are intimate. In a way.

PLACES

Good-bye to a Skyline

The skyline is a mile and more away, and high, and all sorts of roads ascend to it, or descend from it, both straight and deviously winding, and the roads divide the bricks and gables and the unfunctional chimneypots and the shrubs and the fences and the lawns into dense dull blocks of red geometry with a bit of matchbox blue here and there for relief and the dark green blobs of foliage like lumps of teased and dyed kapok.

It isn't very interesting as a vista, but at least it is a vista and I always try to get some interest out of it, seeing I have to look at it most of the time.

The skyline is something else though. Perhaps because it is so high, and so far away, and there is so very much of it—miles and miles and miles—and so very much sky too, and all the shapes on the skyline are delineated as precisely against this enormous sky as paper cut-outs. All that prodigality of space and light is rich bounty in a city—the tender blues and the soft greys and the cotton-wool lumps of clouds drifting about the lightning flashes and thunderheads and rainbows and dawn greens and dusk gentians. In London in winter the sky was as thick and murky as stockpot and the sun swam in it sluggishly, a squashy crimson blob that never struggled higher than the rows of grimy rooftops. I admit that I thought it incredibly romantic at the time, but I can breathe here.

One of the charms of my skyline is its variety. It was wild country once, that's for certain. All these hills were wild. Sandstone. Scrub. Jungle. Up there, miles away, like upturned mops drying out above the domestic rooftops, there are three cabbage-palms in a row. I like them so much better than the poplars beyond, perhaps because they have this grim little air of defiance. They've held out against the taming of these hills. And that's good, because they are a kind of symbol. Convicts wove cabbage-tree fronds into hats for protection against the fierceness of a cruel and alien sun, their children, the currency lads and lasses, adopted the fashion—defiantly too, perhaps—and by the time of the gold-rushes the cabbage-tree hat had become the cult-emblem of colonial independence, of swagger, of spiritual freedom, of anti-imperialism, of individuality. Men would pay as much as ten pounds for a cabbage-tree hat, so prized had they become. Henry Lawson writes of men in the nineties wearing cabbage hats black with age, hats that had been handed down like heirlooms.

Queer how an article of wearing apparel can become a cult-symbol. Black leather jackets or bludger caps or faded jeans or gear or bowler hats. In Greece we wore unblocked woven straw hats and dipped them in the sea and rolled them up to work them into a floppy mushroom shape, and that was cult too. I imagine a cabbage-tree hat might have looked something like that.

Among neat red peaks of rooftops serrating the skyline there are some slate ones too—older, broader, with many more chimneys—and of course the blocks of home units towering up between, isolated yet and rawly new, but flying flags to announce readiness for inspection; their bare jutting balconies give them the look of tall ransacked chests of drawers. Every one of them has been built in the year I've lived here. I wonder how long the few broad slate roofs can last. And I wonder too about the huge concrete building that presents to me a three-quarter back-view of great blank uncompromisingly ugly planes. Ventilators squat along its irregular rooflines like rows of unpleasant fungoids; triffids perhaps, or something similar. I think it might be an old cinema but if it is then it must be on the arterial road that runs along that high ridge, and I have to travel along there frequently and I've never placed the cinema from the front. Perhaps it only exists from the back, or perhaps the front is now disguised as something else entirely. So many suburban cinemas have been turned into something else, or just closed up sadly. That's the end of an era too. Saturday night at the movies, new dress, newly set hair, best blue suit, brilliantine, box of chocolates, clumsy fumbling in the fly-toxed dark. 'He says I am the living image of Myrna Loy.' I've seen women all over the world who must have been told once that they were the living image of Myrna Loy, or Hedy Lamarr or Greer Garson or Ingrid Bergman or Veronica Lake. They were bravely keeping up the style and the eyebrows and the make-up all those years after Poignant in a way, the gallantry of blood-red nails and black-red mouths and the dresses draped in sarong style and a glitter of sequins on the shoulder straps.

When so much is changing—as it should, because change is life and growth and a city is a live thing—it is still comforting, reassuring in some way, to have a church on the skyline too. Not a very beautiful church, rather heavy Lutheran in character, but its spire and its little bell tower are classically aspiring and sometimes the moon at the full jerks up theatrically behind the cabbage-palms and seems to pause a moment to frame the spindly cross in a perfect halo of gold, and on Sunday the chimes are real bells, not electric. I love bells, and this church reminds me of Feldkirch in the Vorarlberg which I first saw on a Sunday morning in the snow and there were such neat plain heavy churches and sober Sunday congregations plain and black against the white, and big black open umbrellas clustered in repetitive curves and bells and bells and bells wild in the cold clean air. And once on a summer holiday in Cornwall I was initiated into the dangerous art of bellringing at the Mermaid Church at Zennor and shot up on the sally rope ignominiously and had to be hauled down by an hysterical vicar. Bells all over the world have told time, have summoned the faithful to prayer, have signalled birth and mating and death, and war and peril as well as rejoicing, and sanctuary as well as catastrophe.

I am looking at my skyline rather intently and in detail just now because I will be leaving it soon. We are moving over that high hill to the other side. There is always a lovely anticipation about going over a hill. Even though one really knows that one is just moving into another dense dull block of red geometry relieved by some blobby green clumps of foliage the skyline is going to be different again. On this one the towers will keep rising. By the time the little girls in their bright uniforms have passed out for ever from the exclusive school up the way the ridges and hills may look medieval. But I hope the bells still ring on Sundays through the blond brick canyons, and I hope those three cabbage-palms still stream against a windy sky. One needs some continuity as well as change.

The Jungle at the Bottom of the Street

On the last day of school holidays, when it was finally my turn to have our two small visitors—my ten-year-old son Jason and his younger cousin Terry—to myself for a whole afternoon, we considered plans with a very proper deliberation and gravity.

At least I did, because in this last year I have been separated from my youngest for school-term periods and so when I see him I am inclined to marvel at the perfectly natural evidences of growth and change: he has put on new layers of fresh bark while I was not watching and is becoming, I suppose, something else. Also, it was their last day, and I was formal with a sense of occasion. I must say they were very graceful about my suggestions, possibly out of that grave and beautiful courtesy which children sometimes surprisingly display towards their elders, or possibly because they had been just about everywhere already and were so gorged with treats that they couldn't have cared less where we went.

What is curious is that I have been looking down from my balcony for a whole year now at an inlet of the harbour below and for a whole year I have noted and catalogued mentally the mood and the colour and the light on the water against the monotonous darkish scrub of bush that fringes it and the unhealed scars of the new developments—although at dawn and dusk these new developments take on a queer oriental quality with brush flicks of light angled along their tiled roofs and the stark planes of their geometry softened by wreaths of harbour mist. And for a whole year I have said to myself that one day I must walk down there and explore a bit.

Agreeably the children said they would like to do that too if I would—and I was humbled slightly by realizing that they knew perfectly well that they were giving me the treat—and so on a spring afternoon we loitered, the three of us, down the suburban hill along the ordinary bus route between the solid brick bungalows set in their groomed spring shrubberies and the not-so-solid blocks of new units set in bare clay just tufting here and there with lawn grass and spindly labelled sticks that will no doubt turn into shrubberies eventually,

98

and we looked over fences and into windows when we could and I noted that the bungalows had frilly curtains and the units straight 'contemporary' ones and I thought how neatly boxed people are these days and then I thought of Rilke walking through the streets of Paris and writing such memorable and moving words about one decayed house that had called to him with such persistent melancholy, and then I shrugged mentally and thought that if there was nothing romantic about these streets there was solidity and prosperity and order and man had established himself quite well and decently on these hills against some fairly terrific odds and was here to say.

And it was just then, still high high above the harbour inlet that was our goal, that we crossed the main road (observing our traffic drill) and through a flame of coral trees and walked into a jungle.

I have never been familiar with the real bush. I grew up in pastoral country and have lived my adult life in cities mostly, so the bush mystique has never touched me. Until now, that is, because it seems a very strange and magic thing to have a jungle at the bottom of the street and to have had it there all along and not to have known about it.

It is a vertiginous jungle, and it plummets in a deep hoop from the busy road down and down and down to a shaved oval of grass that I suppose is used for sport, although how people get down to it is a mystery. Indeed how the grass is kept so velvet smooth is a mystery. We couldn't find any tracks at all, and that was all the more exciting because we had to slither and slip and slide down precipitous slopes of ancient sandstone, clutching creepers and branches to brake our headlong descent, and there was no sky any more and no sound of traffic and we were plunging down through a primeval world that could not have filled me with more wonder if I had been Alice falling down the rabbit hole.

I have been in forests, great forests, Sherwood and Burnham Beeches, and the Black Forest where the wolves still prowl, and the spruce forests that press in on the Fern Pass in Austria, and I have been awed and made sombre by so much majesty.

But this was something else. Older. More poignant in some way. And more formidable because so indifferent. It was dark and cool and quiet as all leafy places are but dry with a curious dryness of air and scent that was bitter and aromatic and the leafiness was harsh and spiky and even inimical and the forms of tree and bush and plant and leaf were primitive forms and the flowers that sparked so palely ragged among the grey down-drooping sickled leaves or the malevolent spikes that were not even leaves were like the first tentative sketches of flowers, not flowers at all yet but strange little desperate sparkings and explosions of something not yet desire but poignant beyond all telling because the desire was there. And once the children trying to brake me tumbled us all together into a bed of leaves dried as hard and fine as razors and smelling of ants, and at eye level, erect and triumphant on a sandstone outcrop, a spike of saffron rock-lily glimmered victorious.

At the very bottom we plunged out of the jungle into a wall, and this was the wall of a building in ruin with around it a series of strange concrete ramps like fortifications pierced regularly with circular shafts and grown over with more wild nasturtiums than I have ever seen together in my life before. There were millions of nasturtiums. Billions of nasturtiums. Cascades and carpets of nasturtiums shouting their noisy brilliance among the silk-fine circles of their veined leaves, succulent green and as big as dinner plates. As though the nasturtiums had decided to take over the whole world, in spite of that shaved oval of grass below them, and beyond it, still a long way away, the harbour inlet and the civilized motor cruisers and the pretty painted yachts rocking on a diamond dusting of sunlight.

Terry said, over armfuls of orange and gold and blazing scarlet: 'There's a waterfall.' And of course there was, but very high, on the opposite side of the hoop which we had descended. So we had to climb to it, they like the wild healthy young animals they are in great bounds and leaps, laughing down at me through the spikes and thorns and sparking bush flowers from huge gold buttresses of rock where they stood poised for flight, spilling all around them wilting nasturtiums that glowed on the golden rock like scraps of torn and brilliant silk.

And I looked for . . . what? Fossils and wings and delicate bones embedded in the ancient rocks. Casts of wormburrows, tracks of crawling things, marks of a raindrop, a suncrack, a footprint so old that its origin could not even be surmised. And yet I needed none of these proofs and evidence to tell me how old this place was. I sat very still in that primeval stillness and I knew all right.

We found the waterfall, and it might well have been a sewer outlet, just as the magical ruin down below might well have been the heart of some sewerage system.

But walking up the suburban street again, scratched and bruised and scarred and scored with our adventure and still quiet with the spell on us, I looked again at the bungalows and the crust of asphalt and brick and I knew that it was only that—a crust. In the immensity of time the works of our hands are the most transient of all.

Pilgrimage to a Possibility

This time it was quite different to the glimpse one gets whizzing over the Bridge, or the slow pan of skeletonic sails billowing gauntly beyond an outward-bound liner still tied to the dock by thousands of coloured streamers. Or even coming over from the Northside by ferry and cringing momentarily under those Hokusai wave-peaks—petrified, one knows, but apparently about to break and hurl the flotsam of cranes and gantries and girders contemptuously into the harbour. (It nearly happened once, and every newspaper reported it with glee.)

This time I was privileged, along with forty others, to make a proper pilgrimage, with informed guides and instructors, around whom we gathered in little restless groups, straining to hear and interpret difficult gutturals, or whirled and eddied indecisively. Should one linger here outside, or follow the purposeful path of the group ahead? Take notes? It was too hot for an autumn day. The harbour was clarion blue and the sky piercingly tender; a briny day of salt and sun that Sydney puts on sometimes like a bit of stored finery, all negligently gorgeous, just to remind you.

How on earth was one to comprehend that vast littered dusty area through which we picked our way with teetering steps and hop-skip-jumps over puddles, cables, torn cement bags, crumpled soft-drink cartons, old pie-crusts, and other objects that it would be better, perhaps, not to investigate? The sea was lapping and gurgling close and the dust scuffed up and settled back on us, making mud-packs on faces already sweaty. Gentlemen removed their jackets. Ladies mopped up. Everyone, vociferously, marvelled.

The explanations did nothing to help evaluate the immensity of the structure that curved its gigantic wave-peaks over us, or even the Cyclopean pre-cast parts that had only looked like building blocks, or bits of a Meccano set, from the distance of the Bridge, but here dwarfed us: we had all shrunk to Alice size and needed a bite on the other side of the mushroom to re-establish confidence in ourselves. The backs of our necks ached from straining up at the sails. After even five minutes the damn things were dominating us.

Yet the stairway, even if it was planned for gods or giants (and I suspect it was), was recognizable as a stairway. Reassuring, somehow. Processional. Aspiring. Even in the rough it led from earth to sky and made the concrete sails accessible. I don't know why a beautiful building in the making has this haunting quality of linking past and future. It is like seeing an old dream change its shape, as old dreams do, and turn into something else.

Mungo MacCallum, in *Nation*, wrote a piece about this Opera House called 'Drawing a Dream'. I can only say *Credo, Credo*. I Believe, I Believe. (Although, in fact, I don't like opera at all, having had far too much of it in my childhood and still getting wildly giggly about flossied-up people singing 'Pass me the salt, please,' or 'Look! Look! Who comes?')

But I thought—no, didn't think, just left myself open and expectant for the unprecedented—on Bennelong Point, with a kink in the back of my neck from looking up at the sails of the Opera House—no, didn't think, just remembered.

And there was this stairway that I saw once, antique, majestic, and golden against a golden escarpment of rock in the wildest shepherd country I have ever known. It rose from nowhere to nowhere because nothing else had survived, no motive or reason, no portico, entrance gate, parking lot for chariots, or, at the top, a palace or temple or fortress or citadel or keep. Just this flight (and it is a proper word) of hewn stone stairs that rose from a shepherd's grazing plot and ended abruptly in the sky. Jacob's Ladder? Stairway to Heaven? We toiled up, playing princes and priests and barbarians, and looked down on a column half buried across two fields: hens were roosting on it, and children with goat bells tied by leather thongs around their necks walked the length of it, arms out-balanced like tight-rope walkers. Later we scuffed the hard earth scummed with goat droppings and found mosaics.

Inside the Opera House it was cold. Raw concrete cold and more puddles. Overwhelming still. The pilgrims milled along unfinished corridors, wearing purple I suspect, and seeking some certain certainty. The explanations went on, inaudible except to the earnest few who had glued themselves to officialdom: figures were whispered over awed shoulders ('Look! There's an owl on it!'): so many tons, hundreds of tons, thousands of tons.

Perhaps, if one blinked twice, there would be the wild brambles of blackberry and the fig-trees growing up from the concrete, and the goats and the roosting hens. Already the reverence was almost suffocating. And time gets terribly twisted.

Suppose—just suppose—that one had been on just such an inspection tour of the Pyramid of Cheops, or the Hanging Gardens of Babylon, or the Temple of Artemis at Ephesus, or the Colossus of Rhodes, or the Mausoleum at Halicarnassus, or the statue of Zeus at Olympia, or the Pharos at Alexandria. All of those wonders of the world were built in their time. So is this. It took computers to work out that these fantastic shapes are based on a simple curve. Somebody invented a safety pin once. And a mousetrap.

Suppose we think of the Pantheon. Suppose we think of Brunelleschi and the great dome of Florence. Suppose we think of Michelangelo and St Peter's. ('If the plan of the construction was changed as some envious people are trying to do it would be the same as if I had done nothing at all.')

Suppose we even think of the Parthenon. Ictinus and Callicrates, in the golden age of Pericles and ten whole years between the agreement and the actual commencement of work on those saffron columns that meet (if you could follow them) at a vanishing point beyond your sight, as you trudge around in the dust.

Suppose we think of the enigmatic monoliths of Stonehenge? The vaulted domes of the Mycenaean kings? The Great Wall of China? Somebody, somewhere, once, to the end of perfection and above the yappings of the mob, spent years and years and years working out the complicated mathematics of simplicity. Who made the first eye in the first needle?

The theory of relativity is simple. Once you've been told about it. So is the theory of the Opera House (but could we please have plays instead?—I mean, rather than Robin Hood on Ice, or the latest M.G.M. spectacle).

There was a man called Erostratus, once, and he burnt down the Temple of Artemis at Ephesus (one of the wonders of the ancient world, you remember) as a way, he said, of getting his name in the history books. No one remembers the name of the architect.

I still thought, driving back across the Bridge, Oh, it is beautiful, beautiful, beautiful.

103

The Private Pleasures of a Public Market

'Excuse me, lady! Outa da way, please! Outa da way!'

He was young and swarthy, with shoulders and arms built through generations for labour. Over his hairy Esau pelt he wore ragged shorts and a huge leather apron studded intricately with metal and hung about with wicked-looking curved picks. On his head a blue beret, worn jauntily. And as my friend Toni and I leapt for safety (or even survival) from his hurtling cart of tomato crates he grinned at us with that joyful unselfconsciousness of a Mediterranean male whose inalienable right it is to appraise every female he encounters—of whatever age or condition.

(I have a woman friend who has lived overseas for many years and she says that this is what she misses most in Australia, aside from somewhere to go for a holiday. She doesn't want to be pinched, particularly, but she feels deprived of that glint of recognition in a passing eye, the gallant salute from male to female: Madam, we are comrades and conspirators, and you know it, ma'am, as well as I do.)

And: 'Out of the way! Out of the way!' (or its equivalent) they yelled in urgent accents of Italian, Greek, Yugoslav, Chinese, and even Australian, as we dodged around piled trucks pulling in from places where still things grow in spite of the drought, stacks of aromatic crates, or jumped hastily from the onslaught of those lethal handcarts—dangerously stacked with fruit and vegetables or more dangerously empty—that shot out from every market aperture with the obvious intent of crushing us down into the mulched cabbage leaves and the trodden mint and parsley that bore every evidence of a progress passing.

What was exciting was that we were involved in the progress, shouting in triumph as it passed, as though these huge market vaults were really Persepolis. It was terribly early in the morning, and every single leaf, blade, shoot, root or bulb had the dew or the earth on it.

I have always thought an early morning market to be a celebration. Demeter, who is the earth and the fruits of it. Harvest festivals. Corn

Kings and Spring Queens. Poetry—'Season of mists and mellow fruitfulness'. We survive on the peasantry of grass (those of us who are lucky enough) and the green of chlorophyll is nothing less than the colour of life. We all exist by that cool and cleanly and most commendable virtue of green. (My husband tells of a Chinese army that lived by every soldier getting down on his hands and knees and eating grass and roots.)

This early morning market was a proper celebration. As proper as Covent Garden or the Portobello Road or Never-on-Sunday Piraeus or co-operative Omsk or Tomsk or dear old unco-operative Athens or even, I suppose, a Chinese field where ragged soldiers grubbed around on hands and knees for a grass blade in lieu of wages and commissariat. If the incense smelled predominantly of crushed cabbage and sweaty leather there were wafts of herbs and spices too, and under that vast ecclesiastical roof whole pockets of air that were sodden with the scent of roses (pink and yellow and red and white and tangerine, and every shade of every colour in between).

And all this abundance, this prodigality of leaf, shoot, bulb and tuber, piled up in scented mountains under the echoing roof of this shouting, tumultuous market, came out of the Russian Steppes, out of the Caucasus, out of the Ice Ages that had frozen everything living everywhere else on earth. Plants came out of Siberian forests and high Asiatic plateaux. They filled Europe, they invaded all environments, they called to their aid ancient winds and modern insects and even birds to pollinate them. They were as ingenious and indomitable as man was, and wherever he has gone they have been there too in some form or other, ready for the plough and the spade and the harvesting.

'Do you think,' said Toni conspiratorially, 'that the Mafia are abroad?' (One is inclined to say 'abroad' instead of 'around' in these scented circumstances: there is a marvellous expectation of the Borgias, or their modern equivalent, sliding in to buy strange herbs for dubious purposes.)

I said I thought they were, and we tracked them down through crates and crates of pink tomatoes and mounds of celery and spinach and prodigal heaps of cabbages like green roses and the more intensely greenly deliciously tight curls of broccoli and tortuously spiked Chinese cucumbers and fresh bean shoots and weird mandrake roots that a little smiling Chinese man said were ginger and the whitely gleaming stalks of spring onions. The greens predominated but the earth was there too. You felt you were being offered your fill—thorn and leaf and succulent cell and indomitable tuber.

We didn't find the Mafia, but we found a swooping penguin flock of nuns, all black and white and with their sleeves rolled up and sugar sacks over their shoulders, bargaining with intense and concentrated delight over pumpkins and marrows and black-purple aubergines and red peppers and green peppers and lettuces all crisp and morning-curled and little pink radishes done up like Victorian posies.

'Out of the way! Out of the way!' the voices yelled, and two nuns jumped, black and white and beautifully hooded, spilling all around them spikes of scarlet gladioli and frantically red roses and little tender bunches of maidenhair fern. (And I wanted desperately for Elaine Haxton or Cedric Flower to be there to record it.)

Toni and I bought garlic in white bundles with the straw stems plaited. We bought Chinese cucumbers, not knowing quite how we were going to eat them but not caring. We were given a crate of lusciously pink tomatoes by my landlord, who operates joyously around those parts. We bought roses of a wicked Inca red, and virginal white daisies and little yellow pom-pom dahlias, and we looked and smelled and sniffed until we were quite intoxicated and fell about saying: 'Why shouldn't I buy this?' or: 'I think I want that,' and each saying to the other: 'Now, really.'

What we really wanted, I think, was to capture the penguin nuns for ever, and we wanted to buy guinea pigs, and white rats with pink eyes, and a beautiful mottled snake as thick as a motor tyre or a garden hose, and a Boxer pup who was yearning in spite of his pedigree, and a white rabbit who looked at us with such a boulevardier insouciance that we knew he'd been on stage at some time.

What we did was to buy hamburgers and coffee in some crummy market joint that was patronized by the men in leather aprons and served by Toulouse-Lautrec ladies in incredible hairdos, and around us everything was still roaring with green life and smelling of cabbages.

There are festivals going on all over Australia now. Perth, and Melbourne, and Adelaide. Culture is being served up, and Royalty, and Greek drama, and Russian poetry, and negro jazz in white ties and tails.

Toni and I, being low-life prone, will take the festival of an early morning market. Any time.

Living in a Neighbourhood

Practically every popular Greek song I know that doesn't deal with the boy-girl bit, either straight or by way of little cypress trees or spring swallows or white ribbons or some other similar device, has as its subject, nostalgic and yearning, the neighbourhood.

No other neighbourhood is or ever can be the same as the one in which one grew up, or lives now, or will return to after exile, or grow old in, or whatever. No other people could be so friendly, no streets so gay, no corner tavern so lively, no music so enchanting, no girls so pretty, no friends so true. And like that. That is what the song 'Never on Sunday' is all about, whatever the simpering English version says, and when Melina Mercouri sings that song she is singing praise of the Piraeus and the harbour and the markets and the football team and the people in the streets and the sailors' dives and her undying loyalty to all this, her neighbourhood, vibrant and squalid and spellbinding.

London, although rather more reticent about putting it to music, has something of that feeling too. Somebody once said that London is less a city than a series of villages, and if you live there for a while you do enter into an emotional relationship with your own village, which might be Chelsea or Soho or Pimlico or Notting Hill Gate or Mayfair or Rotherhithe or Putney or Limehouse or Bloomsbury or Hampstead. Each of these neighbourhoods has its own distinct personality and quality. Each is strongly individual, and its individuality partakes of the people who live in the neighbourhood plus the mixed flavours of its commercial amenities—the bookshops and the barrows and the bakeries and the fishmongers and the gentlemen's hatters and the pubs and the tea shoppes and the espresso bars and the rooms to let and whether the landladies accept coloured gentlemen or not. A neighbourhood is nannies in a square and intense young students and gaudy chieftains in coffee bars and street-corner prophets hurling denunciations and loose ladies being asked to move on and successful actors being seen and decayed and slightly dotty gentlewomen pricing haddock and exquisite women emerging from converted mews to sweep away in silver Jags, and whether a neighbourhood is going down or going up it has a certain intensity in atmosphere and a coherence in spite of its fluidity. The street-corner prophet and the decrepit newsboy and the bird-watcher go on for ever, as does the pub philosopher who knew it when.

I expect this is true of Australia too, or the urban part of it as distinct from the suburban, where I think it would be straining romanticism (even though elastic) just too far to expect anybody to be passionately attached to a service station or a drive-in or a super-market or a chain store or even a bowling alley or a Leagues Club.

Having just moved into a neighbourhood (the first approximation of one I've lived in since I came back to Australia), I've been loitering about in it this last week or so, idling down streets, mooching in shops, listening in on conversations. Getting acquainted, as it were.

It seems to have a quirky sort of character. A blend of the raffish and the smart, a mixture which I, personally, find piquant and attractive.

There are, naturally, the supermarket and the several service stations, which the neighbourhood wears with the air, at once desperately uncertain and desperately gallant, of somebody trying on a false hair-piece for the first time. The face-lift and the false eyelashes may follow, but there isn't enough confidence for them as yet. The old family grocer is still in business, and many other old family businesses too. The haberdasher does *not* sell textured stockings, and I suspect never will, the florist makes up Victorian posies and also corsages of carnations or orchids, there is a tailor whose window is populated by very ancient dummies clad in tacked half-garments of uncertain period and who will carry out repair, make ladies' costumes, or convert double-breasted suits into single, with the new narrow lapel. There are two dressmakers who both create formal wear, ladies' own material made up (or created). There is ironmongery and carpentry and shoe-repairing and laundry and electrical goods, and there are a surprising number of other old family businesses boarded up and looking desolate and flyblown, in limbo as it were, until their metamorphosis into smart boutique or pricy antique shop.

There are lots of those, and interior decorators, and glittering pharmacies and purple-draped hairdressing establishments specializing in colour rinses and wiglets, but there are also terribly exciting and cluttered junk shops and an auctioneer's saleroom which is a treasure trove of ancestral discards and very jolly and hectic on auctioneering days. Every greengrocer's and every milk-bar is attended by quick and voluble Latins with eyes the colour of Kalamata olives, and there are innumerable delicatessen aromatic with mysterious bundles of sausages and fragrant with cheeses and lovely bread smells and positively vibrating with the hum of foreign conversations, which lack restraint. There are two Chinese restaurants, with take-away meals, which should be very convenient while I am still apprehensive about using my science-fiction electric cooker, and a Spanish one that looks too smart to just drop in on. There is a Polish furniture-maker who is a real craftsman, and a folk-singing joint for my adolescent young, and a music-hall where I can't afford to go, and a butcher's shop where, to my astonishment and delight, I was served by somebody I went to school with, all dressed up in a blue apron and looking most unlikely.

Then there is a gunsmith whose shop is pure James Bond and who covets my eighteenth-century pistols which I acquired a little dubiously and have entrusted to him for cleaning, and where I have a discreditable but intolerably heady urge to go and practise target shooting. This is closely linked to the wistfulness I feel wandering around the second-hand car dealer's among all the low-slung beauties of decent vintage that I have never owned and have secretly yearned for as much as everybody else with a feeling for style. Perhaps, in this life, one should cultivate frivolity as well as endurance.

And there is the corner pub. Not just a corner pub, although it looks conventionally hideous enough on its street sides. But behind it there is a garden with tables and benches and geraniums blazing away and a wonderful oak-tree and it is just about the most civilized public place I've found in a year and I shall have a lot of pleasure there sitting in the sun at a slatted table peeling its paint and drinking very cold beer and making out shopping lists and watching the regulars come and go.

Because the neighbourhood is its inhabitants too, and these are colourful, mixed, not easily slotted into one category. There are the housewives, stopping by to meet after a morning's shopping, and there are the selfconscious week-end customers in carefully careless informal wear with the right accessories of poodles or bull terriers, there are workmen in overalls and foreign wanderers carrying airline bags and nervously suspicious expressions. There are the beautiful young, not yet in one another's arms but working up to it, and there are the oldest of the regulars, stubborn, isolated, and resentful, who knew it when.

There is also, in my street, an old brick cottage with two peppercorn trees in front and a rocking horse on the verandah, and further down there are four small children who say hello to me now as I pass by.

All in all, I have the feeling that I am living in a neighbourhood.

PROBLEMS

Progress

'Progress is a wonderful thing,' she said wistfully if somewhat dubiously, watching the Nappy Wash van pull in at a house down the street.

'Everything's made so easy for them nowadays,' she said. No doubt remembering the series of pails for soaking and rinsing and the gas copper and the fiddling little messes of hand-mashed vegetables and steamed brains and the prunes burnt and smelling to high heaven in the saucepan while you rushed out to rescue the nappies from the rain.

It doesn't seem that long ago really. The age before Baby Foods became a business, let alone Pet Foods. The age before aerosol packs and Mr Omo and supermarkets and department stores rivalling Babylon and R.S.L. clubs outdoing it and all-electric kitchens and three-car garages and T.V. sets and T.V. dinners and pace-and-trend-and-jet-setting and expressways and the Gold Coast and Trip Books and computerized services and miracle drugs and miracle cleaners and Mini-Care and Easy-Terms and Built-In and Additives and pre-mixed and pre-sealed and pre-frozen and pre-thought everything. And home units.

Progress progresses more recklessly every day and every month and every year. The thing about it, though, is that it doesn't seem to progress at a uniform pace over the whole range of weal and woe of the citizens who are supposed to benefit by it. Because citizens are affected in their daily lives by more than a technology galloping away triumphantly to ever more marvellous discoveries. They are affected by the pace of progress in education, in political organization, in religious and philosophical thought, in legal codes, in emotional focus, in public and social services.

It is very progressive and forward-looking and pace-setting to live in a new house incorporating the latest in laminations, metal alloys, and miracle plastics, but if the house is plonked down on an unsewered estate twenty miles of travel away from the breadwinner's place of business, ten miles from the children's school, and five miles from the nearest shopping centre (with or without a progressive supermarket), it is problematical how much one is actually benefiting from progress. Particularly if both partners have to work to maintain the pace-setting nest, or if one goes mad with boredom while the other goes mad with tension, and the septic goes wrong anyway.

All sorts of theoretical progress has been made in the education of our children, but in practice free education is anything but, and if the children are to benefit from new equipment, learning aids, libraries, music-rooms, televized courses and all, their parents have to cough up the money eventually. Classrooms have a permanent air of the temporary, buildings are mostly antiquated, inadequate, and bursting at the crummy old seams. A Mirage jet crashes—two million dollars up the spout—and one thinks, with sad resignation: 'That's progress for you. There's another high school gone.'

And talking of aeroplanes, the progress in the high skyways is nothing short of marvellous. It is dizzying to think how quickly and painlessly you can hurtle about the air from city to city and country to country in a nice plastic seat with All Found on a plastic tray. The difficulty lies not in the air, but on the ground, because for some reason the faster you can gad about up there, the slower it becomes down here to get to the airport in time to join the jet-setters, or to get to your actual destination at the other end after you have been progressively catapulted through the atmosphere in record time. The time of transport to and from airports can be longer than the time of flight: one is apt to arrive late, fractious, and de-exhilarated.

Cars have tigers in their tanks and citizens at the wheels so forward-looking that they have practically renounced the use of their legs and the traffic snarls become more formidably tangled and the tankfuls of tigers get all ravelled up into proper cats' cradles and the forward-lookers get all ravelled up in frustration and fury, and one can see no solution to this sort of progress excepting perhaps that they might all melt one day into pools and pools and pools of butter like the tigers in *Little Black Sambo* and the Ministry of Transport could feed on pancakes for ever and ever. Although I don't think there are many people left who can remember how to actually mix pancakes, any more than they can remember motoring just for the pleasure of it.

As progress progresses apace and ever pacier our majestic moral institutions, evolved through deeper thought and longer time, lag sadly in contrast. The legal code is left lumbering behind like an outdistanced behemoth, religion flutters ineffectually and probably suicidally over the flickering flame of the past, emotional focus blurs

114

on such intricate subjects as morals, spirituality, and even reason, explodes into psychedelic spots, and re-settles more comfortably on the television and the dollar.

Progress progresses, the hives of the cities buzz with more furious activity, and public services bog down or are hastily amputated.

Fares go up but public transport becomes more nightmarish than ever. Postage goes up and postal deliveries are cut to once a day only providing there isn't a strike this week. Hospital fees go up and the distraught sick wait helplessly for the privilege of a bed. Wise out-patients allow for half of a day, the completed front of a knitted sweater, the first volume of *War and Peace,* twenty back numbers of *The Women's Weekly,* a whole packet of cigarettes, or a long letter to Auntie Val, to stay their urgency for progressive medical advice or miraculous drugs.

Rates go up and garbage collectors loftily decline to remove anything than cannot be contained in a single regulation tin. Wastepaper collections cease altogether. Bank charges go up but banks are shut on Saturday morning.

Wages go up and workmen can't be bothered to turn up and the cost of living goes up higher than wages and everything costs more for less and for the life of me I don't know quite where progress is progressing but I know I can't keep up with it.

'It's a wonderful thing all right,' she said, and we had a nice long nostalgic talk about the lost pleasures of Friday-night shopping.

On Gathering No Moss

All right, so the Moss family from England stayed here for forty hours, loathed it, and got the first available plane out. I can't for the life of me see what all the fuss is about. Why shouldn't they get right out if they could afford it. They conducted themselves with dignity, avoided publicity, didn't want to talk about it, didn't whinge about it, and didn't leave a forwarding address.

It all reminds me very much of a little poem that a friend recited to me recently, which goes something like this (I hope I've got it right):

La Pérouse sailed into Botany Bay,
Said: 'Merde, alors!'
And sailed away.

Why is everybody so shocked? Who wouldn't get out of Melbourne in a heatwave if he possibly could? Personally I admire them for their strength of character and immediacy of decision. And envy them desperately for their power to act on that decision. I still have the record of a postcard I wrote to a friend at the end of my first week as a migrant in Greece, and it makes pretty sad reading. 'Language impossible,' it says. 'Children cretinous. Contacts non-existent or unavailable. Wish you were here. Wish anybody was here. Can't think why we are.' But most people, including myself, just have to put up with the place in which they find themselves, mistake or no mistake. I remember that the first and only time I ever went to Surfers Paradise for a holiday I sat down in a gutter and howled. But as the holiday had been paid for in advance, and as it had cost what was then to me a great deal, both in money and organization, I felt I had to stick it out, and stick it out I did for two unspeakably hideous weeks, when the sensible thing would have been to cut my losses and turn right round and head for home.

I've been marooned in other places too, through errors in judgment, false propaganda, or lack of the fare out, so I can really appreciate the resolute action of the family Moss.

I have an idea that the shockingness of their action lies in the fact that we go on deluding ourselves about the desirability of Australia as a place of domicile and a way of life and expect that migrants should be grateful for the opportunity of sharing it—not as equals, indeed, because that would be going too far, but somewhere on the fringes of the Great Oz Society, in a crowded slum in the inner suburbs or a still unsewered estate twenty miles out, certainly way beyond range of all those lovely golden beaches that are shown in the migrant brochures, and probably without shops or schools.

'They don't try to fit in,' a commercial traveller said to me in some anger. 'It's their business to fit in to our way, not for us to fit in with theirs.'

I asked whether, if he found himself in a European country, he would adopt the habits and customs of Europeans, and he said that was different.

It probably takes a migrant five or six or ten years, starting from scratch, to catch up to the general state of affluence that prevails, that is, to live in the same sort of house and own the same sort of things that the general population takes for granted. It may take longer. It may take a whole generation. And while he is catching up—I suppose even after he has caught up—he will be prey to many nostalgias, many uncertainties, perhaps many regrets. (I know this to be true, because even after three and a half years, and as a home-grown migrant anyway, I am still catching up.)

And it is more than material things. It is more than language even. It is a social uneasiness, a necessity to clue in, to adjust to a different pattern of life. There is a doctor in Melbourne who runs a clinic that deals mostly with Mediterranean migrants, and this doctor finds that a great proportion of their ills and ailments and muscular pains are due, finally, to the fact that they are missing their accustomed siesta. If your body expects and takes for granted rest in the early afternoon it is going to protest at being deprived of it and forced unwillingly into action. Actually, to digress for a moment, I do believe that it would be sensible for all Australians to adopt the custom of the siesta, particularly in the tropics, where only a puritanical stubbornness or sheer lunacy can possibly explain the insistence on sweltering toil in the very worst part of the day. You can't tell me that anyone could possibly work well in such conditions. How much more sensible to start two hours earlier in the morning, declare the wretched shank of the day closed, and take up for an hour or so late in the afternoon, rested and refreshed. (Here I will confess to taking my telephone off the hook between the hours of two and four in the afternoon, and trying to ignore the doorknocker: I am not always successful, because some people are so incredibly insistent on being seen and heard, whether one wants to see them and hear them or not, but they aren't my favourite people; my friends are considerate enough to avoid me for those two hours.)

There was a time when Australia must have seemed like the promised land to thousands of poor Europeans seeking hope and sanctuary. I don't believe that is true any more. The standard of living in their own countries has risen, and is rising, to such an extent that they are probably as well off materially staying where they are as they would be by trekking across the world, and a good deal better off emotionally in their own familiar social patterns, which are generally richer and more colourful and more satisfying than anything we can provide.

I always ask migrants what they miss most, and most of them miss precisely those familiarities of their accustomed social patterns. That is to say, the corner pub, the street market, the favourite café where one meets one's friends, the sidewalk table where one sits and watches the world pass by, the evening promenade, the ceremoniousness of old rituals, the feasting and the singing and the dancing, the music and the wine.

'The life,' they have often said to me. 'I miss the life. There is no life here.' And I understand that very clearly, because I too miss the life, and it has often occurred to me in the last three years that I am infinitely more isolated and more completely marooned in an Australian suburb than I ever was on a poor and primitive Greek island. Materially I am much better off, but spiritually I sometimes feel impoverished of the gaiety and social ease of Mediterranean living. (Yes, and I know that if I don't like it I can go right back where I came from.)

One Viennese girl told me that what she missed most was somewhere to go for holidays, and I thought this an odd one until I had considered it for a bit. She said that every place where she thought she might like to go was so very far and so very expensive, and in any case the only change was in the temperature and the scenery: the language, the customs, the food, the clothes, the very people, were standard from one end of the country to the other, and she found nothing very novel or stimulating in meeting the same people in a slightly different setting. She was not, I hasten to add, complaining, because she was doing very well in Australia and didn't regret Europe all that much, but she said it used to be such fun to take a train and in a couple of hours be in a completely different country with different costumes and different customs and different language and different food, and she found great refreshment and spiritual replenishment for very little money and in very little time. I could not but agree.

And I suppose I should say here that I am not complaining either, but I do think that the time has come for all of us to stop being complacent about the Great Australian Way of Life, and the Great Australian Climate, and try to understand that it might not suit everybody in the world. In fact, they might prefer the older, more potent societies from which they came. La Perouse, evidently, had not a doubt about it.

A View Through the Punch Holes

A current source of fascination to me and mine is a gas bill, delivered to us, I suspect, by accident rather than design, and demanding payment of the sum of sixteen cents.

It offers, in electronic grey-black on tasteful Op-art grey-blue, a most incredibly elaborate series of computations to support this demand. If you hold it up to the light the detachable portion looks like a skyscraper at dusk with the windows lit erratically. Or, even more perhaps, a piece clipped off a pianola roll. *DO NOT PIN OR MUTILATE THIS PO* (punch hole punch hole) *O* (punch hole punch hole punch hole punch hole) it warns enigmatically and an arrow points emphatically at nothing whatever—at least nothing I can see.

I think it is spooky. Particularly as we don't use gas, I mean. Not that I've anything against gas, I hasten to add, but circumstances just happened to land us up with all electric and we are pretty craven about circumstances. But even if we did use gas I think I would hesitate before making out a cheque or money order as coldly directed just for the sum of sixteen cents. The amount of clerical work seems disproportionate; also, in the case of a money order, our nearest post office is a mile away. Then, too, if one is not to bend the card, a special size envelope is needed. Plus a stamp. The whole thing is obviously uneconomic.

Perhaps one is actually meant to try it out on an old Aeolian Stroud? What would it play, I wonder? 'Tramp, Tramp, Tramp, the Boys are Marching'? Or 'Nearer, My God, to Thee'?

Or, if one did go to all the bother of cheque or money order plus special envelope plus stamp just suppose one succumbed to an irresistible urge to wilfully and mischievously pin or mutilate the *PO* punch hole punch hole *O* bit? What on earth would happen? I have read lately of an American youth—a beardless boy, practically—who, without benefit of superior brain power, vast blocks of stock or even a close relative on the board of directors, became vice-president of a gigantic corporation simply by the happy chance of a golfing buddy in spike shoes stepping on his IBM card one day.

There are certain friends of mine, obviously well adjusted to the electronic age, who think that my attitude towards computered bills and computers generally is ridiculously timid. Computers are here to stay, they point out stoutly, and you've got to learn to live with them. And one friend, indulgently reassuring me (with a sort of patronizing twinkle), swears to me that a computer can only count up to three, anyway, so what's there to be scared of in it?

But what I say is that the centaurs of Mount Parnassus could only count up to *two,* but they managed to abduct a lot of innocent mountain maidens before some narky old crone thought out a way to thwart them. She put an ordinary kitchen sieve outside every maiden's door, and the raiding centaurs, fascinated and frustrated, stayed outside all night, trying to count the holes in the sieve. (I don't know what the maidens did all night. Gnashed their pretty teeth I shouldn't wonder.)

Could one lay computer traps with some similar simple device? According to the latest crop of American jokes (of which I have acquired a frightening collection) a lot of people are trying. From Indians in feathered war dress to suddenly uncertain atheists to plain wise guys individuals are dreaming up trick situations and trick questions to prove computers fallible. No doubt the stories are apocryphal, but the fact that they exist suggests a spreading unease, a sense of profound disquiet, a recognition of the presence of the inimical, even the stirrings of panic.

There are a group of psychiatrists who maintain the theory that jokes serve the purpose of releasing a person's bottled-up anger or releasing a person's bottled-up fear. Hostility and anxiety are emotions that most people must repress most of the time, yet these emotions are basic because they accompany any human being's response to dangerous situations. So we disguise our hostility and anxiety in jokes. The better the disguise, of course, the better the joke, and we can laugh at our own fears and angers.

The fact that there is presently such an incredible spate of computer jokes seems to suggest that there are a lot of ordinary people, just like me, who are either smouldering with anger at automation or scared plain silly. And why shouldn't we be? The infernal machines, an American magazine tells me, are already making movies, catching crooks, translating foreign languages, arranging marriages, predicting weather, setting up type, drawing up blueprints, checking tax returns, navigating aeroplanes, composing music, routing 'phone calls. Even (for the U.S. Post Office, and just wait until our own official moral mentors cotton on to this one) hunting out pornography. You can, if you mistrust your G.P., plug yourself into a machine for the diagnosis of illness or disease. And that reminds me of another computer joke (?) which describes someone being strangled in the arms of a machine. A bystander comments mildly: 'Stupidity bothers it.'

The American John Dempsey, who has compiled the computer jokes, divides them into four categories. First, the computers are human jokes, and he points out here that in many cartoons computers are drawn with primitive faces, arms and legs. Also, in many instances, the computer has broken down: he thinks that people find this reassuring. As a sample of this kind of joke, a repairman fixing a broken-down computer says accusingly to executive: 'Did you ever think of showing it some *love?*'

Second, the computers are anti-human jokes, in which the computer is incredibly big and complicated and the humans are incredibly small and perplexed and foolish-looking. (Boss to computer salesman: 'Nothing big—I just want to replace one wise guy.')

Third, the computers are superhuman jokes. (Man confronting enormous computer: 'What do you mean, "obvious to the lowest intelligence"?')

And fourth, the computers are subhuman jokes, which are pretty optimistic really, and I will stick with, since they demonstrate the belief that human beings are eventually superior to machines. And the one I like best of these is the tale of a man playing chess with a computer, from which smoke is pouring out in great gouts and springs are popping wildly. And the man says, rather smugly: 'I *knew* you'd be a poor loser.'

Now I come to think of it, not one of these jokes throws any light at all on my mysterious gas bill. But in the absence of the Aeolian Stroud, which might play its meaning to me, I think I will take the dare and mangle and mutilate and stick and pin and scrunch it and enclose sixteen cents and post it off before I dare think too deeply of possible consequences. I am feeling a bit defiant, possibly because some sadist suggested to me a machine into which my masters could feed all my favourite phrases and adjectives and programme my few poor ideas and . . . I'll tell you what: I *hate* computers!

On Letting Asia In

We were having a wallow the other night in the nostalgia of a stack of old photograph albums, some of them of wartime vintage.

One of these photographs shows a group of war correspondents in uniform, posed rather selfconsciously near a Chinese temple in Yunnan Province. The temple is shadowed gracefully by an Australian eucalypt, and this does not look at all incongruous. The tree is as right in its setting as the temple.

The correspondents, naturally, look impermanent. They are all middle-aged now—some of them old, even—and some of them are famous and some of them are not, but every one of them would have photographs pretty much like these and every one of them would have, in daily use or in daily view, some personal little oriental object or objects—a jade paper-weight, a personal seal in a black lacquer box, a small Ming porcelain that has become talismanic, a silk scroll, a carved screen, a bronze incense-burner, a set of painted plaster theatre masks or wafer-thin wine cups. Their wives (or ex-wives) would still wear the pink jade and silver and the ivory hair-ornaments. The souvenirs.

What is interesting is that the giant old eucalypt which so gracefully shadows the graceful temple in the photograph began as a souvenir too. There are eucalypts growing all over the plateau country of China, brought back as saplings in pots by coolies returning from the Australian gold-fields, or sent back with the coffins of the dead returning to the *feng-shuei* of ancestral burial grounds.

At the time of the great gold-rushes, thousands of Chinese coolies, mostly from Canton, were brought out here as cheap indentured labour. They were, in effect, slave labour, and as such one might think that their case should have had strong appeal to that embittered colonial mentality that was so basically concerned with the plight of the underdog.

What happened in fact was that the unfortunate Chinese were assaulted, stoned, mobbed, robbed, beaten up, murdered, and even scalped for the novelty of their pigtails. Three of the worst outbreaks of mob violence on the gold-fields were organized against the Chinese diggers.

Although this savage reaction could have been caused partly by ignorance (the reviled coolies were suspected of bringing leprosy and smallpox into the colony, of following heathen practices, of luring white women into opium dens and there indulging in unmentionable, and even unimaginable, vices), the real basis of the Australian attitude was undoubtedly economic rather than racial. The earliest union work-codes excluded Chinese, Kanakas, Japanese and Afghans, but accepted American negroes, New Zealand Maoris, and all half-castes born in Australia. The bogy was not colour prejudice, but cheap labour.

Anyway, as we know, the Chinese problem (plus the problem of the Kanakas working the sugar plantations in the north) resulted, at the turn of the century, in the establishment of the principle of White Australia as a national policy. Complete exclusion was impossible because of the thousands of Chinese already in residence, some naturalized, some with other forms of domicile rights, but all future policy was determined by the Chinese problem, geared to the Chinese problem as it existed then and extended to other Asian groups.

Until World War II we seem to have had an ambivalent attitude towards our Asian residents. There was, on the one hand, something mysterious and deliciously sinister about the thought of opium dens, incense, joss-houses, gongs, heathen ritual and such. Brocades and pigtails and long fingernails and oriental inscrutability and Fu Manchu. And on the other something so whimsical about Johnny Chinaman with his market garden, his painted vegetable cart, his fantastic way with the most soiled garments, his cabbalistic laundry tickets, his politeness, his neatness, his baggy pants, his lisp, his deference. But whether whimsical or sinister, superstition clung around him like an almost visible aura. 'You must have crossed a Chinaman.'

But we were British then, and Asia was still the 'Far East' or tea caddies and chinoiserie and mandarins and warlords and silkworms and traveller's tales.

It was not until World War II, when that group of correspondents were posing themselves by the tall eucalypt on the Yunnan plateau (in between getting on with the job of reporting the war effort of the fourth of what were then called the Great Powers), and the Japanese were sweeping down through the islands above us, that Asia was metamorphosed dramatically from the Far East to the Near North. The most alarmingly Near North.

Indeed our national policy might be dedicated to the proposition that we stay, racially, as we are—98·7 per cent European excluding Aborigines (although it seems doubtful whether the Aborigines are going to go on meekly submitting to exclusion)—but since the end of the war it has been impossible for any one of us, as Europeans, to ignore the fact that two great continents, teeming with the differently coloured skins that comprise half the world's population, lie between us and home base.

One has been very conscious in Europe, over the last decade or so, of the emergent black races, of the problems of Africa, of the American negro, of the race riots in Notting Hill, of the Jamaicans pouring into England.

Coming back to Australia one is even more conscious of Asia. Not as the Far East. Not as the Near North. Not even as Our Neighbours. One is conscious of Asia as the place where one lives.

Asia is in our daily newspapers, in radio broadcasts, in television discussions. Asia is in the minds and mouths of our politicians, economists, churchmen, militarists, moralists, reactionaries and visionaries.

Asia is in faces in the street. Faces at parties. Faces in class photographs at end-of-term at school. Asia abounds in our every crowded place of learning, in schools and universities and hospitals and technological institutes. Young Asia. Eager, absorbent, ardent enquiring Asia. On quota still, on restricted permit, but here for long enough for us to know them if we will, and for them to know us. Long enough for the exchange of ideas and the reassessment of national values. Long enough, most importantly, for the young to form friendships that might and could endure.

And, anyway, ideas can not be excluded by immigration laws, and Asia is with us in ideas wherever we look. Look at the cars in the streets, look at your tape-recorder or your camera, observe the trends in entertaining, in daily living, in fashion even. Every chic woman I know has at least one dress of Thai silk. Sukiyaki has taken the place of spaghetti at the clever party. Modern interiors are graced with paper lanterns, or lanterns of filigree brass, screens are a must, and furniture of cane and bamboo. Rock gardens are more stylish than herbaceous borders.

Ideas, like the eucalyptus tree, take root and grow. Watching the young together, Asian and European, I hope profoundly that they are exchanging good souvenirs to plant and profilerate everywhere.

This Way to Megalopolis

It is January again. January is a month for hangovers, bad tempers, avoidance of bank managers (who are likely to have hangovers and bad tempers too), self-deception, dishonest spiritual audits, impossible resolutions, and agonizing reappraisals. January is also a month for astrology, predictions and prophecies—a sort of field month for old Mother Shiptons, disguised as professors, architects, city-planners, sociologists, and other such crystal-gazing folk.

This January we are another year closer to the millennium, and this is considered a good enough peg to hang anybody's prophecy on. About how it's going to be, I mean, when two thousand dings up on the calendar and the computer and the End-of-the-Worlders totter out to meet their maker and even the cynics search the sky for a sign or a portent, however modest, to mark the turn of another thousand years of human endeavour.

That is, of course, providing the cynics and the credulous alike can find a snippet of sky to search. What with air traffic and space garbage the firmament is likely to be fairly cluttered, and, besides, by the year two thousand it is confidently predicted by those who should know that most people will be living (if you call it living) in the towers and turrets and canyons of Megalopolis, where sky-gazing might be difficult.

What price Megalopolis as a way of life? I suspect it's going to be a high price for most, although there are already millions and millions of people living in such colossal civic congregations as metropolitan Tokyo, metropolitan New York, and Greater London who seem to have accepted the megalopolitan way passively enough. At least on the surface. It is possible they might all have the screaming heebie-jeebies underneath and accept their gibbering substratums as normal too. Like: 'Don't everybody?'

Out Australian Megalopoles will be slightly coy in comparison. It is predicted that only five and a half million drones and workers will be accommodated in Greater Sydney, and about the same number in Greater Melbourne. Still, those population figures are bound to rise in the first fifty years after the millennium when the word gets round that the Greatest in the Southern Hemisphere is booming. We might expect urban populations to rise to seven millions, or even eight.

Whether all those millions will be pursuing Aristotle's city ideal of 'a common life for a noble end' is dubious, but then it is also dubious whether any individual life for whatever end, even an ignominious one, will be possible either.

I don't want to be too pessimistic about Megalopolis. After all there have been cities and cities and other cities for seven thousand years, and for seven thousand years they have functioned as temples and fortresses and capitals and markets and factories and cultural centres. And, importantly, as emotional focal points for their diverse citizens. The clever, the literate, the creative, the beautiful, the cunning—those with which to give and those with which to take—have always been attracted to the vigour and intensity of urban communities, and through history that vigour and intensity so stimulated the citizens' experience as to bring about the most remarkable advances in all fields of human activity and lay the basis of all modern civilization.

Every variety of political experiment, from monarchy to communism, has been practised in, and from, cities. Every city has created its own distinct and individual personality, from the moral order of the Greek city states—symbolized in magnificent buildings and public assemblies—to the foetid luxuries of Babylon.

Cities have always been legends too, and the legends have lingered in words and songs and dreams and inexpressible yearnings long after the cities have returned stone to stone and dust to dust. Where does Atlantis lie? And Eldorado? How many miles to Babylon? Was it really passing brave to be a king and ride in triumph through Persepolis? How tall were the topless towers of Ilium?

The names are music to romantics. Samarkand, Trebizond, Bukhara, Baghdad, Isfahan. . . .

This mound of dust and shards is Jericho. That one Ur of the Chaldees, the city of Abraham and sandy safety vault for legendary treasures—the golden helmet, the battle standard, the loosened funeral ribbon. The buried cities of Homer are revealed one by one and the world is dazzled by the reality of their fabled marvels. The stories and songs sang true after all.

In the ninth century A.D. the bloody-handed Vikings, driven out of their own north lands by the shifting of the herrings' feeding-grounds, set out to find the vast rich city of their heroes and their stories and their dreams. 'Miklagard' they called it, and sought this Miklagard in England and Scotland and Ireland and France. And some of them travelled southward down the rivers of Europe and came at last to Constantinople, glittering with gorgeous domes and spire and palaces, gold-encrusted and jewel-studded, so rich beyond all their dreams that they thought they had by-passed storied Miklagard somehow and come instead to Asgard, the home of the gods.

> That is no country for old men. The young
> In one another's arms, birds in the trees. . . .

The magic of that city—'hammered gold and gold enamelling'—still haunted Yeats nearly a thousand years after.

I wonder if any passionate dreams and yearnings are likely to centre on a city that will be honeycombed all the way from Newcastle to Wollongong. The perfect city, Aristotle maintained, was one of a size where the cry of a single herald could be heard by every citizen. And certainly all the really creative cities of history have not been very big.

I feel that in spite of all the well-intentioned efforts of the planners such a sprawl as Newsydgong is likely to become will not be coherent. Will a citizen be expected to feel loyalty and pledge allegiance to the whole, or only to a part? Obviously he will have to work out his labour and his leisure within the small concrete compass of his allotted cell, or subdivision, or development, since travelling space on the freeways and expressways will necessarily have to be allocated by priority. Any space, all space, will be at a premium, state-owned and rented out only, again on priority. Perhaps some citizens will live and die within a single cell.

Will they be sustained by the knowledge that they are parts of Newsydgong, the Great City? Its marvels, though inaccessible and unencompassable by an ordinary citizen, will be loudly and ceaselessly trumpeted through its length and breadth by innumerable mechanized versions of the herald. We are the Greatest! Every citizen will know that somewhere, somewhere, to the north perhaps, or the west, there is a centre, a focal point, a seat of administration, where the loftiest towers of all soar serenely around the Harbour, that brilliant spread of uninhabited wetness that was the beginning, sacred to Saint Cook and scene of solemn ritual. Perhaps, one marvellous day, an ordinary man might even see it, as a reward for long service in his own Development, or as a prize in one of the compulsory state lotteries that will one day in the future finance such needed projects as sewerage and garbage disposal and postal deliveries.

He could even be lucky enough in his lifetime to win a trip to a fabled Beach, where the great and the wise and the honoured and the filthy rich will be allocated whole houses with Space around them and walk as they please upon precious sand or stroll under rare natural trees, those curious survivals from another time.

He will have been told that there are other Spaces over the horizon somewhere, quite open Spaces, but he will be sceptical about this story, as sceptical as about that other story that in the other time, the time before, the dead were allocated great Spaces all to themselves. Who will be able to believe such a thing? The city stretches for ever, and even if a man were lucky enough to win a travel priority he might travel all his life on such a quixotic quest as to find open Spaces, or a different horizon either.

And why should anyone want more than the knowledge that he is part of Newsydgong, living a common life for some end that is the lofty affair of administration? Perhaps the end will be sewerage and garbage disposal and a water supply that will function both mornings and evenings for the allotted hour. Perhaps the end will be to be able to cross a freeway without a written permit stamped by authority, or even to ride on one through development after development after development, cleared at last of the familiar landmarks of the garbage mountains (or middens) awaiting conversion in the garbage factories, and each development smelling sweetly of its own fumes to the greater glory of Newsydgong.

I suspect it won't be for the common man to say, in any case. But in the unlikely case that I am still alive come the millennium I think I will gleefully count my hoard of city memories, big cities and little cities, squares and fountains and bookstalls and cafés and shops and lanes and columns and shards and pubs and bridges and men digging holes in roads and lovely encounters and bright red buses and barrow boys and flowersellers and flea markets and churches and chimes and trees and parks, and happily bequeath the possible glories of Megalopolis to my less fortunate descendants. They can have the beastly place.

Towards the Millennium

Hurry hurry hurry! Only thirty-three shopping years to the millennium! Plan *NOW* for Utopia. Or Judgment Day.

Think of all the things you'll need. Like space visas, procreation coupons, individuality injections, identity kits, deep-freeze coffin permits, priorities for the state psychiatric clinics, subscriptions to fun things like the Kill-or-be-Killed Klubs and educational things like the electronic memory banks, water-tight (oops!) leases on plankton patches in various oceans, desalination plants in others, reserve tanks of unpolluted air, security safes for your replacement parts (kidneys, lungs, heart, brain, etc.), tickets in the jackpot job lotteries ... or so the visionaries, soothsayers, and old Mother Shiptons say, anyway. There are some Jeremiahs, naturally, who say that all we'll need is a sling-shot apiece and a hole in the ground, but let's be optimistic enough to believe that there is time, even with only thirty-three shopping years left, to buy what we need for the great celebration, and that the great celebration will, in fact, take place.

After all, at the celebration of the last millennium most of our ancestors thought that their time was up, and were probably quite surprised to find themselves staggering on into the Dark Ages. And I have read that as the last century turned into this one it was widely believed that mankind was entering into the Age of Enlightenment, when, in fact, Europe was about to explode cataclysmically. Personally, I remember most vividly that when Elizabeth the Second ascended the throne of England all good Englishmen rejoiced at the prospect of the New Elizabethan Age, and I wonder whatever happened to that!

I mean, I don't think it is wise to be absolutely arbitrary about actual dates for either universal disaster or universal reformation where the human race is involved. Not unless we can standardize the human race in time, that is, and although we are making a pretty good effort in this direction there might be some rebels who will resist and hold out for individuality, variety, and flexibility, perhaps even truly believing that they are more faithfully fulfilling the designs of evolution. And there are bound to be some reactionaries who will haver and waver mistrustfully about novelty of any kind, and stubbornly stick to the old and to them reliable ways. There are such people about now and there is no reason to suppose that there won't be then, only more proportionately to the enormous increase in world population.

Thirty-three years is not really all that much time. Nearly half of the population of this country was alive thirty-three years back the other way, and there were visionaries then, and soothsayers, and prophets, and old Mother Shiptons busily predicting the time we live in now.

And in spite of the Pill, and the Computer, and the Bomb, and the Television, and the Astronauts, and the Affluent Society, the predicted marvels of the Alibi Age have not been as many or as truly marvellous as was confidently expected at that time, nor does mankind generally seem to be much better off for any of them. The same monstrous inequalities still exist between the Haves and the Have-nots of the world, and nature still goes on strewing her human gifts around with a staggering partiality.

Thirty-three years ago a liner made the trip from Australia to England in thirty days. As far as I know a liner still does. In spite of fins and gadgets there has been no revolutionary improvement in the manufacture of automobiles, only more automobiles. The predicted heliports for city travel are still predicted, as are the continuous belt pedestrian pavements. Women's clothes, which were shocking to all moralists thirty-three years ago, are still shocking to all moralists, but nothing of a really revolutionary nature has appeared on the fashion scene either for women or men. It is not usual for gentlemen of business to wear shorts to their offices, let alone togas or something equally comfortable, and that ridiculous article of apparel, the tie, is still considered essential, though it beats me why. Skirts go up or down, but women's clothes reveal the same dreary conservatism; I can't see a mass movement towards the sari, or, at any rate, away from girdles and bras and stockings and heels.

Thirty-three years ago there were killer diseases, and there are still killer diseases. For the first time, this very year, somebody has at last found out something about what an aspirin does to the basic metabolism. Thirty-three years ago there were slums, and there are still slums, just as slummy as before if not slummier. There have been some advances in architecture and domestic design, but these have benefited the very few: most people live in much the same sort of house as people did thirty-three years ago, excepting, if the house is new, it is probably not built as well. Thirty-three years ago youth was going to the dogs, and youth is still going to the dogs.

Thirty-three years ago there were visionaries who saw the Dead Heart of Australia as an inland sea, and all the desert blooming: I've just been reading an article predicting much the same thing for the millennium. Thirty-three years ago the cities were draining the countryside of youth and talent, and the cities still are. Thirty-three years ago the Yellow Peril was a bogy to many Australians, and to many Australians it still is.

The Haves of the world certainly have more of most things, more money, more education, more leisure, more novel gadgets, more fears, more worries, more desperations, and the Have-nots of the world have less, even of what they had before, and while everybody agrees that this is a disgraceful state of affairs the Haves are no more eager to share with the Have-nots than they were before this Age of Wonders.

My youngest child will be exactly the age I am now when the millennium comes. I doubt if he will walk into either Utopea or the Judgment Day, with or without a collar and tie. I suppose he will take for granted certain comforts and luxuries that I do not. He will probably take for granted certain discomforts and disadvantages too that I do not. It is not likely that he will holiday on the moon or emigrate to another planet. For what he gains he will pay proportionately, in the thirty-three shopping years left to him.

Our human environment is changing, without a doubt, but erratically, and if the human intelligence is changing this is erratic too. In our blunders and errors and self-delusions, in our audacities and visions, we will jerk on our evolutionary way, not towards Utopia, perhaps, but towards something that is still quite unpredictable.

What Will I Tell Your Father?

The night music around our way is quite literally a siren song. I suppose it is like that anywhere near an arterial road. One wakes so often on an eerie wail of warning to the sense of some shapeless disaster. The wail swells to a shriek and fades and swells again; the sound of outrage threaded through the nightly squeal and yelp of tyres. Police? Ambulance? Where? Who?

I don't know why the sound of sirens seems to be fraught with more peril by night than by day, and have no statistics on the ratio of daytime accidents to night-time ones: perhaps at night one is more danger-conscious, especially if one has children, and the children are out in cars.

And despite all of one's gravest forebodings, it is more likely than not that one's children are in cars, and often the cars are old and not absolutely roadworthy, and if they are not old then they are probably new and fast. Too fast for adult peace of mind. Too dangerous altogether. Sometimes lethal. This time? Next time? Never send to know for whom the siren screams.

It's no use telling yourself that the odds are against it. It happens. In some house somewhere a telephone rings, or somebody blunders down the passage to a midnight knock and opens the door on a policeman. There is a mangle of metal on a road somewhere, and maybe a mangle of flesh on a casualty stretcher, and eighteen or nineteen or twenty years of hope and promise doubtful of fulfilment.

There will be at least a couple of thousand people killed on the roads this year. Many of them will be young. I had a terrible letter from Melbourne recently with a description of the last hours of one of them. His spine was smashed and his ribs had punctured his lungs and he lay on the road for two hours before help came and he died that night on the operating table. If he had lived he would never have walked again. For a period of time that night my correspondent thought it was his own son who had been injured, and his letter has this awful duality of anguish—a real and present grief for the boy who died so wastefully, and the aftermath of the agony he suffered for his son, whose mutilation and probable death he had to accept before the nightmare relief of identification. A nightmare because there was guilt in the relief too. Yet how could a parent not be glad that his own had escaped?

There is a woman friend of mine who is so truly terrified of the combination of youth and automobile that she has forbidden her teen-age daughters absolutely and without exception to drive with any boy in any car whatever. If they go to a party they go by public transport. Naturally the girls find these conditions maddeningly restrictive and frustrating, and see themselves as martyrs to absurd and unreasonable parental prejudice.

But unless one takes a stand as firm and unequivocal as that there seems to be little one can do. Except pray. The mystique of the automobile exerts a positive and powerful thraldom even on the unwilling. A car was a convenience once. Now it is a social necessity.

I have been made most painfully aware of this over the last eighteen months while stubbornly holding out against all the social pressures, direct and indirect, that are at work every day to the end that this family, too, should keep more in its garage than packing crates and cabin trunks. We have become a nuisance to those friends who feel obliged to pick us up and deliver us home again, and virtually lost to others who live so far out as to make this sort of thing impractical and taxi fares beyond us. We are objects of wonder to local shopkeepers who look on in disbelief as we stagger off with loaded baskets on two feet instead of the more usual four wheels. Sometimes one has a sneaking feeling of deprivation. The empty garage is a reproach. Is it fair to take up all that space for storage when there is another tenant's brand-new car standing out in the weather every night?

I learned from one of the Sunday papers that a garage these days is not a luxury but 'the essential guardian of one of any family's major investments'. *Any* family? That's a pretty sweeping assumption. And yet when I think of it there isn't a family of my acquaintance that doesn't own at least one car: many of them two.

One of the garages illustrated in this article was described as looking like a garden pergola. I thought it looked more like a heathen temple. And I have an idea that that is what garages are becoming as automobiles, more and more, tend to dominate their owners. I think it is positively creepy that our garage is as big as our living and dining areas combined, at least twice as big as any of the bedrooms, and five times as big as the kitchen. We are cramped for space, but there is generous provision for our non-existent car. A 'major investment' to be sure, but then I would consider children to be even more in the nature of major investments, and in any new block of flats or units children obviously don't rate anything like the 'essential guardian' area. Not even real playing areas, although I suppose children could play in the streets if the streets weren't taken over by the automobiles.

A Californian-born friend of ours, son of a migrant Greek barber, once described to us his first sight of his wife (at this time she was riding a donkey a little way ahead of us, with a child straddled in front of her, a red poppy in her hair, and the saddle-bags loaded with picnic food).

'She was fourteen years old,' he said, 'and her hair was blonde and her legs were long and her clothes were the sharpest I'd ever seen and she was driving a white Cadillac to school. It was the dream, man,' he said. 'It was the genuine American dream.'

The Australian dream too? Our daughter (blonde too) has gone ahead and got a driving licence, empty garage or not. She nags about a blue Sprite in a used-car lot up the road. Every Come-Alive, With-It, For-It commercial endorses her.

Kids and cars. Cars and kids. What on earth is one to do? It is already too late to forbid or deny. The infection is deep, virulent, and has reached epidemic proportions. Go man, go girl, with the wind in your hair. The power and the thrill are temporary. Temporarily, also, you are lethal. As well as vulnerable.

I began this article because of a telephone call from an acquaintance whose husband was abroad on business. The status Mercedes, which she never drove, was used—with parental permission—by her son, who drove it out one night, turned it over three times, and left it an unrecognizable and irreparable heap of junk metal.

Fortunately the kids escaped with minor injuries. One with a dislocated finger, and the other—the driver—with a leg skinned rather nastily.

The mother is still distressed. But she is mostly distressed at her own reaction to this near-catastrophe. Because, she said, after the first shock her mind wasn't running along 'Thank God you're alive' lines, but on the junked Mercedes and her husband's loss of face at golf club and office. And all she could say, over and over and over again, was:

'What will I tell your father?'

This Side Idolatry

'And what does it feel like to be a teen-age idol, Mr Lust?' Thus, winningly, the lady reporter.

'Well . . . I dunno . . . I mean it don't make that much difference, really. I was idle before I was a teen-ager.' Thus, perplexed, the oafish pop-singer.

This is part of a Peter Sellars' sketch that used to make me laugh until I cried. But presently . . . well, I dunno. Have you noticed how often, and how glibly, the word 'idol' is used in newspaper headlines and on newspaper billboards? And in connection with whom? T.V. idol. Screen Idol. Sports Idol. Teen-age Idol. Who on earth are we idolizing? And to what end? I know a number of people who work in the mass media—television and films and radio and journalism—and most of them are nice people and very hard-working people, and some of them are detestable people but still hard-working, and I can't think of a single one of them absolutely suitable to be set up as an object of worship, although most of them, at one time or another, have been referred to as such.

An idol, according to my dictionary, is an image of a god or a saint, or an object to which or through which worship is offered. Or, an idol is the image of a heathen god. Or . . . (dictionaries are always rather fun, because they give you so many alternatives, and so ambiguous, like the Oracle of Delphi) . . . an idol is a source of error, a fallacy, an insubstantial apparition, a phantom due to reflection, as in a mirror.

Now, in spite of that conversation Moses had on that mountain, people always have, and probably always will, set up idols to worship, as the poor old fellow found when he came down and saw what they'd got up to in his absence. As a matter of fact I've always wondered about that calf totem, reminiscent as it is of India and holy cows, but then there is hardly an animal in nature, from the Egyptian scarab to the Hindu elephant, that has not somewhere been worshipped as a god. The totem, as object or symbol, became a useful sign of relationship and distinction for primitive people, and lapsed, in the course of civilization, into a mascot or emblem, like the lion and eagle of nations, the dove and the fish and the lamb of nascent Christianity, the elk and the moose of fraternal orders, and those dumb animals that are used to represent the elephantine immobility and mulish obstreperousness of American political parties. The ferocity of the first human gods was probably carried over from the animals they replaced.

Small boys are still quaintly encouraged to gather around the totem of the wolf. And if you want to see totemism in a primitive form you have only to go to a Head of the River day . . . the totems, in this case, being colours rather than animals, but the worship is absolute and the ferocity of the tribes gathered about their totems formidable to witness.

And talking of ferocity it is even more formidable to witness a horde of young girls in process of worshipping their current idol in the flesh. They are like those Abyssinian tribes who ate the fish they adored and said: 'We feel the spirit moving within us as we eat.' Or they are even more like those Maenads who tore to pieces the God-King on the day appointed and bolted him down, raw, to the end of fecundity and the continuity of all living things.

I think I understand this. In some atavistic way I expect we all understand this, and in some atavistic way we are all idolators. I just question the validity of our contemporary idols.

To what possible end do we worship, for instance, a young man who changes gramophone records at a radio station? Quite likely he is a very worthy and hard-working young man, but what on earth does he represent in virtue, or power, or terror that we should set him up as an idol? And my newspapers say that we do. Or, for that matter, a young woman, comely certainly, who reads the weather reports on a television station or announces the coming programmes? These young women do their jobs very well, and very dreary jobs they must be at that, but why, because they read weather reports and announce programmes efficiently, should we worship them? What do they add to our common stock of wisdom, faith, belief, and righteousness? How can it help us, in the difficult business of getting through from the cradle to the grave, to know what their diets are, or their opinions on premarital sex, Vietnam, the Bomb, contraception, marriage, or anything else for that matter?

Public entertainers of talent are a little more understandable as objects of interest, but I will still stop—as Ben Jonson did even in respect of Shakespeare—this side idolatry. Entertaining is a job too, and the people engaged in it are proportionately outstanding, competent, or mediocre as in other professions. They are, when you know them fairly intimately, just as muddled and questing as anybody else, and not at all profound or illuminated by the fact of four wives or three husbands or an adopted child or a series of spectacular nervous breakdowns or another swimming pool or a child-bride or a new contract. Or do we worship them actually because of the four wives or three husbands or the nervous breakdowns and the swimming pools and the new contracts? Are we worshipping Success? And is that what Success means to us?

If one of the more popular newspapers is any guide, and I suppose it must be because so many people buy it, we, like the Americans, also worship the female mammary gland. That's fair enough, I expect, as the fount of life is fitting as an object of idolatry. Provided it functions. What seems weird is that the ones presented to us, on page after page after page of nasty grey print, are completely unfunctional presently and never likely to be otherwise in the future. Of course people have idolized sexual symbols since time began, or people began, rather, and very properly too, since the race would peter out entirely if it was not fertile. But our idolization of sexual symbols has nothing to do with fertility. Only momentary titillation. I don't mean the nymph shouldn't have her place in the scheme of things, because she does and always has and always will have, but so does the maiden, and so does the mother, who are the other two forms of the triple goddess. If the world is to go on, that is. Or do we really want the world to go on? Do we care a damn whether it does or not? Are we concerned any further than scrambling through our own brief parts as titillated as may be and with as many material comforts as possible?

It might be a good idea to examine our idols. Have we set up a golden calf to worship, or is it only plastic, spray-painted gilt? Or even a source of error, a fallacy, an insubstantial apparition, or a phantom due to reflection, as in a mirror?

The Kingdom of Shod

Once upon a time, like now, because they tell me there is no time like the present and anyway I have been accused of writing too much about the past, there lived, and live yet because there is no way out of it, an ordinary family in an ordinary unit of the Kingdom of Shod.

The Kingdom of Shod is so happily constituted that every ordinary family earns enough money to buy lots and lots of things called consumer goods with which to adorn its dwelling and the persons of its members, to promote ease and relaxation in their everyday living, and to excite envy in the breasts of their neighbours who are thereby impelled to buy even more consumer goods to prove that nobody is better than they are anyway.

This is very good for the economy of the kingdom because practically all of its subjects are employed in the manufacture of the said consumer goods and this is very desirable because employment means money and the subjects need money to buy the consumer goods which they are so busily producing to be consumed. So everything goes round and round very merrily, but just to make sure that nobody ever has a surfeit of consumer goods—and think how terrible that would be: why, everything might stop!—all consumer goods are so designed that they fall to bits very quickly and have to be replaced with newer and therefore more fashionable consumer goods which excite even more envy in the breasts of neighbours who are thereby impelled. . . .

Are you getting sick of this? I am.

When I dragged on my jeans this morning I found that the zip had stuck again and this annoyed me more than somewhat because the jeans are fairly new and the zip has been sticking since the first time I wore the wretched things.

A number of choices were open to me. I could say to the devil with it and go through the day with one hip provocatively exposed. Or if I felt shy about the exposed hip I could wear my shirt (or rather my husband's shirt) outside my pants instead of tucked in (I happen to like my shirts, or my husband's, or my son's, or whoever's shirt I am wearing, to be tucked in). I could take the damn pants off and get to work on the zip with a pair of pliers. I could go up to the shopping centre and buy a new zip and come back and unpick the jammed one and replace it—a finicky and infuriating task that doesn't bring me on at all. Or I could throw the fairly new jeans into the cupboard to join the silk pants and the jersey pants and the houndstooth pants that all have busted zips too and wear a skirt instead if I could find a skirt with a zip that worked. What I did, neurotically, was to open my mouth and scream in rage and frustration.

Now, I don't think I am an unreasonable person and I do understand the unwritten laws of the Kingdom of Shod as well as anybody else and I know that what I was expected to do was to go out and buy a new pair of jeans. But I like the ones I've got. And I like my silk pants too, and my jersey pants, and my houndstooth pants. And I like my lace suit and I like my black velvet hobble skirt and all the other garments I can't wear because their fastenings don't fasten any more. Or because their buttons have fallen off, or their seams have disintegrated, or their linings are dragging. One doesn't expect a

138

zip fastener to outlast the garment as it used to do (my husband has a zipped flight bag that was made in Cairo in 1944 and the zipper still works), but is it too much to expect that a fastening does its job of fastening an article until the article wears out?

In the Kingdom of Shod every article of wearing apparel actually needs remaking upon purchase if you are to feel safe in it. Every seam needs overstitching, every loose thread needs firm ending off, every button needs securing (buttons particularly, and particularly if they are unusual ones, because if you lose one you will find it impossible to match and have to replace the lot with different buttons entirely).

If the garments are cheap and mass-produced I suppose that one must expect some carelessness in manufacture. But this sort of shoddiness is just as apparent in quite expensive clothes—linings that drag, hems that fall down, seams that come adrift, buttons that hang by one thread. In the make-up room of a television studio recently I noted with grim interest that the centre-back seam of the Star's gown (and I know where it came from too and who made it and approximately what it cost) had come apart in three different places and that she had a run in her stocking. I noted this as the wardrobe girl was struggling with the hook of my own dress because the thread loop for the hook had come unstuck and just at the moment I saw that I had a run in my stocking too.

I have experimented widely with stockings. I have bought all the advertised brands, the run-resistants and the ladder-locked, the stretch ones and the reinforced ones, the expensive ones and the cheap ones, the ones for that dewy bride who deserves only the best, and I have never found any yet that lasted out more than three wearings —excepting for a very expensive pair of fine Italian flowered stockings that have lasted two years and the thick-textured stockings I wear all winter long and the next winter too and put away for the winter after that. We all know that it is possible to make ladderless stockings, and in fact it has been possible for twenty years, but we all know the laws of the Kingdom of Shod too. I am not sure now when I watch the television commercials for stockings whether I am howling with laughter or howling in good earnest.

And how about those hook-on suspenders that unhook themselves with malice aforethought at the most embarrassing moments? I know I'm a bit careless, but I can't be the only woman who has dropped them on studio floors, under dinner tables, in bathrooms and other people's cars. And what can you say but 'Oops!'? And the straps that give suddenly, and the elastic that gets tired just at the moment when you are depending on a bit of support, and the lethal bit of wire that decides to pierce your heart instead of holding your shape?

I seem to have carried on overmuch about wearing apparel because I got started on those damn jeans of mine, but I could, without much provocation, go into full cry on the subject of household necessities. Like the fancy door handles that rattle instead of turning, the rubber sealing in the aluminium window frames that buckles so that the windows won't close, the new refrigerator that drops chrome fittings into the red-cabbage salad, the switches on the electric stove that just go round and round so you don't know off from on, the towel rail that falls off the wall, the taps that drip, the plumbing that fails mysteriously to function or else over-functions to flood level, the cheap plaster that jumps out of the wall because the door bangs because those fancy door handles don't work, the cupboard door that falls off its hinges, the elaborate light fittings that crash because nobody but a contortionist could change a light bulb in them without disaster, the switches that won't switch, the washing machine that won't spin. . . .

It is fortunate indeed that in the Kingdom of Shod everybody earns enough money to replace everything. Otherwise we might be tempted to cook on charcoal, and to light the darkness with candles or kerosene lamps, and to fasten our garments with old-fashioned buttons or hooks and eyes. Or safety pins. Except that safety pins bend these days.

On Being a Culture Vulture

The other day I was interviewed for television on that old chestnut of why Australians go away. Actually, I thought it was why, having gone, Australians should bother to come back. And I thought too that every possible thing must have been said on this subject, but apparently not, so here we go again.

Why does it so still rankle and niggle? Why does a man choose to live in the country rather than the city? Or the city rather than the country? Why does somebody say: 'The Mediterranean is my spiritual home' and somebody else say 'Wagga Wagga'? And somebody else say 'the Barrier Reef', or 'Upper Kurdistan' or 'the Maldive Islands'? Indeed, why not? I had a letter from a gentleman who finds the Canaries much to his liking, and again I thought, why not?

There is a lovely poem of John Donne, a gentleman who somewhat takes my fancy (being dead doesn't count in this, as I am sure you all know). Anyway, he wrote this:

> Is the Pacific Sea my home? Or are
> The Eastern riches? Is Jerusalem?

Well, I felt that he felt that it didn't matter, 'whether where Japhet dwelt' he wrote, 'or Cham, or Shem'.

I think you dwell where you dwell and build firmly with the bricks to hand. And if it happens to be Australia it is Australian earth and mud and bricks and the lot, nor do I think it peculiar that some people decide to leave it and go play with some other mud. When we were little kids we all stood against the kitchen door and had a book put on our heads and our parents measured out our height to see if we had grown half an inch or one or two, and if we had caught up to our brothers and sisters, and if you want to go measure yourself against Europe I see nothing wrong with that at all. You might be even taller than you thought.

What I find is peculiar is the attitude of some people when you come back, having measured yourself (and maybe found yourself a bit short on the European kitchen door), who say, like patriot vigilantes: 'You were a traitor for leaving. But you are a coward for returning.'

Personally I never know whether they are blaming me for failing, or blaming me for trying. Nobody ought to be blamed for trying.

Culture, as I understand it, comes from the Latin *cultura*, meaning a cultivating, meaning agriculture, rearing of plants and animals, production of articles of commerce which are due to animal or vegetable activities or functions. We can talk, for instance, about the culture of rice, or the culture of cotton, or pineapples, or cabbages, or even babies under the cabbages, or rose-bushes if they happen to be girls.

The culture of human beings might be something different. It might be the result of mental training. It might mean the refinement of taste, the keenness and balance of intellect and judgment. It might mean a quality and elegance of manners.

When we speak of a country's culture, or the culture of a civilization we usually mean its art and letters, its architecture, its handicrafts.

141

We talk of folk culture and we talk of mass culture. So that culture could be, in fact, the way of life of a community. (As a matter of fact that's what I think it is.) So Australian culture might well be venetian blinds, plastic flowers, feature walls, rolladoor garages, television personalities, pop groups, rotary clothes hoists, pubs and horse-racing and surf-boards and supermarts and commercial palaces. Also the clubs, which are our version of temples. (As a matter of fact I was taken into the stockmarket a little while ago and I thought that was the closest thing to a heathen temple I'd ever come across: outside real ones I mean.)

And this, of course, is the image we project. Our very own identity. Because whether you will or no what survives of a civilization is its buildings, its art, and its literature. We read with some titillation of the Greens and the Blues (or was it the Reds?) careering around the stadium of Byzantium, but what we actually go to see is Agia Sophia.

What do we know of the trade in currants or oranges of ancient Greece? Indeed, what do we care? We have the Parthenon, and the Temple of Aphaea on Aegina, and Poseidon in bronze (and he must be the most beautiful male man ever sculpted in the world) and the Charioteer of Delphi (he might be the second most beautiful but a bit camp for my tastes), and we have the theatres of Dionysus, and Epidaurus, and Herodes Atticus, and that is enough. And if it is not enough we have Pericles' funeral oration as well: 'Future ages will wonder at us. . . .' And, golly, wasn't he bang on right!

What do we care about the oil trade of Renaissance Italy? Nothing, and less than nothing. We care about Michelangelo, about Bernini, about da Vinci. We care about Dante, as we care about Chaucer, who, most extraordinarily, popped up at about the same time. (And, indeed, I sometimes wonder what divine breath blew over Europe just about then, when you consider the Romance poetry of France, I mean, and all at the same time.)

So what do we care about the Japanese car trade? Or nickel? (Yes, I do understand that in that heathen temple they are all going potty.) But shouldn't we be caring about Russell Drysdale and Patrick White and Peter Sculthorpe? Shouldn't we be going down on our filthy bended knees and thanking the dear Lord for the ones who actually came back to us?

The gentlemen referred to above are all successful and therefore eminently respectable. Even though they went away and came back. That's just our luck. They might have preferred Barbados or California

142

or the Black Forest. They might have been sick to death of struggling and being called arty types. I don't think it matters much. Because they would have been what they would have been wherever and whatever. I'm not sure that locale is all that important.

Alexander the Great was offered three hundred elephants by an Indian king for one philosopher. There is no record of the eventual deal. But when I read my daily news-sheets I do think we might offer three hundred kangaroos for one Bertrand Russell or a Macneile Dixon just to come and say a few commonsensical things to us.

Like: 'Go away by all means and find the taproots. Find the Parthenon, find St Peter's, find St Paul's, find Poseidon and Mary Magdalene and Ghiberti's gates to paradise, find architecture that is simple and harmonious, rock cubes growing out of rocks, find flowers and sun and wine and dancing and laughter, find love if you will.

'But don't feel you are an awful failure if you should just so happen to want to bring it back.'

Outside the Fence

A woman of my acquaintance, and of approximately my age, got up one day not long ago from the executive desk she had occupied for quite a number of years, put her papers in order, and walked out whistling (if not absolutely confidently, at least gallantly).

'Enough's enough,' she said. 'If I'm ever going to be a writer it's time to get on with it.' And by this act of renunciation, recklessness, audacity, courage, or what you will—foolishness if you like—she joined the sparse, scattered ranks of the outsiders.

And many people said to her: 'Have you gone *mad*?' They said it with bewildered eyes and a sort of suppressed ferocity in their voices, as if she had offered them a deliberate affront.

Indeed, what she renounced was considerable in the way of comfort and security. She had a job which carried prestige and responsibility. She was well paid and highly respected. She enjoyed all the advantages of good health, good looks, mental alertness, and the protection, in times of sickness or doubt or trouble, of the very influential group of people who not only paid her for her outstanding qualities but actually seemed to appreciate them in human terms. Moreover, she liked her job, which she found to be not only interesting, but emotionally rewarding.

So, perversely, she left it, to take up the lonely, precarious, and completely unprotected life of a freelance writer.

Even as a confirmed and addicted outsider I sometimes wonder what on earth this infection is that is so virulent as to make apparently sane people exchange the security of the social stockade for the dangers and difficulties and perils and pains of the wilderness beyond the gates. One's very sense of survival (which is so terribly strong) should keep one where the living is safe and the guards posted and watchful, where there are patterns and rules for the regulation of one's daily life and the chain of authority is definite and established.

Because it is a wilderness outside. No trails, except for the ones you blaze yourself in fear and hazard. No organized protection—only your own vigilance. The rules are those that you make up as you go along, and your survival will depend upon your ability to discipline yourself finely enough and harshly enough to abide by them. No one will make a decision for you, the consequences of the ones you make will fall upon you absolutely and entirely, and it will be impossible to pass the buck, because, outside, there aren't any takers.

Neither is there an expense account, or sick leave, or paid annual holidays, or the use of a company secretary or a company car, or petty cash, or a mailing service, or an office telephone on which you can make private calls you don't have to pay for, or extended pleasurable luncheons whose duration is excused under the heading of 'important contact', or Christmas bonuses, housing loans, superannuation, pension schemes, retirement allowances, or any of what are so nicely called fringe benefits.

It seems to be generally true that if you have a real talent of any sort there will be some company, corporation or syndicate who will pay you for the exclusive use of it. It should follow, logically, that if you are worth so much a week to an organization you must be worth considerably more to yourself, on the principle that an organization is bound to be making a profit out of you; why employ you otherwise?

I used to believe this implicitly, and went on believing it for years against all the frightening evidence to the contrary. Because the fact is that most outsiders (with some dazzling exceptions) earn considerably less with considerably more hardship than they would have done if they had stayed inside, kept their scepticism, derision, and raging dreams to themselves, and, tongue in cheek (I've often wondered what that expression actually means, and have come to the conclusion that insiders keep their tongues in their cheeks as a prudent safeguard against sticking them out at authority), climbed up the promotion ladder in logical and/or sycophantic rungs.

Also, by quixotically going outside, you relinquish the protective blanket of your company's name, which is, after all, so damnably superior, commands instant respect, and, in the mind it falls upon, conjures up massy piles of gilt-edged securities, mahogany board-room tables, and distinguished authoritative gentlemen wearing the right suits and smoking the right cigarettes and carrying the right briefcase as they board the right airline or climb into the right car to go home to the right house in the right locality to be greeted by the exquisitely coiffed little woman and the breakfast cereal children (so much has advertising done to us).

Outside, stripped of all that, you are nothing but your miserable, tentative, sometimes bold and sometimes hopelessly despairing self. Any outsider who has tried to raise a bank loan, or even to buy something or rent something or acquire something on hire purchase, knows this. The benevolent unction of greetings over, the questions begin. The moment you answer 'self-employed' a mist of suspicion glazes the eyes of your status-suited interrogator and his mouth purses in dubiety. If you continue with 'painter' 'actor' 'writer' 'poet' 'sculptor' or any of the other deadly outside follies the dubiety changes to a real, if agonized—because he is status enough to know that he should respect culture—hostility. Have you contracts? A continuity of work? Who will guarantee you? I have nothing but my brain and my hands. And nobody will guarantee, nobody could guarantee, that they will continue to function efficiently.

As the companies, corporations, syndicates and chain stores take over this land of Australia, which used to be the stamping ground of the individual, I don't know whether I want to weep or cheer at every little family business holding out and maintaining its standards, at the sight of one lonely weatherboard shop standing in a cleared waste where some new syndicate palace is scheduled to rise. (How long can he hold out? Is he doing it for profit, or from belief?)

It's hard to go it alone now. One is penalized for it. Brutally, I sometimes feel. And it is so easy to give in, knuckle the forelock (if not literally any more, spiritually for certain), accept (or pretend to) a different set of values, and live status and safe for ever after.

145

I have another woman friend who was born an outsider, of splendidly non-conformist parents (wild, they were). And she, outsider that she was, came into the stockade in her young womanhood from motives of real anguish—she had a couple of children to support. And for seventeen or eighteen years she has hired out her talents to masters, kept her tongue in her cheek instead of her thumb to her nose (which becomes her better), firmly suppressed all her bred-in insurgent tendencies, and brought home the rent. A couple of weeks ago, and again from motives of real anguish, she, too, like my other friend (who is childless and therefore has nobody to hurt but herself), turned her back on the stockade and walked out into the awful solitude of individual endeavour.

This piece I am writing is probably a good luck and a good wishing to both of them, and to all the others who are outside, cold and free, instead of inside, warm and fenced. We can't win, of course. But there is a certain grim little pleasure in the fact of holding out, and, who knows? one of us—or even some of us—might score a bit.

The Last Days of Prometheus

This morning at breakfast I was the object of much mild merriment and irreverent impersonation because last night, for the third night in succession, I fell asleep in front of the fire.

Personally, I think that going to sleep in front of a fire is one of the nicest possible things to do, and I am glad beyond telling that this is an old house and an old fireplace and it was built when a fireplace in every room was quite usual and workmen knew how to construct chimneys to draw properly. There were five fireplaces in this house originally. We sacrificed the one in the kitchen to an electric wall oven, and the *art-nouveau* affair in the main bedroom to a built-in dressing table, but we were stubborn about the remaining three, although the builders so took it for granted that we would be boarding the useless things in that they cracked tiles and dolloped plaster and paint about over the marble with complete insouciance, and were astonished when we demanded care and preservation.

146

It isn't that they are particularly pretty fireplaces, unless you have a taste for Edwardian (I'm developing one fast). This fireplace in the study has a mantelpiece and an ornate surround of mottled brown marble, and inside it are olive-green tiles and a perfect frenzy of cast-iron framing a grate that won't take anything bigger than ten-inch blocks of wood and fairly small lumps of coal. But it is astonishing how much heat such a small fire throws out, and how it draws the young—with books, Scrabble, chessboards, knitting, homework, records—from their own quarters to ours. A few weeks ago the elder two were out most nights: now they stay at home, roasting chestnuts, and giggling at me falling asleep, and bickering about whose turn it is (while we have a guest) to bed down on the study sofa.

The other evening, making a foray out under the back deck for wood (split telegraph poles are what you get: I wonder what we will use when the supply of telegraph poles burns up?) I looked around at the old rooftops of tin and slate and tile and all the new blocks of units that don't seem to have rooftops at all, and the forest of stink pipes, television aerials and chimneypots climbing away and up and over the far ridge, and in all the areas that I could see there were only two other chimneys smoking. And when I came inside again I jumped in positive terror when my youngest hurled a lump of coal too enthusiastically into the grate: because what would happen if the back-plate broke? Where could one replace it? Who could mend it? We've been having considerable difficulty even in finding an ash-tray—of any size, let alone the right one—to fit this old-fashioned grate. Suppose the grate itself was cracked or damaged? Where would one go to get another?

Oh Prometheus, I thought, you've nearly had your time, man, and you too Agni, and Zoroaster. And as for Hestia of the Hearth, you, my girl, might as well move out and take up your pitch from now on in the barbecue or the incinerator, because those are the only places where any sort of flame will be lit. It has been decided that you are a dirty, messy lot, and nobody has the time or the inclination to go on cleaning up after you when a switch can turn on more nice constant unvaried heat than you capricious immortals ever provided in the five hundred thousand years or so of wonder and terror and reverence and ritual and worship and ceremony embodied in a live and glowing spark.

I wonder how it began, really. Lava? Lightning? Something awesome, certainly, inexplicable, mysterious beyond terrestrial explanation. But how did those something-less-than-men learn how to use it, how to control it, and, most wonderful of all, how to make it

147

themselves? Probably they didn't for millennia. A charred log will burn for a long time, and the fire could be preserved if the tribe or the group stayed in the one place. You could even experiment with it if you were game enough.

But if you were nomadic—and the widespread distribution of our ancestors, those carnivores who were more than apes and less than men, through regions of great seasonal variations in temperature, seems to indicate nomadic habits and the habit of fire—you would have to take your fire with you, or find some way or renewing it. Some hot coals, maybe, carried in clay or a hollow of thorn-brush? A slow-burning twist of bark? William Golding, in *The Inheritors*, has his pitiable little family of Neanderthals transporting their fire from the summer quarters by the sea to the winter quarters in the inland caves in a container of clay, and there in the cave refuelling the few coals with breathless relief.

A profound and sacred mystery, fire. More than warmth, more than comfort, more than illumination, more than protection from wild beasts. A tool. You could use it to help turn yourselves into men. You could drive game with it. You could even change your physical environment. You could make plains and grasslands and open stands of forest. You could fertilize soil with the ash of it. And later you could turn clay into pots, and bricks, and abstract copper and tin from coloured stones and make bronze out of them. You could make iron. No wonder you worshipped it, and tended it, and served it, and sacrificed to it and in it, and made legends and stories to explain it and propitiate it and dedicated virgins to its eternal perpetuation and protection from contamination.

The Greeks say that Prometheus stole it from the gods, just enough to make the pith of a fennel stalk smoulder, and he brought the fennel stalk to men. Zeus was so angry that he punished Prometheus by chaining him to a rock where an eagle feasted on his immortal self-renewing liver, eternal feast and eternal torment. It's a very nasty story, but I expect we must suppose that fire was so important it was meant to be an Olympian prerogative: the Olympians were often unpleasant about much more minor matters. Funny, I was looking through a *Time* magazine lately and there were a whole series of Sidney Nolan's paintings of the Prometheus legend, and I remember the winter all of Nolan's Greek myth painting started, when we used to huddle around a tin filled with charcoal embers until the point of near asphyxiation: you had to throw a nail in, or put a piece of silver paper on top to absorb the fumes.

Later the Master of the Fireplace on Hydra built us a lovely masterpiece (behind a sheet so that his assistants wouldn't learn his esoteric art) and when it was unveiled it was a white plaster cone with a ledge around it and it looked like a witch's hat. It was made like that because the Master of the Fireplace had learned his art from his father who had learned it from his father who had learned it from an exiled Russian who built his fireplaces (behind a sheet) the way he remembered them at home.

Oh dear. Looking at all those smokeless chimneys I feel quite desolately that there might never be another generation of Masters of the Fireplace. Will there even be Masters of the Firelighting? Some lingering race memory of flints and pyrites and fire-drills and two sticks? I mean, just in case the switches fail some time. How grim and uncomforting that somebody could even grow up and live a lifetime and die without ever having roasted chestnuts or prodded glowing coals or made dream pictures in flames or listened to the fire sounds —the crackling and the hissing and the sighing and strange whimpering of a knotted log—or just dozed off, as I do quite often. And as I will, I expect, for as long as the back-plate lasts, and the supply of telegraph poles, and the old fence palings for kindling, and Hestia is good enough to stay on my hearth. Prometheus, I expect, has gone in for nuclear fission.

Reflections on a Dripping Tap

I knew it was all too good to be true. I knew something would happen. And of course it has. Trickle trickle trickle in the washbasin. Drip drip drip in the kitchen sink. Seep seep seep over the laundry floor. The plumbing will have to be adjusted. Or—mercy!—there might be stains, which is all very well if the porcelain belongs to a landlord, but absolutely unthinkable if it is your own, and brand new, and not yet paid for.

Plumbing is a fairly mysterious business to me, but then so are most other household amenities, or necessities, or whatever they are called these days. I'm sure I don't know how a telephone works, or an electric switch, or a refrigerator, and I suppose I should really find out if I intend to go on living with these marvels instead of retrogressing entirely to a world of cleft sticks and pine cressets where I sometimes feel I more properly belong.

The thing about a dripping tap, though, is that once you have lived in a place where water is precious you become actually unnerved by any wastage of it. I mean you can't quite take for granted that there is plenty more where that is coming from and there really isn't any necessity to put a saucepan under it to collect the drips for the flowers. And you can't ever again take a long long shower or rinse your hair more than twice without feeling guilty. And you can't quite restrain that mad little leap of sheer pleasure and thankfulness you feel when a storm breaks and the rain crashes down and you want to run out in it and stand with your face turned up and your mouth wide open, rejoicing. And the taste of water will always be of special interest, because rain water does taste different from spring water, and one spring differs from another, and if you have to buy every drop you drink you become a connoisseur in no time at all and expect cold water, fresh and sweet-tasting, to be served in a frosted carafe with all your meals and without necessarily a headache powder to go with it. The French disagree with this, I know, but then they live in a place where water is plentiful, and so don't value it as highly.

It surprises me rather that most Australians don't value it more. I know everyone is very conscious of its scarcity when there is a drought, but then they all forget again (except the poor food-producers, I mean) as soon as the headlines revert to scandal and the garden sprinklers can be turned on. And yet we live in the world's driest continent, and of all the terrible problems besieging the human race there is none more pressing than how to supply water to a world actually running dry of it. Water to grow food and more food, water to make the arid and stony places fertile, water for the expansion of industry, water for the amenities that we have come to regard as necessities. Of all the earth's billions and billions of acres, less than ten per cent can be used to grow food, and all for the lack of water. One gets an Ancient Mariner complex thinking about it.

By the beginning of the next century there will be something like six and a quarter thousand million of human beings demanding at least a crust of daily bread. That is to say there will be so many if there

150

is a decline in fertility. But if there isn't there are likely to be seven and a half thousand million, and most of these will be in the developing countries, where the food problems, and the water problems, are most acute. Asia, which used to export cereals, now has to import them. India is in the grip of famine. Most of this poor old wrinkled, desiccated earth is parched and gasping, including this terribly ancient place we call Australia and can't populate and can't bring ourselves to share and can't make fruitful without water and water and more water.

At one time, in London, I used to read regularly at the British Museum, with the idea that one day I might write a novel on the beginnings of civilization. There is nothing like a bit of overweening ambition when you are young. I didn't ever write the novel, of course, but I did become fascinated by the development of the great civilizations on the Tigris and Euphrates, and on the Nile too, and came to understand that civilization, what we call civilization, was only possible when man learned to control water instead of being controlled by it. Once he learned to irrigate—and who, who, who, I wonder, I have wondered ever since, thought that one out, and was he honoured for his invention, or stoned, or made into a divinity or a scapegoat; or was it one man, or generations of men?—the villages of reed huts became towns, and the towns became cities, and there was a surplus of food for trade, and communities could support people not actually engaged in food production, such as scribes and scholars and artists, and there was leisure for the pursuit of wisdom and beauty and knowledge instead of total engagement in mere survival.

Trade began on the waterways of the world, and the exchange of cultures, and the dissemination of ideas, and exploration, and discovery. I have always been excited by rivers, and find lakes—even the most beautiful of them—dull, because they aren't going any place, and rivers are. Rivers have mystery and majesty and individuality too, and the power to bless and destroy, and are still held to be sacred by many peoples in the world.

I know a man who set out once to travel on, or at least see, every great river in the world, rather like some people collect luggage labels, and he saw most of them too, from sweet Thames flowing softly to the gorges of the Yangtze, but he hasn't collected the Volga yet, or the Amazon, or the Jordan either I think, and he may be fibbing ever so slightly about some of the others, but I don't think so, and anyway he talks very well about them and it seems to me to have been a very interesting thing to have done. And it was he who told me too of the courts of the Mogul emperors which were air-conditioned by water flowing over exquisitely lacy grilles and splashing across paving stones where ferns grew among the silk divans and the piles of cushions and the tables of ivory and ebony, and I thought then, and I think now, that I would like that very much as a domestic arrangement. I learned Xanadu off by heart at that time so I could chant the bits about the sinuous rills and think about stately pleasure domes.

What I do have as a domestic arrangement, though, is this dripping tap that is driving me quite dotty with gloomy reflections about the future of civilization, which, having begun with water, might very well end for the lack of it, and indeed cleft sticks and pine cressets might be terribly in again and water-diviners sacred kings. In the meantime what I had better do is call the plumber.

The Long Hot Days of Summer

Last night I lay awake for a long time, listening to the wind. It keened at first in a melancholy sort of way, like a lament for something irrevocably lost, and this, while sad, rather suited my mood (I had been playing that lovely disc of Salli Terri with Laurindo Almeida and Martin Rutherford over and over and over for hours before I went to bed, and I could hear the Faure pavan in the wind, and the yearning Dowland galliard, and it all hurt rather, but exquisitely).

But once the mood was fixed and I was having a nice nostalgic wallow in it the wind changed its note from a keen to a querulous whine, like some old black gamp at a wake who has taken offence at a chance remark from an unfeeling relative, and the whine persisted disagreeably and grew higher and nastier and more insistent until it rose to a scream—not a scream of anguish, either, but of implacable vindictiveness—and the scream ascended (or escalated perhaps) in decibels and sheer malice until I thought I might even scream too, in defiance probably, or on that old principle of: 'If you can't beat 'em, join 'em.'

I had the most horrid imaginings of the Furies, and remembered that if I bit off the end of one of my fingers and threw it to them it would placate them for a bit. (One does have very peculiar thoughts in the night, I find.) Fortunately sleep took me over before I was maddened enough or resolute enough to do this, and although the scream seemed to go on in my head all night at least I awoke with my hands still in working order, and just as well too because I have need of them.

But the scream was still carrying on. *Is* still carrying on. I have been watching in nervous fascination this demonic wind at work in the tossing, tortured suburban shrubberies that form so large a part of my instructive view. The air is tumultuous with whirling petals of oleander and frangipani, up on the hill the three cabbage-palms I like so much are streaming, and every rotary clothes hoist for miles around is spinning dementedly—although not at the same speed or even in the same direction, which is not to be wondered at when one looks down at the weathercock (shades of St Peter) on the garage next door, which is quite frenetic with doubt.

My own hoist of washing is slapping and tugging frantically in a wild bid for freedom from the restraining pegs. It will go sailing over the neighbouring wall pretty soon I should think, and in my present mood of exasperation I feel inclined to let it, and it can lie in the mud if it damn well pleases (and there will be mud because it is going to rain before long).

I know that I am not alone in being violently affected by weather. Aunt Glad's corn responds, and the bunion on the unhappy left foot of the lady upstairs. The petulant businessman who so rudely digs you in the ribs as you try to board a bus is probably having rheumatic twinges, and when the day is humid and sticky artistic Norma's moral climate wilts accordingly and she wonders, dismally, if art has been worth the sacrifice.

One of the first of my many astonishments in London was to see, in Piccadilly, a tall man in brown robe and sandals, with a long white beard blown back, storming down the street with his fists upraised and shouting as he charged along: 'Will it *never* be warm?' I didn't understand then about London eccentrics or the London climate. I did later.

About 2,500 years ago Hippocrates, who is called the father of medicine, wrote a treatise called *Airs, Waters, and Places,* which demonstrated his deep concern with, and interest in the effects of climate on man's comfort and health, and for a long period of history

Hippocrates' original thoughts about environmental factors were the only ones that men took into consideration in explaining disease phenomena. It was only with the impact of Pasteur's discoveries in the latter part of the nineteenth century that medical studies veered from the investigation of man in his environment to that of bacteriology.

Lately some scientific gentlemen have been veering back again, drawn irresistibly to the obvious, that is to say, that man's physical environment affects him. They have, naturally, given this old truth a nice new name, bioclimatology, which is erudite enough for anybody, even these days.

Of course weather affects people. The influence of the climate on Earth—human, animal, and plant alike—is overwhelming. Whole cultures and economies have been shaped by it, civilizations have risen and decayed because of it, the erratic glittering brilliance of northern literature could be due to it, the milder satire as well as the romanticism of the English movements, the laziness of the south. Even speech patterns could be formed by it. There are some phonologists who say that a cold climate encourages greater energy of articulation while a warm one leads to relaxation of the speech organs (relaxation of just about everything, I would think, from observation and experience—it is not for nothing that all southern races have some succinct phrase that demonstrates a willingness, even an eagerness, to put everything off until tomorrow, or preferably the day after, while the northern ones are tense and terrifyingly energetic in mind and body).

Weather has malevolently spiked the most grandiose dreams of conquest. It decimated the army of Cambyses the Persian by blowing up a sandstorm in the Libyan desert, just when he had conquered Egypt and thought he had the game by the throat. Weather drowned thousands of the troops of Alexander the Great who had been foolish enough to camp in dry gullies in Pakistan. Weather scattered the Spanish Armada. Weather, in the form of relentless cold, turned back Napoleon's troops from their Russian conquest (as it did Hitler's supermen 130 years later) and, in the form of mud, so delayed his attack at Waterloo that Blucher's Prussian armies arrived on the battlefield in time to execute a flanking attack (and Victor Hugo wrote: 'A few drops of water . . . an unseasonable cloud crossing the sky, sufficed for the overthrow of a world').

This has been an unseasonable summer in Australia, they tell me. That's what they told me last summer, which was just as diabolical

154

with caprice and mood and malice as this one; furies of wind and rain alternating with days of enervating humidity, and nothing predictable except discomfort in one form or another.

Whatever happened to those long hot Australian summers that I remembered so well for all those years, when my mother would sit on the verandah behind the fuschia bushes (hosed down for coolness), and my brother and I, amazed at such lethargy, would race for the burning sands and the cold clean depths of the sea, and rejoice in the sun day after day and week after week, living and growing in it as in our natural element.

Perhaps those summers never existed really and memory is playing one of its tricks. Or perhaps—and if this infernal wind doesn't stop I *will* scream—the climate of the world is changing.

Or perhaps it is true what was whispered to me from behind the hand of a little old lady as we stood together on a street corner a couple of days ago, stranded and drenched (and my new hairset flattened and wet and clinging):

'It's the bomb, dear. It's the bomb.'

A Breath of Fresh Air

Professor Renwick, Director of Research of the Hunter Valley Research Foundation in New South Wales, is reported to have returned from the Water for Peace Conference in Washington with one of the most unpleasant predictions it has ever been my unhappy lot to note.

He is alleged to have said that before very long there won't be enough water to go round, and we will probably be drinking water that has been re-purified after having been used several times already. It will be grey and misty-looking and taste strongly of chemicals. But he consoles us by assuring us that it is quite safe to drink, so safe, in fact, that American hospitals are already using water that has passed several times through the sewers.

Goodness, how much nastier is civilization going to get in the name of progress? Although, in this country, sewers are in even shorter supply than water, so mercifully we might well lag behind in this latest refinement to modern living.

But what intrigued me most (in a grisly kind of way) in Professor Renwick's statement was the implication behind his comparison of water with air. 'Water is getting like air,' he said, and—no doubt to emphasize how very ordinary and practical re-used sewer water would become—he pointed out that people even now spend money on installing air-conditioning plants to 'get air at a certain quality and quantity when they want it'.

You don't think there is anything sinister in that? Air-conditioning, we know, is a fact, and makes many office buildings more comfortable, but most of us, privately, get along pretty well breathing whatever happens to be in the atmosphere and thinking no more about it. Our doctors sometimes recommend a 'change of air' and send us (if we can afford it) to the sea or the mountains or the dry inland to breathe something cleaner or purer or more beneficial or just different.

Because air can be very different indeed. There are constants that we breathe wherever we are—nitrogen, oxygen, argon, neon, helium, krypton, xenon, hydrogen, methane, and nitrous oxide. Then there are the variables, that change with place and weather —water, carbon dioxide, ozone, formaldehyde, sulphur dioxide, nitrogen dioxide, ammonia, and carbon monoxide. And dust. Soil dust, salt dust from ocean spray, volcanic dust, plant dust, pollen dust, bacterial dust, meteoric dust, and the dust particles from vehicle exhausts and belching industrial chimneys. Not to mention thermo-nuclear dust.

Our man-made production of dust and poisonous gases has been prodigious in the first half of this century, and we promise well to out-do ourselves in the second half. In areas of heavy industrialization amounts of two hundred tons of dust per square mile per month have been recorded. Catastrophic smogs are already history, killing off thousands and leaving thousands more with chronic respiratory ailments. (I gasped through the London horror smog of 1952, when four thousand people died as a direct result of exposure to concentrated contaminants.) If we go on so fecklessly fouling up the air then it is indeed predictable that air-conditioning, in the cities, will soon pass out of the luxury bracket into the domestic essential. But we might go even further than that.

If you are hypnotized, as I am, by the gimmicks and gadgets of contemporary living that are advertised in the back pages of the biggest and glossiest American magazines, you will have noticed that the fastidious can already purchase clean air in cans. Special air. Salubrious air. Air from Florida, air from Arizona, sea air, mountain air, desert air, air scented with pine and spruce and ozone and flowers. All right, it's a gimmick. For the moment. But I have also heard that right here in Australia there is an enterprising individual busy bottling the air of the Blue Mountains.

Well now. It is a gimmick that may well catch on. As modern life becomes more and more like a feverish squirrel cage harassed men of affairs, instead of going away somewhere for a change of air, might find it more convenient to have the change of air home-delivered. Not that re-conditioned stuff, but the real thing, the salt whiff of the sea, the sharp tang of a mountain morning, the clean dry air of the plains. Particularly if the air could be supplied in big quantities. As a commercial idea I think it has great possibilities. Hospitals would come in on it for their respiratory patients (the rich ones anyway). Faddists would fall for it. Really smart parties would be designed around the air tanks. Night in the Simpson Desert. Afternoon on the Gold Coast. Champagne breakfast in the champagne air of New England. Crisp cold invigorating air for the working hours. Languorous tropical air for the viewing of etchings and other evening sports.

Naturally it would come pretty expensive at first, but soon huge factories would be set up for bottling and tanking. And one has seen all too clearly how the rich man's indulgence becomes his necessity, especially as the would-be's follow as the night the day, and the unthinking follow the would-be's, urged on by the fervent missionary zeal of the evangelical advertisers, and finally what had been a desirable luxury becomes an essential.

Naturally when this happens architecture will have to be adapted. New houses and blocks of units will be hermetically sealed and built around storage tanks, from which a range of breathing air will be piped into rooms by a selector button. The design of automobiles will change radically to allow for tanks. There will have to be pedestrian kits with respirators, emergency kits, and holiday packs.

By this time bottled air will be big business, part of the G.N.P. Every country in the world will be exporting and importing air in the fiercest competition, and advertising will plug every variety from rarefied to foetid (perverse tastes will have to be catered for too . . . at a price). But as air pollution increases, as it will, there will be less

157

and less good air to bottle. Higher tariffs will have to be imposed to protect native air, and the rich will pay astronomical prices for imported luxuries. Himalayan Heights for Hallucinations. Louisiana Swamp for the breath of heavy Southern passion.

In the meantime old-age pensioners, widows, basic-wage earners, and the ranks of the underprivileged will have to breathe toxic sludge. That is until some sharp promoter dreams up a campaign to make bottled sludge fashionable among the pace-setters avid for new kicks. London pea-soup, Los Angeles smog, Manchester broth, Liverpool chowder, Detroit dust—one whiff and you're sent, man!

But as the sludge is used up (there will be monopolies, and huge reserves held to force prices up in the name of the Protection of the Air Bottling Industry), air will have to be rationed, which will invite black-marketeering and a further rise in prices for a breath of anything breathable. The Have-nots will need to adapt their lungs to a greatly reduced air intake or die gasping. They will adapt, of course, or enough of them will adapt to begin a curious new race of people, slow, wheezing and pigeon-chested, bluish in colour, but perhaps capable of surviving when the big bang comes and the rest of us are wiped out.

Do you think I am writing science fiction? I hope I am. But then once upon a time nobody would have considered it remotely possible that they might have to drink water that had been through the sewers.

I remember that my father used to say that the air of our home town was worth a quid a whiff. I hope he was as much of a crank as I thought then. It would be awful if he was prophetic.

DILEMMAS

A Room of Your Own

Virginia Woolf (of whom I am not all that much afraid—I mean only a bit because she did write deliciously) said that no person aspiring to be a writer should even contemplate a literary career without the prerequisites of five hundred pounds a year and 'a room of her own'.

The five hundred a year is a bit of a hoot these days, but I wish I could recall her distinguished shade to tell her how fervently I agree with her dictum about the room of one's own. I wish this, not in anger or rage or frustration (having used up all those emotions years ago and not wanting to exhaust myself further and to no purpose, because anger and rage and frustration have availed me nothing), but quite wistfully really (although not with complete resignation—I'm not that far gone yet).

Just a little while ago I overheard one of the chess players down at the other end of the room (that is to say about ten feet away from where I am working) ask of my son, with a quite interested glance in my direction: 'What is your mother writing about?'

'I don't know,' said my son, and of course there was no earthly reason why he should, because he is not a clairvoyant and in any case his mother didn't know either.

At that moment a sports car roared up outside the block of flats, and another herd of young swept in as boisterously as an equinoctial gale to sweep my daughter off to some jollity or other, and suddenly the living-room (which is the only place I can put my desk) was seething with ebullience, and the girls were clattering backwards and forwards down the hall to put on different clothes, or to exchange the ones they were wearing (I don't know why; I thought they looked very nice in their own), and so the boys had to wait while the girls shrieked and giggled in the bedroom, and because they had to wait they obviously thought it polite to make conversation with me, and while this was going on the landlord called to see me about a cleaning lady he had heard of (and whose ministrations I await with the ardour of a girl longing for love), a blast of rain spattered against the windows

161

and I remembered that there was washing on the line and had to tear downstairs to retrieve it because there wouldn't have been any towels for anybody otherwise, or clean shirts, or pyjamas for my hospital-incarcerated husband, and while I was pelting upstairs again (they were yelling down at me that I was wanted on the telephone) I thought wildly of Virginia Woolf, and also of something somebody said to me only the week before:

'You must live such an interesting life,' she said, 'and meet so many interesting people.'

One of the interesting people I know is a television producer, who maintains that one should never permit the public to even peep behind the scenes of a performance. He says that mystery and illusion must be maintained. The curtain parts, the show is played, the curtain closes again, and that's all the audience should be allowed to know about it. It makes me think of a gully-gully man producing chickens from the most unlikely places and beaming as blandly as a heathen idol.

Actually I have always thought the show behind the show to be as interesting—if not more so—than the show itself, and in this respect I do indeed live a very interesting life, although not quite in the way my acquaintance of last week imagined, and certainly not according to Virginia Woolf.

The show behind the show, as far as my own little performance is concerned, is high comedy with Heath Robinson devices in the way of stage machinery.

To begin with I live in a flat, and in the second place I share it with two teen-agers (the third child being boarded out for the period of crisis). Theoretically this is all quite sound, since the flat has three bedrooms, and is agreeable enough and convenient enough as flats go, being so modern as to be fresh from the builders' trowels, and the teen-agers of sufficient years to make the whole arrangement tenable —three people living, as it were, communally, but you in your small corner and I in mine and all that.

Practically, it works out quite differently. (And I am for teen-agers rather than against them so this is not a particular grizzle or whine: as a matter of fact I am quite inordinately fond of my own, and agree that this is their temporary home just as much as it is my temporary home and they are entitled to bring their friends also.)

However. This is the sort of thing that happens. Last week I had to go to Melbourne on a business trip, and having been pressed rather

162

hard by circumstances (and weather, over which I have no organizational powers) I left the flat rather messy, and with the washing (which I had got up early to do—I mean five o'clock in the morning early) in a laundry basket, with instructions that it should be put out on the line as soon as the rain stopped, and further instructions and directions relating to kitchen refuse, old tins and bottles, hospital visiting, and all the rest.

Two and a half days later I arrived back, glowing with the pleasure of unaccustomed luxury, and bearing a sheaf of flowers gorgeous enough for Joan Sutherland. Also a guest from the south.

This is what greeted me:

Twelve dirty milk bottles, and two half-empty ones growing penicillin. Four unmade beds. One kitchen of which the sink and every available service was stacked and heaped with unwashed plates and cups and glasses. One laundry basket exactly where I had left it but with the damp washing gone mouldy. One ironing basket tipped up across a floor. Four cartons of bottles and tins that had been added to rather than taken away (and too late too late: garbage collection had been and gone). One filthy bathroom. One living-room littered with discarded newspapers, articles of clothing, piles of records, coffee cups, punched cans of lemon drink, and a perfectly strange teen-ager lolling on the sofa and conducting a conversation on the telephone. One desk from which the typewriter (which is my livelihood) was missing, but to which had been added innumerable lists of chess scores and other esoteric data, while my mail and documents had been shifted to the floor. One refrigerator and a whole set of cupboards empty of any sort of provisions for the week-end (and too late to buy any) excepting for a dozen eggs and two pounds of butter (it is extraordinary what little purchasing power ten dollars has, although my daughter had, I noticed, a jazzy new slacks suit).

Two horror-stricken faces. And two voices crying in dismayed unison: 'But we didn't think you were coming back until *tomorrow!* We were just going to start cleaning up.'

'Well, why don't you?'

A giggle from my daughter. 'Because you're back now.'

Getting Away From It All

Dame Edith Sitwell once wrote, in an article for the *Daily Mail:*

'If Judgment Day arrived and the secrets of men's hearts were discovered, those hearts would confess their sins without a qualm. But one hypocrisy they would cling to. They would insist on the fact that they had enjoyed their holidays, no matter how frightful the experience would have been.'

Of course people insist that they enjoy their holidays. Holidays cost time, money, organization, argument, compromise. Nobody I think, excepting perhaps the carefree jet-set, can just drop everything and go on a moment's gay whim. For most people getting away from it all is circumscribed by it all from the very beginning, by office rosters, by that exasperating and frustrating equation of time and distance divided by cash, by available accommodation, by seasonal booking loads, by family schisms on choice, by the necessity for holiday wardrobes, by good advice and bad advice, by passports, papers, insurance, pet-sitters, plant-waterers, renewal of locks and hinges, post-office arrangements, and getting the desk cleared up.

All this is hard work. People (ordinary people that is) usually begin their holidays in a state of complete exhaustion, and the more exhausted they are the more imperative it is that every precious day should count. In any holiday there are only so many of them to work the expected and demanded magic, to soothe, to heal, to relax the shrieking nerves, to unravel the tangle of a whole year's decisions and indecisions, to clarify the half-desires irresolutely sought, the half-fears that have only been half-vanquished, the partial attainments partially achieved in perplexed dissatisfaction. One demands of a holiday that it be more than a balm. One expects to be renewed in some mysterious way. One expects to return with the problems solved as well as the suntan and the colour slides and the stock of funny stories.

Holidays are more than a bit unreal. Unsettling. Not only is normality fractured, which is risky for normal people, but a definite time-limit is imposed. Whatever the place and the situation and the plan one has chosen, it is temporary. Whatever one has decided to do one must do it as hard as possible because there's an end to it and the end is in sight from the beginning.

People on holiday become greedy of experience, variety, excitement. Consciously or unconsciously they are out to get their money's worth, and their time's worth, and their months of planning's worth. Even if the holiday is the quietest possible, and the aim of it nothing more than to loaf around, one is, in fact, loafing with intent and can spend a prodigal amount of emotion in the doing of it. A succession of days that are less than felicitous for loafing can arouse emotions that range from irritation to the profoundest melancholy, because they are wasted days, paid for in advance and now proved worthless. Irretrievable also.

In the season for it the world is seething with people restlessly fleeing from the familiar to the unfamiliar in search of release or renewal. Prodigious amounts of money are outlaid on seasonal nomadism. Shipping companies and airlines flourish on it, travel agencies make fortunes out of it, advertising revenues grow fat on it, whole countries gear their economies to it, sleepy ports and quaint hamlets are entirely disrupted by it, miles of virgin coast are deflowered for it, industries are built on it, new towns spring up because of it, social patterns are shattered by it. And highways made nightmarish.

It is a long time since I did much in the way of holidaying myself, but Hydra during the years I lived on it appeared to be the holiday goal of half the world. It is quite curious and instructive to earn your daily bread and conduct your daily affairs in a resort, where the faces change daily and your social contacts, however lively, interesting and intense, are of a purely temporary—and therefore illusory— nature. This, of course, makes for variety and excitement, but also for mad mental whirlygigs and eventual exhaustion. Because the one certain thing about holiday-makers is their inability to accept, or even comprehend, that everybody else is not on holiday too.

The holiday-maker is greedy to fill his limited days with the utmost in experience, novelty and pleasure that can be squeezed out of the situation. If you are a permanent summer host, as I was, and as anybody is who is fool enough to live permanently in a summer resort, you are going to be squeezed too in the process.

Because your holiday guest expects, disarmingly and quite relentlessly, that your time and your expertise as well as your house and your friends and your (to him) enviable way of life will be entirely at his disposal. After all, he is only asking you to give up a lousy little week or a fortnight or whatever to guide him, advise him, arrange for him, introduce him, interpret for him, explain to him, and to keep up with his holiday pace. It is impossible for him to realize that you are still recovering from last week's relentless pleasure-seekers, and that as soon as he is crammed with enough gorgeous holiday experience and second-hand stories to dine out on and reminisce about (and plan to come back to) for the next year, you, the host, will be airing the beds and washing the sheets and stocking up the larder and painfully stretching your welcoming smile for the new lot due in on the morning steamer (or coach or train or aircraft) and the new lot will be exhausted too from all the planning and travelling but anxiously eager to make every single vacation moment pay off.

I will admit that a great deal of this is self-inflicted. But the friends of the friends of the friends were not, the ones with little notes of introduction or verbal messages or just vague hopes based on stories or rumour who landed on one's doorstep with rucksacks, suitcases, cameras, and expectations, needing drinks, food, guides, interpreters, hotel rooms or just good advice.

I think if one is to be at the receiving end of holiday-makers one should really make it pay off on a proper business basis. Although I know a young woman who rented a beautiful villa on Hydra and set herself up in the professional hostess business, and as far as I know she entered into the holiday spirit so absolutely and wholeheartedly that she ended every season in the red financially, involved romantically, and quite quite shredded emotionally. She said it was a great way to live. But then she was young and obviously had stamina.

There were other holiday-makers (and still are, I've no doubt) of the faster-moving variety, whose object was to 'do' as many places as possible in the time available to them. These impinged upon my life only incidentally, since they never had more than a day—and some-times only a few hours between steamers—to wring the island dry of its history, economy, local customs and quaint folklore, to snap the colour slides, buzz off a few feet of film, raid the tourist shops, write the postcards and be off. I suppose that they sorted out where they had been when they got back home and had the colour slides developed and ran their movies for captive friends. And I'm sure they had some shocks in the process.

Because I still remember, and still with dazed disbelief, an American gentleman in dazzlingly gay gear, hung about with more cameras, meters, recorders, dilly-bags and gadgets than I have ever seen before, standing on the waterfront of our small Greek island and demanding of the donkey boys that they bring him a camel instead. It turned out, upon fascinated enquiry, that he had lost a whole page of his tour schedule and confidently believed himself to be in Egypt. I thought then that it probably didn't matter much either way: he could check it all out with the travel agency when he got back home.

I do know though, personally, that on any tour you are bound to miss out on something. And according to your home-bound and envious friends, it is always the most desirable experience, the most breathtaking sight, the most sublime work of art. So, after my first European tour, which lasted five weeks and ranged through the natural, historic and artistic marvels of France, Austria, Germany and Italy, I was mortified to discover that I had, in fact, missed the Signorelli frescoes at Orvieto, and therefore, according to my friends, might just as well have stayed at home. You can read anything for the Signorelli frescoes—a tomb, an inscription, a painting, a view, a regional wine, an obscure restaurant, an unforgettable character. Even a season. Because if you went there in the spring you can be quite sure that your friends will commiserate with you on not having been in autumn.

I do realize that this is beginning to read as if I am conducting a spiteful one-woman campaign to spike the well-earned enjoyment of hard-working folk who have saved and planned arduously for a few brief weeks of leisure and relaxation.

Actually nobody believes in leisure and relaxation more devoutly than I do, although I suspect that leisure and relaxation are infinitely more beneficial if they are completely unearned and you can wallow in them without worrying about how much good they're doing you. That's only a theory, of course, engendered out of wistful observation of the idle rich, as distinct from the busy rich, who only enjoy being busy. There was a lovely heiress from Texas who trailed around the Mediterranean for several consecutive seasons and she seemed to enjoy herself very much making a desultory investigation of the romantic and erotic habits of young and handsome fishermen, shepherds, muleteers and deck-hands in comparison with the romantic and erotic habits of young and handsome painters, poets, actors, students and philosophers. She was the most relaxed person I ever saw. And she said she was having a dreamy holiday. Just dreamy.

That's another thing about holidays, of course, and I don't think that advertising is entirely to blame for it. The expectation of romance.

Advertising certainly encourages the expectation, but even without it (if you could possibly imagine life without it) there are so many novels, stories and films based on holiday encounters that even the most normally timid and unassuming and shy and unadventurous people are subconsciously prepared for that magic moment of recognition (ship's deck in moonlight, airport terminal in fog, customs barrier in snow, white beach in hot atmospherics, hotel foyer in jet-setty modern, strange restaurant in candlelight) that is going to change their whole lives.

It is encouraging, I suppose, to know that the romance does sometimes happen, but from what I've seen it usually happens to the beautiful, the young, the extroverted, the confident, who get it all under normal circumstances anyway. And—again strictly from observation—I have noted that while unfamiliar surroundings are conducive to the romantic encounter, the time-factor involved in all holidays usually curtails the encounter to a brevity that is nothing short of maddening. If the magic moment of recognition doesn't come off by the end of the first week there is only frustration and disappointment ahead. So much chance is involved, like arrival and departure dates (why didn't you arrive sooner, later? oh damn the office roster!), previous bookings (how can you change your accommodation at this point?), previous companions (how in hell can you shake off the dreary bunch who seemed so interesting yesterday?), previous arrangements (why oh why did you let yourself be talked into that excursion when you might have been going on this one?). You have to be lucky or fated to meet the beloved of your dreams in the right place at the right time and with all your holiday arrangements conveniently coinciding. On the whole, I think, it is more satisfactory to find the beloved first, in the normal course of your normal days, and make your holiday arrangements together.

But in spite of disappointments, frustrations, minor or major hysteria or melancholia, I expect that people will go on optimistically, year after year, and season after season, getting away from it all. And it all will wait patiently until the traveller returns with his quite irrelevant suntan, colour slides, and confused or disturbing memories.

This week the brilliant plan of buying an island, investing in a charter schooner, growing bananas, developing that unspoilt beach that nobody knows about, is real enough. Next week the dream will have become cloudy, distant, and not really attainable, and it will be impossible to recapture the sun-sodden indolence of the days. You will

168

sigh at your desk and pick up your telephone and your problems. Next year. Maybe next year the romance, the glamour, the adventure will be actual. Just like the travel brochures promise. It's worth another dream or two anyway. And, who knows, against all logic and reason, you might even enjoy your holidays. I do hope so.

Bachelor Boys

He said, my friend of twenty years ago, that being a bachelor boy at fifty-plus isn't such a big deal after all.

He said the freedom's beaut and all that, but as a divorced man he still has enough faith and belief in the institution of marriage to want, sincerely, to have another and better go at it. In fact, I gather from talking to him (or letting him talk to me, rather, which is the way these conversations usually work out) that he is not fundamentally damaged by a marital break-up, but ready willing and able—even, perhaps, actually anxious I thought—to give it another try, keeping in mind all the lessons he has learned.

He is not what you would call a wary man at all.

But he said that the world of the divorced was strange, different, alienated from normality. He said it was very very lonely. He said that the social pattern, here in Australia, was to invite people in pairs, like animals to the Ark, and that if you weren't respectably paired off you were a social embarrassment, if not a downright danger.

I did have a talk about this once with a bachelor girl, also divorced, at a time when I was enduring a spell of enforced loneliness, and I do believe it to be true. If you are not part of a conventional male-female relationship you are likely to be overlooked on the invitation list.

Males, still, have a greater social freedom here than females. (He, my friend, ceded me that one.) They can drink in a pub alone, they can go to a theatre alone, they can, in potentially romantic or other-wise interesting situations, initiate conversation. They can, in fact, be active where females are still supposed to be passive.

But he said he thought it was damn funny the way the arch eyebrow, the racy story, the sly whisper behind the hand burgeoned and blossomed in the world of the divorced.

169

He is a good cook, this friend of mine, and he likes to—I suppose also he needs to—entertain. But he said that it is quite extraordinary that his male friends invariably arrive at his parties minus their legal partners and plus some kooky irregular. He is not actually objecting to this, and concedes that it might even have some advantages, since his situation could make him extremely receptive to the charms of unattached and pretty women, and with the most honourable intentions. He really is optimistic about the possibilities of the conjugal state, and would prefer to do the rest of the journey in double harness rather than single.

He is also personable, has a good job with quite a lot of prestige, status, what you will, attached to it, and I think might fairly be a good mark for a girl with her sights set on security, sophistication, and some elegant trappings around the fundamentals of eating and sleeping. Age differences don't matter so much these days, as witness Frank Sinatra and Cary Grant, and a girl could do much worse than to settle for solidarity, comfort, maturity, and a tolerance learned out of experience.

But where the kooky irregulars leave him cold, he said, is in their studied languor. Look, he said, with fervour and possibly justice, I might spend two days preparing an exquisite meal. The courses will be as near perfect as I can make them, the wines will be as near perfect as I can find them. I will happily be my own butler and footman and wait on everybody and pour the wines and light the cigarettes and remove the plates. But, he said. But. No matter how decorative my female guests, no matter how compliant, no matter how romantically exciting, don't you think that one of them, just once, might pick up a teatowel and bog in with the cleaning up?

I asked him, with some temerity because he was so really incensed, whether he believed that a woman's place was in the kitchen. I reminded him that many women spend so much time moiling and broiling in their own kitchens and over their own sinks that they might reasonably expect, on a gay night out, to be exempt for once. I know that I personally do not expect my guests to wash up after my dinners: on the other hand I don't expect to wash up after theirs, either. And that is a lesson I have learned, hard, by playing Greasy Joan to too many clever male cooks: he whips up the unpretentious little sauce and you scour the pretentious pot; he decides on something fanciful like sliced prickly pear and you are left with the spines in your fingers.

He (my friend) said that was different. He said that the young ladies he was talking about, in the sly, arch, racy, permissive world of the divorced, did not generally moil and broil in their own kitchens: it was doubtful, he said, whether they even had kitchens. They expected to be dined and wined out, with all the candlelight and trimmings. They expected their cigarettes to be lit, and the hock glass changed for claret. They expected the attention, the sweet words, and the soft music. In return they provided decoration.

He was, in fact, quite bitter about the limbo in which a divorced man finds himself, and it echoed the considered opinions of my bachelor girl-friend, also divorced, who said that practically every man who had ever taken her out, or who she had cooked a meal for, took it for granted that bed privileges went with the meal. She finally couldn't stand the social climate here and took herself off to America, where I hope, sincerely, that she will be accepted for what she is and not for what people think she ought to be.

As for my divorced male friend, bugged by the teatowel and the litter of prawn shells, unwashed glasses, dirty saucepans, sticky plates, overflowing ashtrays, and languid ladies lolling about decoratively and unfunctionally, he's getting married again.

She's fifty, and they like each other, and they've bought a little property where they are planting native trees and shrubs. And he says that she can cook just as well as he can, and she's not frightened of a teatowel, and with a bit of luck he might never again, as long as he lives, have to give one of the gay bachelor-boy parties for the regular males and the irregular females, with a nod and a wink to accompany the main course.

He says, all told, he's a pretty happy man these days, and very optimistic about the future, and marriage, and going on in double harness rather than single.

But he says he would be grateful if I would pass on to the lovely languid kooky girls that a teatowel in the hand is worth the kinkiest clobber in the boudoir.

I think that this is a rather nice story, and I am pleased to pass his message along. I have a feeling that he might even be, simply, decently, nicely, one of the happiest people I have had the good fortune to meet.

I Haven't a Thing to Wear

'But I haven't a thing to wear,' I said in dismay, and turned the lovely lovely invitation over and over, already teetering towards rejection and the gloomy pleasures of self-martyrdom.

And they said . . . ! But I won't tell you what they said, except that they said it succinctly and quite explicitly (they are most articulate, my lot), and as a result of what they said I found myself in town with four hours between appointments to find something to wear and a cheque-book to pay for it and the knowledge that I'd better not show my face in my own door again if I didn't. Actually I felt quite exhilarated and reckless, and I knew precisely what I wanted (which, of course, I had known all the time—in the back of mind, that is, unacknowledged).

I wanted something cool, casual, disarmingly simple and supremely elegant. The sort of thing the Contessina wears at luncheon on the marble terrace, languid among the ancient urns and the slow dappling fall of vines. The sort of thing the Honourable Gillian doesn't wear to Henley, either because her mamma thinks blue is more suitably girlish or because she's on the Carnaby Street kick. The sort of thing every woman wishes she was wearing when she sees somebody else wearing it. You know the sort of thing.

And the day was hot hot hot. Humid hot. Sticky hot. It was like breathing steaming flannel—mildewed flannel at that—and I marvelled that so many women looked so cool and fresh in those stifling city canyons: my hair had gone limp and sweaty after ten minutes and my linen suit was wilting and the palms of my hands were wet. It wasn't really the best day for shopping, and if my need had not been urgent and my mood reckless I would have given up and found some air-conditioning and a nice long tinkly drink instead.

As it was I set my course for the department stores, because every one of them carries the clothes of at least one designer I like, and, besides, they often have exciting surprises. So of course I shouldn't have been as surprised as I was to find the department stores, on that suffocating day, to be jammed, floor after floor after floor, with rack after rack of corduroy garments and velvet garments and tweed

garments and woollen garments and knitted garments and garments
of leather and fur. 'Don't you have any summer clothes left at all?' I
asked, and the salesgirls, fanning their hot flushed faces and shifting
about uncomfortably on their swollen feet, looked at me as if I had
dropped in from outer space. 'These are the *autumn* collections,
madam,' and I said yes, evidently, but it was still some way to autumn
(this was February) and could I buy something more suitable for the
weather, and they said I should have been at the summer sales because
there had been some wonderful bargains but now they wouldn't have
any summer stock again until winter.

I thought this quaint but not absolutely satisfactory for my present
purposes and after spending a great deal of time in department stores
(mostly because it was cooler inside than out and anyway I was being
methodical), riding up and down on escalators among simply hundreds
of cool fresh women carrying bulky parcels of tweed or velvet or fur
or woollens I thought I had better dismiss department stores altogether
and start in on the boutiques, which were more likely to have the sort
of thing I wanted anyway.

This city is filled with boutiques. Arcades of boutiques. Streets of
boutiques. Boutiques tucked away in unlikely basements or on the
second floor back of office buildings. And all the boutiques were filled
with corduroy, tweed, woollens, knitteds, leather and suede and velvet
and fur. I walked blocks. I walked miles. I systematically explored
every arcade, basement and office building. I walked until my hair was
plastered in wet strands around my face and my underclothes were
stuck to my skin and my linen suit might as well have been Ned Kelly's
armour and my feet were beginning to swell hideously and painfully
and I thought if I didn't sit down I might faint and that I was probably
going mad anyway because all around me all the time were women
looking cool and fresh and not at all distraught going into boutiques
and coming out of boutiques carrying bulky parcels of corduroy and
velvet and woollens and knitteds and. . . .

I sat down in a plastic and formica cubicle under painted palms and
drank cold lemon juice and smoked a hot cigarette and mopped my
smeary make-up and tried to reason it out. Because surely I couldn't
be the only woman in the city who needed something cool to wear?
Evidently I was. Other women obviously planned their summer
clothes in the middle of winter and didn't get caught out. And I
thought fiddlesticks to that because everybody gets caught out some
time. Suppose you'd just arrived from a cold climate and simply

173

didn't have any cool clothes to wear in this one. But then I had arrived from a hot climate a couple of years before and hadn't had any warm clothes and just had to freeze for two months because all the shops were filled with summer collections. Then suppose one was going on a trip to a hot climate and wanted a stunning outfit? Obviously if you didn't have the stunning outfit already you would have to go without. Or else you had a marvellous little dressmaker just around the corner who would copy anything from the Paris collections or the American magazines. I don't have a marvellous little dressmaker around the corner. In fact, I have had packed away in tissue paper for the last two years about twenty yards of fabulous French fabrics and Greek embroideries just waiting for that little dressmaker I haven't found yet.

Well, I thought, never mind any more about what the Contessina would wear to lunch on the marble terrace, because if the Contessina hasn't got it hanging in the cupboard already she's out of luck. I decided that this dreadful day would be a lesson to me in providence and planning, and that never again would I wait until I actually needed a garment before buying it. With the temperature at over a hundred and the humidity getting up towards a hundred too I wondered what the Baroness would wear to lunch in the great hall of the Schloss, all drenched with rose and gold reflections from the glazing logs on the hearth.

I needn't have worried. Because if the Baroness is not out-and-out kinky in her tastes, if she is more than seventeen years old and bigger than a wraith, she's out of luck too. Have you ever, on the most sweltering day in summer, tried to struggle into the suffocation of a size twelve corduroy designed for a pre-adolescent? In a fitting room with strip lighting that reveals all too clearly all? No, I don't want to remember the rest of that day. I arrived for my appointment beaten, humiliated, sweaty and swollen-footed, carrying two pairs of winter shoes that I don't need and that probably won't fit anyway once my feet go down. If they ever go down.

And as for that lovely lovely invitation for which I set out to outfit myself coolly and elegantly . . . it rained buckets that day and the affair was cancelled.

Australia Day

'But what is Australia Day anyway?' my daughter asked, and it was a fair enough question as it turned out.

The kitchen at this time was pullulating with neighbouring young in varying stages of sunburn and nose-peel and bluebottle stings, all wearing summer uniform of faded shorts and shirts, bare-footed, skinny and hard and with their teeth coming down like half-lowered blinds, and their eyelids too with heat and the bliss of holiday undiscipline.

Ten-year-old Michael said he thought Australia Day was the Anzacs, but Bill said no it wasn't, it was something to do with becoming a Commonwealth, and one of the other kids said it was nothing of the sort but the anniversary of Captain Cook discovering Australia, and somebody else said it was Federation, but nobody seemed to know what Federation was, and anyway it was obvious that none of them was teased very much by the question because they drifted out after a while into the heavy building heat of the summer morning and climbed the splintered palings of the back fence into somebody else's yard and I could hear the pup, Pal, barking and the voices chanting the ritualistic phrases of the game they have been playing lately: 'Crocodile, crocodile, can I cross the river?'

I suppose if it wasn't school holidays, and Australia Day fell in term time, they would each of them be involved in parades of some sort, or assemblies, and the breaking out of flags and speeches from headmasters and prominent citizens about our glorious heritage and founding fathers and all that. Or maybe not. It's awfully difficult to make our founding fathers out to be anything else than . . . shall we say . . . reluctant?

Driving out from Sydney on a week-end lately I looked at the bush again for the first time in a long while, and it frightened me. So intimidating it is, so apparently monotonous, so uncompromising in colour and texture. It does not beckon or invite, as green woods do, and coppices, and noble forests of beech and oak and larch and fir. Its mysteries are not of the romantic order, but freakish, spiny, spare,

175

and unearthly strange. And so utterly indifferent. I thought then about the reluctant founding fathers and how it must have seemed to them, rejected of their own familiar country, rejected of their own familiar society, but never so utterly rejected as by this utterly rejecting landscape that they had never even asked to see, let alone to engage in combat for sheer survival. From a real adversary courage flows into you. This adversary is too awesome: it simply does not care.

Out beginnings are, at the best, ignominious. Little to celebrate in the founding of a colony that was founded only because it was so far away that it could be conveniently forgotten. Founded parsimoniously, grudgingly, without aspiration, enthusiasm, or the high wild audacity of reckless vision. Founded to clear the hulks and prisons, to forestall the French, and perhaps to grow flax.

At a party the lady exquisitely silvery from glittery head to glittery fingernail, like a living statue to grace a Roman Emperor's banquet, or, more contemporaneously, a toy for Silverfinger (there must be one, or, at least, there must have been if 007 could have kept at it for a bit longer), recalled, with some emotion, the splendours of Bastille Day. A Francophile this one: she had, one gathered, travelled. I sympathized, having some pleasant private memories of Bastille Day myself, and being a bit of a sucker for a bit of *gloire* any old time. In between sips and bites we hummed at each other snatches of the 'Marseillaise'.

Our American friends, when reminded of Australia Day, talked of the Fourth of July, emotionally also, as Americans away from home so often do. We sang snatches of 'The Star-spangled Banner'.

Our children talked of Greek Independence Day, and this time I got emotional, remembering the blue and white flags snapping at every masthead and the silly toy cannon blasting off on the headland and the bunting blowing and the monastery wreathed in plaited laurel and the herbs strewn and trampled on the marble courtyard and the marching feet and the schoolchildren ranked and chanting and the white bows like helicopters on the thick black hair of the girls and the boys' ornate caps with Athena's owl of wisdom picked out in sequins and the speeches and the poems and the soaring oratory and the pride of the ceremonial garlands around the marble throats of the heroes, disdainful on their tombs. We sang snatches of the Greek national anthem.

Alas, we Australians haven't a hope of competing in this field of intense nationalism. We are not yet clearly enough in focus. We do not

176

have the heroes, nor the race memory of resistance, persecution, plunder, glory, unspeakable barbarities and unbelievable heroisms. We do not have the shining belief, the unshakable conviction out of which the heroes and the songs are made. We are uneasy, tentative, unsure, a little sheepish still as to our origins and uncertain of our destination.

Certainly we know we are the best in the world and we live in the finest country that ever was and we have a climate where other countries only have weather and our beaches are the beautest and our way of life something to be emulated by ignorant foreigners and our soldiers are the bravest and our characters the greatest wags and our girls the prettiest and our clubs the biggest and our families the decentest and our racehorses the fastest and our sportsmen the most sporting and our beer the most ambrosial and certainly we've come a long way and now we have something called progressive stability which is going to make the future even beauter than the past and we'll have even less to worry about then than now, not that there's any need to worry anyway because we're a democracy and we have democratic elections to put these jokers in Canberra to do the worrying for us. That's what they're paid for, isn't it?

As for this Australia Day . . . we're as patriotic as anybody, but it's summer after all and the kids are on holiday and the beer's in the frig. and the Holden's in the garage and the week-end's nearly here and we know we are the most enviable people on earth so why get out and wave flags about it. Makes you feel silly, anyway.

And down in the yard the inheritors, certain of such certainties and untroubled by Anzacs, Captain Cook, Commonwealth or Federation, chant their cryptic question: 'Crocodile, crocodile, can I cross the river?'

Here There Be Jabberwocks

Lately I have been intrigued by a news item datelined Bujumbura (Burundi) which tells of the unhappy fate of the Mwami Ntare V, who only last July dethroned his father, Mwambutsa IV, and now, at the age of nineteen years, has in his turn been unseated from his throne by his own Prime Minister, Captain Michel Micombero, who has declared Burundi to be a republic.

Burundi, as I am sure everybody knows more certainly than I do (I have always confessed to my weakness in geography), was a constitutional monarchy, which, with its neighbouring republic Rwanda, used to form the Belgian U.N. trustee territory of Ruanda-Urundi.

It seems ironic that the dethronement of the young (and, one suspects, somewhat hasty) Mwami Ntare took place at a time when he was visiting the Congolese capital of Kinshasa as the guest of President Mobutu for the celebration of the Congolese Republic's first anniversary.

Africa has always seemed to me to be more mysterious than most places (if you don't know any geography most places are pretty mysterious anyway) and at this moment in time it is more mysterious than ever, what with people being throned and dethroned and setting themselves up as Leaders, and states and principalities and kingdoms splitting like amoebas or joining together or changing into something else entirely. How can one possibly—even if one was reasonably informed, I mean—keep up with the domestic policies of Gabon, Gambia and Ghana, let alone the republics of Togo and Mali? Or—I ask you—Chad? The Malagasy Republic has a prettily whimsical ring to it, but I have no evidence that it actually exists. And who could possibly believe in Tanzania? Tanganyika and Zanzibar sounded credible, even to me, but Tanzania? Which is what they have turned into, or at least this is what I am told. It sounds like the setting for an operetta. And what on earth is the point of changing Uganda to Buganda? I darkly suspect that these things are done merely to confuse and mystify, while potentates, panjandrums and prime ministers get on with their plotting under the cover of newly set up Ministries of Rejuvenation and splendid uniforms and tenders for national flags and anthems (as a matter of fact I wouldn't believe a word of any of it excepting that I know a man who earns nice loot drawing gaudy stamps for emergent African states: the newer the state the bigger and gaudier the stamps).

Anyway, conscious as I am of my lamentable ignorance, I have earnestly and diligently set myself to swotting up on Africa in preparation for the day when there will be black peers sitting in the House of Lords as well as black potentates being deposed at home. The peers, I think, will be more permanent. But after a couple of days with the World Atlas of the *Encyclopaedia Britannica* I think I have probably only just begun on what will turn out to be a life work. Heaven knows, the republics are difficult enough to memorize, what with them changing all the time, but you should just have a go at sorting out the prefectures and provinces. The imagination seethes. Do people really live in Batha and Biltine, Logone and Salamat, Mayo-Kebbi and Moyen-Chari? What unspeakable magic is performed in the Cercles of Dosso and Konni? Or Woleu-N'Tem? Do adventurous travellers, travelling however hopefully, ever really arrive in cities called Aboso and Accra, Antalaha and Antsirabe, Majunga and Mananjary, Fez, Rabat, Oujda, and Chari-Baguirmi? Is there a Governor of Gojjam? And what opportunities there might not be for adventure and romance in the Region of Quert—a billion-dollar spectacle, I shouldn't wonder, when the movie moguls hear about it.

In this mental state of boggle and bewilderment, however, I believe that I have found the clue to understanding Africa, and it lies in the nonsense verses of Messrs Edward Lear and Lewis Carroll, which aren't really nonsense at all but quite brilliantly prophetic sociological treatises. And if any of you are tackling this particular problem I would advise you to save a lot of time by reading up again on the Jabberwock and the Hunting of the Snark, and the Jumblies, and the Dong with the Luminous Nose, and the Akond of Swat, and all the rest.

If there can be a Mwami of Burundi then the Akond of Swat ceases to be comic and takes on a real identity. He is, of course, the grand panjandrum of all. The Dong, with or without the luminous nose (which I take to be more in the nature of a symbolic attribute anyway), is probably a traditional title bestowed on the most prominent grandee, and carrying with it immense political power. The great

179

Gromboolian plain (where awful darkness and silence reign, you remember) obviously refers to the place where bad potentates go—in direct contrast to the Land of Tute, which must be a sort of Happy Hunting Ground.

The Quangle-Wangle I interpret as a tribal deity, whose abode is fixed by legend in the Crumpetty Tree, which is the meeting place for the tribal elders, known as Snarks. The female elders, or dowagers if you will, who are so immensely fat that they have to be literally rolled along, are called Boojums. They are very influential behind the scenes, and implacably opposed to the introduction of the Jubjub Birds—the Jubjub Birds being those blonde English typists that panjandrums-presumptive, studying at Oxford, are apt to marry, often inadvisedly.

These marriages are encouraged with great cunning by the Bander-snatches, who don't study at Oxford but at the London School of Economics, and with the most subversive intentions. They are, in fact, the deposers of potentates and panjandrums and are for ever plotting frumiously at coups and counter-coups with the Slithy Toves, who are sinister foreign agents and adept at administering the torture of the Attery Squash, which has never been known to fail with even the most obdurate. The Bisky Bat I take to be a game introduced long ago by the Mome Rath, who was a very famous Englishman who had lived in the country for twenty years and spoke the language like a native. (Mome being an honorary title, like Gom, which stands for Grand Old Man.)

The Pobble Who Has No Toes might be the tribal scapegoat, or, on the other hand, pobbling as such might well be a ritual mutilation. I am still working on this interpretation, and will let you know later how I get on.

In the meantime, with the young Mwami of Burundi still in mind, I have just remembered a fable which I believe to have real significance (as most fables do). It is told that there was once an African king whose prevailing passion was for splendid thrones, of which he bought a new one every year, by mail order from William Whiteley's of London. One year his throne was reproduction Louis Quatorze, and the next he fancied Surbiton Contemporary, and so on. But he could never bear to let a good throne go, either in case he got around to using it again or because, once he had sat on it, it was sacred. I don't really know. But he stored his thrones, year after year, in the loft of the Royal Hut, until the accumulation was so great and so heavy that one day, while he was sitting in judgment in a fancy affair of black sculptured leather, the loft collapsed, the thrones fell down, and the king was squashed like a bug beneath the symbols of his own power.

The moral of this story, and I think all potentates would do well to remember it, is that people who live in grass houses shouldn't stow thrones.

The Party

'Look,' they said, 'you don't have to do a thing. We'll fix everything All you have to do is put on your gear and come to the party.'

So I said, all right, I was game, but would they please keep the guest list down to twenty or so because obviously the house hasn't enough space to take more comfortably and we are terribly down on glasses. And be responsible for Cleaning Up After. Actually I was rather pleased at the prospect of a party, and felt that it was very satisfying to have finally graduated to the ranks of those happy parents whose young are capable of organizing their own parties thank you very much.

It is with a deep and abiding sense of horror that I look back on those interminable years of nauseating bunny rabbit invitations, coconut ice, apple-bobbing, pinning the tail on the donkey, musical chairs, lucky dips, and clapping-hands-till-daddy-comes-home. What exquisite relief lies in the realization that one is finally immune from snot-nosed whingers and spoiled screamers and those sly little dears in rosebud wreaths and tap-dancing shoes who always go through the drawers and pry in the closets and expose every nasty skeleton to their mammas later, their mammas being the sort of mammas who never have anything nasty in their closets and always have a Punch and Judy show or a magician for their children's parties.

And then the years of vainly attempting English nursery-type parties in a foreign land, where custom and curiosity triumphed over guest lists, and little Dimitri and Rita and Costa and Aphrodite were liable to turn up expectantly three hours early bringing cousins of first and second degree, godmothers, aunts, and aged grandmothers in shawls who expected preferential treatment and the biggest slice of the cake.

181

And after that the vigilante years of policing the Postman's Knock and wondering whether you ought to frisk the boys for suspected vodka flasks, because the innocuous punch seems to be having a peculiar effect on sweet little Norelle, who has passed out in the bedroom in some disarray, and how are you going to explain *that* to her parents? Also, what is that scuffling and giggling in the locked bathroom? Should one permit the game of Sardines? And what on earth is going on in the toolshed?

Never never again, I thought smugly, and wondered if anybody would Smoke Pot or do anything really excessive and anti-social, but on reflection I thought probably not, because if they were planning an orgy-type party they would scarcely choose to have it here or invite me to it. However, I had heard that one of the proposed guests had been initiated, or intended to be initiated, by the Maharishi, and he might feel it incumbent upon himself to meditate not only transcendentally but publicly. I was glad we had a number of records of sitar music, and evening ragas, but regretted that there was no betel-nut to offer; perhaps he would bring his own.

Such a lot of telephoning went on through the week that I thought it advisable to warn them again about moderation in numbers, and they looked a bit sheepish and uneasy and admitted that the numbers were sneaking up a bit, but as they had separate groups of friends it was really difficult, and after all the house was really quite big, and anyway I wasn't to worry. Everything would be all right. So I didn't worry any more, except to ask them what they intended to do about food. They seemed a little nonplussed at this, and explained that nobody ever did anything about food at a student party. A few chips and biscuits and olives, maybe. What about drink, then? Oh, not to worry, everybody at a student party brought his own.

I thought this was a very novel, if undemanding, way of giving a party, and had a sudden deep nostalgia for Toni, my dear friend Toni, and the Christmas parties that Toni and I used to give in the vintage days of our youth. Oh, the swags of ivy and the thousand white daisies that we plaited into garlands to disguise the dreary walls of our shoddy post-war flats. The Christmas angels that we fashioned from candles and corks and pipe-cleaners, with cellophane wings and sequinned Byzantine robes. The pies and the patties we baked for days, the mountains of grapefruit and pumpkins that we stuck all over with toothpicked olives and cheese, the oysters kilpatrick and the trays of savouries that were so beautiful to look at that it hurt us to

182

offer them. A Christmas party in our youth took a week to prepare.

The times, as Bob Dylan has pointed out, are a'changing. Or maybe Toni and I were wasters of it.

Anyway, with those long-ago parties in mind, or perhaps because I just can't resist pratting in, I did persuade them to let me organize some food, and order a few flagons for getting things under way, and a team of them worked happily all the afternoon making savouries and clearing space for dancing and putting rugs and cushions out on the deck and sorting records, and when it was all fixed it looked just as though there was going to be a party, and this satisfied me, so I put on my party gear and sat down to wait for it.

They began to arrive in twos and fours, some I knew and some I didn't, and they all seemed very pleased to see the food and the first flagon emptied in no time at all. Introductions were quite conventional for an hour or so, but after that it was apparent that there was a kitchen group and a living-room group who didn't seem to know each other at all and didn't want to, but before I could do anything about it another lot arrived and they had various bottles which they seemed intent on secreting in unlikely places, behind things and under things and even in my study, where I had been doing a bit of secreting myself of various little odds and ends I wanted preserved, like a couple of decanters and a carton of cigarettes. Soon there were fifty or so of beards and dundrearies (which seem to be terribly in) and long-haired girls and short-haired girls wearing very with-it clothes, like striped shimmies with hanging knickers to match, and the record-player was going full blast, although nobody was doing anything excessive or interesting yet—perhaps because they were too busy eating the food and emptying the flagons. By eleven o'clock there were more than a hundred, including a group of flower people in beads and bells and a girl who went upstairs to change into purple drapes and put a hydrangea in her navel. The flower people seemed to be extras with transcendental instructions to keep in perpetual motion, in one door and out the other, which was pretty difficult since everybody was playing Sardines willy-nilly by this time in every room of the house, and there were more arrivals heaving and shoving through the front door and looking so like the people who were heaving and shoving in the kitchen that maybe they were extras too. A young soldier who had been telling me how he was going to make a fortune in Vietnam selling emu feathers to the Americans said he thought all university students were stuck-up slobs. I think he was morose at having his beer pinched. Nobody knew anybody any more, although somebody was kind enough to say that he thought my husband, hung about with the prettiest girls and being waited on hand and foot, looked quite like the writer George Johnston. I said I thought so too.

I retired, defeated, at half-past two. There was a little light lute music on the deck, the kitchen rocked with inventive and frighteningly energetic dance, folk-singing was whining and wheedling in the living-room, and Zorba's dance proceeded awkwardly in the hall. Nobody was smoking pot, or doing anything excessively anti-social, and there was no sign of meditation, except perhaps in the glazed eyes of the young man who had kept his whisky flasks strictly to himself. They all seemed to be having a wonderful time.

I think it was a good party as parties go. But I just thought, drifting off to sleep with the thought of the Cleaning Up After, wasn't it nice when the crud left over was only jelly and hundreds and thousands, and their mammas came to collect them promptly at six, and we all clapped hands till daddy came home?

Box About, Boys!

In the curious, illuminating, piecemeal, scandalous, and absolutely delicious collection of biographical sketches known as *Aubrey's Brief Lives* there is one tale of Sir Walter Raleigh that I like very well.

It is told at third hand, like most of Aubrey's tales, but it has about it that sting of absolute veracity that survives even three times re-telling, or six or ten if it comes to that.

When Sir Walter Raleigh was a young man, and still only Mr Walter, he was taken to dinner by his father into very great company. His father had been censorious of young Mr Walt, calling him a 'quarrelsome, affronting creature', and Mr Walt had promised to behave himself 'mightily mannerly'. And so he did, sitting next to his father and demure through half the dinner, when at a lull in the conversation he told loudly and publicly such a pointedly bawdy story of his father as could only be told, I suppose, in the sixteenth century.

'Sir Walt,' writes John Aubrey, 'being so strangely surprized and putt out of his countenance at so great a Table, gives his son a damned blow over the face; his son, as rude as he was, would not strike his father, but strikes over the face of the Gentleman that sate next to him, and says: *Box about, 'twill come to my Father anon.* 'Tis now a common used Proverb.'

Fathers all, it has taken four hundred years or so, but indeed that 'damned blow' has come around to you at last.

Your authority is no more. The young efficiency experts say in American accents that you are too old. Too old to keep up the pace. Too old to re-learn the new efficiency ways. Too old to re-employ. Too old at forty-five, or even forty, to be of the slightest use in the computerized, systematized, pressurized, promotioned, break-neck world of contemporary business.

If you are employed you are a liability, and grudging forbearance is the best you can expect. If, through no fault of your own, you are presently unemployed, you will be whistling a desperate whistle before the time-and-motion boys consider you for even the lowliest air-conditioned inglenook.

A hair-piece will not help you. Nor will the most strenuous course of body-belt massage, judo, karate, or squash. Neither will an unimpeachable record of twenty or thirty years diligent and exacting service in the employ of other, older, pre-with-it masters. The lynx-eyed lads can see through that lot in a blink. You are too old, Father William. You are not a viable proposition. In fact, you are a business discard. Garbage, dad.

I was watching a gaggle of them (the lynx-eyed time-and-motion enthusiasts, I mean) on the television one night not so long ago, positively radiant with still-youthful confidence and vitality and dedication to efficiency and Admass, and diffusing regret too that there was no longer any room for the over-forties. *Sincere* regret. Too bad, dad.

A chill wind niggled along my over-forty spine. Box about, I thought, 'twill come to me too anon.

It was not the first time I had thought about the over-forties. When you are over forty you become all too conscious of a diminution of energy, a hesitancy in mental reflexes as well as physical ones, a sort of creeping caution in actions that were once instinctive and heedless. Nature, of course, never meant us to live so long, but then we are likely to be living longer and longer, re-plumbed, transplanted,

185

pumped full of chemicals and rejuvenating pills. A man of forty may be only half-way through his mortal span (or endurance test) and if he is a half-way reject what on earth is he to do with the other half-span?

There are some over-forties I know, or have known, or have heard or read about, who bravely refused to be humiliated or boxed about by the 'damned blow' of rejection, and re-created their lives with inventiveness and the most defiant glee.

It occurs to me here that they were all people who had lived most of their working lives under the great strain and tension of not being basically dedicated to the work they were doing, or material success, or status, or the profits of their masters, or expense accounts, or credit cards or the other fringe benefits of business bondage. No matter how diligently and responsibly they had laboured they had remained at heart unconvinced. Their jobs were not also their hobbies. Those sorts of people haven't got a ghost of a chance in the super-pressure syndrome. Cover up as they will their slips are bound to show.

Now the ones I am talking about all took risky and heady action before the axe fell or the 'damned blow' landed. Since their jobs were not their hobbies they turned their hobbies into jobs, and as far as I know every one of them, unburdened of his defensive camouflage, revealed the creative, optimistic, happy and successful person he had been all along.

A tired solicitor became the jolliest host of a Cornish pub, a banker with a love of boats and the sea built himself a schooner and lives now by chartering around the Mediterranean, a pressured executive who liked to watch things grow began a nursery garden, a high-priced woman P.R. found she could live more serenely and just as lucratively by writing at her own pace about the things that really interested her, an alcoholic newspaperman with a fine taste for houses and antiques made himself a happy half-million in a few years by indulging in his hobby of restoring and refurbishing houses, an unexceptional secretary started a travelling library and a new exhilarating life, a husband and wife commercial team (guessing perhaps that their time was up), took to collecting beautiful shells in the sun and making them into jewellery.

I have only listed the people I have known personally, and not all of them at that. I have heard of dozens more. And there must be thousands I don't know about.

And thinking of those people I feel much less creepy about the ruthless efficiency boys and I am reminded of another story which might be just as apposite to the subject as Sir Walter Raleigh.

On Hydra there is a legend about one sheer golden rock of terrifying height and majesty. It is said that in the times of the earliest settlement when food was scarce and living frugal there was no place or room for a man who had outlived his usefulness to the community, and it was the duty of his eldest son to place his father in a large pannier basket, load it onto a donkey, and lead the donkey to the high rock, where the son tipped pannier and father and all into the sea below.

But there came a day when one old man already in the basket and poised on the edge of the rock said to his son: 'Don't bother about heaving the basket, son. I'll jump over myself.' And the son bewildered, said: 'But, father, custom is custom. This has always been done.' And the father said: 'Yes, but it's a very finely woven basket, son, and it seems a pity to waste it on an old man like me. After all,' he said, 'you'll be needing it yourself before long.' And the legend says that the son led the donkey home, complete with basket and father too, and that was the end of that custom.

So box about, boys, 'twill come to you too anon.

The Masculine Look

The earliest advice I ever had on men—the nature, capture, and holding of—came from my mother, agitatedly beating the soap-saver in the washing-up water (the kitchen being the place where intimate chats were most likely to take place: when one could corner her for an intimate chat, that is, because she usually scuttled at the hint of an embarrassing question).

Some of her ideas seem curiously devious and even dishonest in retrospect, but then she did her nature study and essayed her first snares and traps in the Edwardian era, when cunning and dissimulation were part of every girl's equipment. Diplomacy, she called such tactics. 'They're easy to outwit if you flatter them enough,' she said, and her soapy hand flew up to her mouth and her golden eyes glinted with wickedness. 'Forked radishes,' she said. And giggled. And left me confused.

Dearie, dearie me, what a tangled patch of radishes a girl has to weed through before she learns anything at all about the vegetable. Or beast, as some say. Although in my heyday of radish-picking radishes were recognizable as radishes, in spite of minor variations. The wartime crop of young men wore uniforms, or if they didn't wear uniforms they wore drab suits with wide lapels and baggy trousers or equally drab sports clothes with equally baggy trousers and wide lapels. They did not wear perfume and all of them had their hair cut short back and sides so you could see the shapes of their heads and whether their ears stuck out like jug handles or not, and altogether, once you had established your own particular taste, it was fairly simple to do a quick sort through and a rough classification before you got down to the serious business of final selection.

These days I think it must be increasingly difficult for girls to even know a genuine radish when they come across one. So many of them seem to be camouflaged as something else entirely. Sunflowers, or artichokes, or pale lost lilies. And then, to confuse matters even further, real lilies are apt to pretend to be honest radishes, which is terribly sneaky and leads to all sorts of misunderstandings. Although girls have told me that they develop a sort of set of antennae or radar device after a while and find it simple enough to see through all the protective camouflage.

Now I read that the broad-shouldered, chesty look—which used to be the hallmark of the genuine article—is definitely out and the slim-line wasp-waisted look is definitely in, aided by hair-pieces, hair-sprays and lacquers, toiletries of all kinds, complete make-up kits, and heaven knows what other artful deceits. If one is to believe the advertising copy for the newer lotions and colognes, conversation between men and women is likely to come to an end entirely. One whiff of Centaur or Ebb-Tide or Bilge or Sump-Oil and the lady swoons away and never gets to know—until it is too late—whether he has a brain in his head as well as an irresistible aroma and a slim-line appearance. Personally I don't believe the advertising copy, and I think the men are fooling themselves rather than the girls, who will only pretend to be fooled when it suits them.

In fairness to the males, however, I suppose it is about time they had their proper share of the advantages of which we women have availed ourselves for so long and with such deliberate intent. The game becomes more exciting when the protagonists are more evenly matched, or it does if you are half-way honest.

Anyway, if you look back through history, the present trend towards masculine foppishness is not new. Until the dreary, smut-laden and hypocritical time of the Industrial Revolution, when a middle-class of merchants and factory-owners began to dictate fashion—even to the previously foppish upper classes—by their own narrow puritanism and distrust of display and extravagance, men have always been popinjays.

Such splendid gear they've decked themselves out in too. Silks and satins and furs and velvets and harlequin tights and doublets and slashed cloaks and trailing robes and perfectly smashing hats all dripping with feathers and lace collars and starched ruffs and nankeen breeches so tight they couldn't bend their well-turned knees and high-heeled boots and knots of ribbons and embroidered waistcoats and capes and tabards and gorgeous jewels and powder and beauty patches and paint and wigs and ringlets and lovelocks tied with bows and perfumes by the gallon.

And with all this adornment of their persons they seem to have been sufficiently masculine to be doughty warriors and dashing pirates and lusty lovers and prodigious life-livers. Life, one suspects, was so short and filled with hazard that appetites were kept pretty keen, and personal vanity and display were simply an outward expression of an inner exuberance. If you are likely to end up with a rapier through your throat it is nice, I think, to have a bit of lace around it and an effective cloak to grace the final fall. The Montagues and Capulets would only have been Italian street-gangs without their tights and peplums, and Hamlet a crazy mixed-up kid, ripe for a psychiatric ward.

I have some splendid prints of the Klephts, the Greek guerilla fighters who harassed the Turks from the mountains for hundreds of years, and these gentlemen, whose heroism cannot be doubted, wore their hair flowing down over the shoulders of their jackets, which were embroidered in red and gold and decorated with rows and rows of silver buttons. Their pleated skirts were bound with tasselled scarves and their shirts frilled with hand-made lace. They all have the faces of brigands, and sometimes I am ever so slightly in love with them. Byron, of course, saw the value of this get-up very quickly, and he was a gentleman who had more than a little success with women.

The Elizabethans, too, seem to have been a virile lot. But could you possibly imagine them sweeping the Spanish Main and tossing off sonnets and outwitting foreign ambassadors and laying their heads on

189

the block in double-breasted suits? Certainly not. They needed all that flamboyance and bombast to carry things off, whether a gallant speech or a few chests of Spanish treasure or one of the Queen's ladies-in-waiting or a head still on the shoulders.

And talking of bombast reminds me of a very interesting piece of information which has come my way. The word is derived from the universal use of padding, or bombast, in this time of gallantry and derring-do. Bombast could be horse-hair, flock, wool, rags, flax or cotton, and Elizabethan men used it to pad their doublets and also their breeches. Bran was used too, because it was light, but was regarded with suspicion and mistrust after the unfortunate incident of a courtier who had a hole in his breeches from which the bran ran out in a steady stream as he bowed before the Virgin Queen.

It was pointed out a long time ago, and rightly, that 'there is no new thing under the sun'. So on the whole I think it is good that the males are getting back to a bit of bombast about their persons. Life will be more colourful, and I suspect—for the girls weeding through the radish patch—much more fun.

Old Acquaintance Be Forgot

One of my more philosophical friends gave me a most intriguing piece of information the other day. In fact the more I think about it the more intriguing it becomes. He said—and he said this with conviction even if he was a bit vague about where he picked up his information—that in a seven-year cycle every cell in a human body replaces itself. So that, he said, every seven years everybody actually becomes somebody else entirely.

I think I really do like the thought of this perpetual changing of identities or seven-year disguises and intend to propagate it with passion, if only to convince a number of people whom I have picked up here and there in my life that I am not that one at all any more but quite a different one and in fact they don't presently know me.

This seems a very harsh thing to say, particularly as I like people rather than not and am usually touched that anybody should remember me from some other place and time, even if they are really remembering somebody else (once you understand that you are different every seven years a lot of embarrassing memories are easier to bear, because it was, after all, that other one who was so gauche or juvenile or stupid, or even the one before that).

I know that there are many people who make their friends at school, in the immediate neighbourhood, at sports or social clubs, and go on through life without adding more than a very few others to their own select and exclusive coterie. And this seems to be a very tidy arrangement. But for really gregarious people the process is not so comfortable or orderly. Gregarious human beings are terribly prone to acquire other human beings—often for no better reason than a whim or a passing fancy—and, of course, to be acquired in turn, because all human communication works on a two-way switch. Sometimes this sort of impetuous or flirtatious commerce leads to a real and lasting and deepening intimacy that proves to be rewarding out of all proportion to the initial dalliance. On the other hand it is wise to remember that human acquisitions are much more difficult to discard than last year's bad bargain in the way of fashion; you can't pass them on to the St Vincent de Paul.

Long sea voyages are terrible traps for the easily tempted (even for the not-so-easily tempted). Shipboard life is really limbo, and that engaging couple with the fund of amusing stories should properly be left there. When the madness of landfall seizes everyone and address books are being swopped about with mindless abandon write their names in your own little book if you must, but for mercy's sake don't let them write yours. As sure as fate they will turn up, a pair of strangers with whom you have not a single interest in common. Worse, your name in their little book is a sort of promissory note on your acquaintanceship, which they can—and probably will—trade in the open market place. And sooner or later acquaintances of the acquaintances will present that note for payment.

I still remember how one of these chance and chummy shipboard interludes resulted, eventually, in a full-scale invasion by forty-seven members of a travelling congress hell-bent on entertainment and information and convinced, on the authority of the shipboard acquaintance, that we were not only able, but actually eager, to supply it.

Of course it isn't necessary to travel about on ships to entangle yourself in a hopeless ravelled snarl of intimacy with the most unlikely people. If you are prone to it one place is just as dangerous as another. Pubs and parks and bus queues and ferries and dinner parties abound with temptations. A face intrigues. A glance is sharp with interest. Somebody smiles at you confidingly. And before you know where you are you are at it again.

One London dinner party of no more than ordinary convivial interest—at least that's what I think in retrospect, because at the time we must have behaved very rashly indeed—sparked off a chain reaction of acquaintanceship that still explodes intermittently after all these years and over all that distance and long long since the appearance, voice, witticisms and even the name of the original acquaintance have blurred out of real remembrance.

She must have traded pretty well in the market though (nastily, now, I suspect she dined out on us for quite some time), because the immediate post-party chain reaction was the most energetic and crackling I have ever known.

For several summers after, the regular morning steamer from the Piraeus would disgorge Oxford or Cambridge students with rucksacks, maiden aunts with sketchbooks, various distressing people of the type known as 'fringe', earnest academics, city men out of uniform, the old Chelsea guard with aberrations at the ready, used-car salesmen, minor aristocrats, pasty poets, debs and debs' delights, useful relatives, discarded nannies and old retainers, all of whom beat an eager and purposeful pathway to our door and knocked there until admitted, crying the name of our dinner acquaintance as an infallible Open Sesame (unfortunately just at lunchtime too because that's when the steamer came in).

There was a German professor who talked even us into a stunned silence and borrowed all our Greek reference books and never sent them back again. There was a young sprig of the nobility who borrowed our signed copies (sentimental) and didn't send those back either. There were two young ladies of Notting Hill Gate with five children between them and libidos as loose as their dirty and travel-stained shifts. There was—and I shudder still—a Dane who played a trumpet and had genetic theories. There was an American poet of some beat renown who drugged himself into somnolence at our kitchen table and couldn't be woken up properly for two whole days. There was another American poet who got into the kitchen and talked for a week and made a play about it which went like a bomb off-Broadway (he at least did something so I forgive him his trespasses as I would hope he forgives us ours).

192

But one thing they all had in common: they had misjudged the amount of money they would need for an island holiday (our dinner acquaintance having assured them that we had said it was fantastically —but fantastically—cheap) and needed cheques cashed.

There was—and if I wasn't in full cry I would leave him to the oblivion where he properly belongs—a Jamaican gentleman with an Oxford accent who pretended he was an African chief and wore a feather in his hair and a flowered loin-clout over his jeans and had the names and the address all right on his list which covered four foolscap pages in very small writing and was starred like a Michelin Guide against the names of people who were good for meals, accommodation, financial help, plain help, or sundries. To my everlasting humiliation we had four stars.

He came up the cobbled lane under an excited police escort, and following him was a cowed Welsh girl with bare feet, two rucksacks on her back, and a divine dark baby on her hip. (The baby, they said, had been born under an oak-tree in Wales, and I believed them.) The last I ever heard of them was that the Welsh girl was having her second baby in a cave on Crete and the gentleman with the feather had been deported, and I thought it extraordinary that so many stars had burnt out.

My mob say I am being very nasty about all this (brought on, I expect, by having to sign a cheque for an acquaintance to get back to the other side of the world). But what I say is that in the future I intend not to be more cautious but to be less cautious in human exploration. After all, to paraphrase a recently celebrated remark by a lady columnist: 'Some of my best friends are acquaintances.'

The Rule of the Olds

I am an Old. I didn't know about it until quite recently and I find it quite distressing. I mean, I've never been an Old before, nor, if I had thought about it, which I didn't, would I have considered it conceivable that I should be so labelled. I've never known such a place for pinning labels on people. You're not a Young, lady, so you must be an Old. Go buy yourself a fancy hat and a pair of winkle-pickers (so becoming to the Old legs) and make up a bridge four and join a women's club of an educational nature, take up a charity, put on a white nanny's uniform and play bowls.

I don't think I will mind so much being really old. Old age carries authority and can be terrifically stylish. Colette could paint the sun and the moon on her raddled old face and get away with it, that Gothic belle Sitwell went in for fancy dress and many jewels and firmly ordered martinis for elevenses, and I have always admired the other Gothic lady, the Baroness Blixen, who got to look like a heathen idol in her old age, and subsisted entirely on oysters, fresh asparagus, wild strawberries, and the finest Moselle wines. Why not? For myself I fancy a red wig and a parrot and a silver-topped cane and a fund of *risqué* stories with which to regale my grandchildren, who are bound to adore me.

But what really distresses me most about being an Old here, now, in Australia, is that I just might, quite inadvertently, be identified with the bigots, the moralists, the reactionaries, the disapprovers of the Youngs. The Olds who rule, who instruct, who admonish, who warn, who exhort and preach and censor. The Olds who must envy the Youngs with a bitter corrosive envy to go to such lengths of prurience and authoritarianism.

Unfortunately there seem to be so many of them in this country, and so much more firmly entrenched and inflexible than anywhere else I can think of. They are parents and often teachers, they fill the pubs and the clubs and the shire councils, they hold high public offices, they wield the big stick of authority. And they know best. Because they're Olds.

I sometimes think they are rather like the dinosaurs, surely the most stable society the earth has ever known, a society so resistant or impervious to change that they refused absolutely to go even one little mutation towards adapting to it, and died out, sluggishly and torpidly, in the creeping cold they had been too inflexible to acknowledge, saying, no doubt, in outrage and disbelief and dinosaur language: 'Whoever would have thought it?' Or maybe nature was just sick of them.

Not that there is much fun in being an Old. It's one of nature's nastiest practical jokes. (I wonder if it was any fun being a dinosaur?) Olds have coronaries and ulcers and dyspepsia and rheumatism and hernias and haemorrhoids and hysterectomies. And bad-tempered livers. Olds (it's one of the signs of becoming one) begin listening fearfully and compulsively to the working of those interior organs that control their very thoughts, absorbing, secreting, expanding, contracting, quivering and pumping and sucking and blowing ... the whole sluggish, viscous, wave-lie motion of life on which they (and I too, of course) are floated inexorably towards the ropy hands, the hairless freckled skull, the abdominal itch, the stringy blotched wattles, the skinny shanks, the grinning set of clackers, and the dull and plodding reasoning that passes as Olds' wisdom.

Cyril Connolly once said that inside every fat man there was a thin one screaming to be let out. Perhaps inside every Old there is a Young, screaming too. For a second chance at it. Alas, there never was but one. That's the joke.

In the whirlwind climate of change we live in I sometimes think that Olds are really migrants in the Youngs' territory, the Youngs having been born in it and not knowing any other. It is a territory where the only valid passport for the migrant Old is tolerance and an attempt, however groping, however muddled, towards understanding the queer tribal customs of the natives. And of course no communication is possible without at least a smattering of the colloquial language. 'Flog 'em!' and 'Run over the bastards!' belong to an outdated phrase-book, and do nothing to establish goodwill. In fact, such nineteenth-century phrases are more likely to bring about active hostility.

Not that I think those little punks are always right. Sometimes, mercifully, they are terribly, devastatingly, wrong. Sometimes they are irritating beyond endurance. Sometimes, like any other migrant in a foreign country, an Old can become so bewildered he can despair of ever reaching even the glimmer of understanding.

But what the Youngs have is time on their side—if the virtuous Olds don't exterminate them first, and everybody else too. Time to adjust their balances and their values, time to learn, time to experiment, even time to devise a new set of rules to replace the old rules, the Olds' rules, the rules that don't apply any more in this explosive, exploding world of shattered morality and fractured faith and all too bitterly plausible cynicism. Any game to be played has to have rules, but the Marquess of Queensberry is anachronistic on these side-lines.

The Youngs, I do believe, even have time—if the Olds allow it them—to discover razors and toothbrushes and soap and the pleasures of hot water.

And they have all that energy, energy to burn, energy to spare, energy to squander, energy to create. Create what? Good or evil? One has to make a blind act of faith here, they are so strange and barbarous and beyond comprehension at times, this McLuhan generation.

I don't believe for a minute that it is possible for a migrant Old to become thoroughly acclimatized to the Youngs' culture patterns. The gap is too great. And there is something infinitely pathetic about an Old trying to pass as a native Young, like those desperate women who spend two days a week at the beauty parlour and put sticky tape between their brows at night to keep the fear-frown at bay and resolutely wear minis in spite of their knees and their nobbly shin-bones, and the hearty males who risk rupture and worse by strenuous exercise, and the lonely terrified ones who expend all their energies going faster and faster to keep up with the trendy movements and the trendy jokes and the trendy gear until they fall down dizzy and defeated, like those old predators who tiredly litter the fashionable rocks of the Mediterranean, sans everything but their pale-blue Mediterranean gear and their laboriously acquired suntans. Poor old wrinkled pachyderms, come to their elephants' graveyard at last.

But those, of course, aren't the Olds that rule. The Olds that rule don't try to pass as Youngs. They have grown thick defensive skins over the Youngs they actually were once, the more easily, I suspect, to idealize themselves.

'When I was young,' they say. 'When I was young. . . .' When they were young decency prevailed, and chastity, and obedience, and King and Country, and short-back-and-sides, and children honoured their parents and were dutiful to their elders and accepted advice and sixpence a week odd-job money and braved the University of Hard Knocks to get where they are today, established pillars of society, powerful, secure, rigidly rooted in outmoded and inapplicable concepts, stern guardians of public taste and public morals. Knowing best. And like the English of another generation refusing absolutely to learn a word of the native tongue. It is the business of the dirty foreigner to learn ours.

'Dirty' is one of their favourite censures. Dirty, immoral, beat, vietnik, peacenik, quasi and pseudo, irresponsible lunatic fringe, ratbag, hippy, druggy, junky, disruptive minority, tool in the hands of outside influences, feckless, rootless, heedless, improvident.

To be dismissed with a spiteful quip as not quite human. Or to be punished severely for the crime of being young in the most frightening time ever to be young in. 'Flog 'em!' 'Run over the bastards!' Spy on them, pimp on them, club them, fine them, gaol them, conscript them. How dare they not accept what the Olds, knowing best, have decided is good for them? How dare they ask questions? Think for themselves? How dare they be disrespectful of authority?

How dare they be young in the time of their own youth, which just happens to coincide with complete social upheaval?

No, I don't like rape packs either. Or gang-bangs. Or hoodlums or thugs or vandals. The casualties, the social cripples, lacking the will and the wit to keep up with the terrifying acceleration of knowledge and skills and ideas. The bewildered dullards who see only the permissiveness and not the challenge. The human drop-outs pitiably divested of any identity and lacking adequate mental equipment to keep up the required fierce pace for successful survival, informed by nothing but the mass media of sensationalism where sin and sex are rewarded if they're fashionable enough, and if they're not at least are newsworthy and more exciting than anything that happens at the milk-bar. They're resentful all right, but I suspect they don't really know of what. Being casualties perhaps. Being wounded. Being failures.

All casualties are nasty and messy and offensive. Once upon a time every small town had at least one village idiot.

I am an Old. I find it quite distressing, but must accept it with what grace I can muster. I must accept that I shall never again walk to the manner born in the territory of the Youngs. But since I don't want to subdue it, or conquer it, or devise repressive legislation against it, or rule it, I hope I will be allowed to walk freely as an interested foreign observer, though maybe a bewildered one sometimes. I might even be allowed to trade and barter. Experience for new ideas and a glimmer of understanding.

I have an idea that the ruling Olds are so frightened of the Youngs because the Youngs are the future, and the Olds know that they're not going to be there, knowing best. As a future it is at the moment dicey. The spiteful hide-bound we-know-best Olds have seen to that. They may even yet blow the future into smithereens rather than miss out on it. I wouldn't put it past them.

I am an Old, true enough. But with a long exciting run for my money's worth, or my imagination's worth, or my talent's worth, and no desire to rule. Perhaps it is a symptom of being an Old that I think it is infinitely harder, in the present inclement climate of greed and repressiveness on the one hand and woeful human deprivation on the other, to be a Young, inheriting it.

Feeling Slightly Tilted?

One of the joys (or despairs, depending) of writing this column is the mail that Terry the postman shoves in to my letterbox every day (or under the door if it's raining: Terry is an extra special kind of postman, the singing, whistling, cheerful, obliging kind you would think had gone out of fashion about a generation ago).

Now and again I grizzle about mail, but sometimes a communication lands up on my desk that sings for me so sweet and clear, person to person as it were, that I turn giddy all over with enchantment.

One such communication came to me quite recently, and so very person to person that I think it would be improper to mention names —at least without asking—and I hasten to add that I have never actually met this gentleman although he lives in the same suburb and I shall certainly meet him in the near future.

Well, wouldn't you want to meet somebody who has invited you to be the first woman ever to know her place in space? And actually tells you the trick of doing it?

My correspondent is a disciple of that admirably lunatic sixteenth-century Danish astronomer Tycho Brahe (I only say lunatic because most original people are so regarded, always have been, and I expect always will be) and he has invented a most pleasing device of brass which he calls an Educational Apparatus for Depicting the Ecliptic Plane & Motions of Members of the Solar System. He sent me some photographs of this device, and it is indeed a very pretty thing, like the most graceful brass sculpture, and of course I want one, not only to know my place in space but because I delight in such things for their own sakes. If I were allowed I might easily palisade myself all about with shadow clocks, sundials, astrolabes, sixteenth-century nocturnals, hour-glasses, water clocks, telescopes, star charts, and such charming fancies, and finish up by building a small Stonehenge in my back-yard to measure the equinoxes. And the fact that I never know what day it is, let alone what time it is, has nothing whatever to do with it. I am thinking, or reeling, in cosmic terms now, and in this I am encouraged by my letter and the mental exercises it lists as a preparation for my proper appreciation of my spatial self. I quote:

'Imagine the little earth globe is held by your fingers. Could you orientate this (approx.) so that lines between points on it are parallel to corresponding lines of the world on which you stand (sit, lounge, lie)?

'To develop a wonderful awareness of "your place in space" it is essential that you are able to do that one—and the one that follows—spontaneously. And if you don't already know it I can tell you it is really extremely simple.

'Imagine—again. Imagine. Imagine. Imagine.

' "Imagination is more important than knowledge. . . ." (Shakes.? Einstein? Clift?).'

Well, Clift has always been pretty strong on the imagining side, and she's been practising with such intense concentration that while she can now twiddle the world between her thumb and forefinger like a connie ready to fly for the agate she is apt, in so doing, to burn the carrots to toffee and let the bath run over and forget that there is somebody still waiting at the other end of the telephone. Still, it's enticing stuff, isn't it? I will go on:

'Look at 'the beautiful little earth globe again. You are an Outer Space Creature (O.S.C.) gazing with auto-focusing, ultra-super-telescopic eyes at an infinitesimal Charmian Clift. Do you notice that of the 4,000 million humans aboard, only C.C. is standing upright? That she, and she only, is on top of the world? Do you see too that even the person standing beside C.C. is slightly, ever so slightly, tilted?'

The person standing beside me says he knows all too damn well that he's tilted, and more than slightly at that, and that living with me would be likely to tilt anyone not possessed of more than mortal powers of maintaining equilibrium. I am not entirely sure what he means by that but I haven't the time just now to consider its implications too deeply because I must get on with my exercises. Like this one:

'You are still the O.S.C. hovering in his U.F.O. (How far distant from earth and in what direction?)

'Now look beyond C.C., just above her head and about one degree southward. See that hot blue star? A further one degree southward and 40 million times further out in space—observe the yellow star? Note that this one is about five times larger than earth's sun and that there are at least 160 planets revolving about it? You can see that many of these have an atmosphere somewhat similar to earth's? And

199

those strange buildings house living things? Of course they do? You know this just as surely as C.C. knows that somewhere on earth, at this very moment, another umbilical cord is being severed.'

Got that one? Well then, because I'm being generous I'll give you just one more:

'Invert the photograph (i.e the earth. You are again an O.S.C. in his [her, its] U.F.O.). Your U.H. (Upright Human) is now a passenger aboard a ship 450 miles south of Mount Pico in the Azores. Can you see that clearly? Can you decide what time he has? And the date? See the changed direction of the planets? And do the planets now turn clockwise or anti-clockwise?

'Of more interest may be the passenger—the U.H. From his conversation and behaviour can you learn that he is an anthropocentric? Of course you can, and of course he is. Note also that this U.H. is a top politician—a national leader who supports the invasion of Vietnam too. A king of nut. He (and most others aboard as far as that goes) is completely unaware that straight down between his feet stands (hangs?) C.C., the budding astro-physicist.'

Well, there you are. Do you wonder that C.C., hanging upside down and gazing into limitless distances with auto-focusing, ultra-super-telescopic eyes, is entranced? When I was a little girl I would often star-bake at night in the confident expectation of finally turning silver, and star-baking I would look up into blazing majesty and I would sometimes feel that I might fall off the turning earth and into the sky, falling very slowly, falling away in to something else entirely. And it is joy beyond telling to recapture that child's intuitive perception of herself in relation to heavenly things. That is why I am sharing my lovely letter with you. In case, I mean, that you too might like to have a try at living spatially.

Who wants to be a clumsy old astronaut anyway? To think of them burdened with all that cumbersome equipment and blundering around blue heaven is to make one feel leaden. It is so much more thrilling to do it alone and untrammelled and hear the stars whine out like wires and feel the spin and wheel of the celestial fun-fair and join in the cosmic revelry. Luna Park was never so good.

But if you tilt please make sure you don't tilt too much. You might —oh dear!—fall off.

WANDERINGS

The Centre

If you come to the Centre, as I did, by air from Adelaide, the surprise of it is infinitely more surprising than you are prepared for, even though you have prepared yourself by much industrious homework on the geology of the place, its flora and fauna, climate, characters, myths, legends, yarns and tall tales.

You get there already visually bruised and aching, tender in the sensibilities with the effort of belief in the awful innocence of your country so exposed to your inspection, drinking cold beer and eating more airline chicken and advancing your watch a half-hour. You are a little shamed and uneasy, as though you have taken an unfair advantage, and you think of the explorers crawling like maddened lice across that vast wrinkled anatomy, crazed by thirst and dreams and the radiantly tender pink blushed on beckoning hills. From twenty thousand feet the hills are like fat squishy tumours, or dried out scabby ones. Benign compared with the incurable acid-wound of Lake Eyre, steaming corrosive white and vitriolic after placid Torrens, where, all unknowing, Swift set the longitude and latitude of Lilliput. Gulliver sprawls defenceless for your microscopic examination. Pitted pores. Dried-out capillaries of watercourses. Culture slides of viridian clotting thick creamy yellow. Wind ridges raised like old scars, and beyond them the even arid serrations of the Simpson Desert, dead tissue, beyond regeneration.

And yet, the tenderness of the pinks, the soft glow of the reds, the dulcet beige, and violet seeping in. The landscape, after all, is alluring beyond reason. Voluptuous, even. You could abandon yourself to it and die in a dream, like those savages of whom Kafka speaks, who have so great a longing for death that they do not even abandon themselves, but fall in the sand and never get up again. Such unearthly beauty, one knows—and still yearns—is fatal. It is a landscape for saints and mystics and madmen.

And after that the vibrant shock of being terrestrial again, bucketing in toward the Alice in a Landrover with the air singing clear and thin and sweet and your lap filled with the strange flat podded pink flowers that are clumped beside the road and under the ghost gums and the wattle. You could not have foreseen that, nor, with all your homework on the history and geology of the MacDonnell Ranges, could you have foreseen the lilac beyond the red and the gold, floating in a boundless clarity where perspective is meaningless. You accept that the mountains are as old as the convulsions of the earth. They had suffered a sea-change before life crawled on the land. They were old, very old already, when life was new. They were worn down and weathered before such as we were even heralded by creeping things. To see them is to know that they could not possibly be less ancient than that. A thousand million years at least it takes to make something so rich and strange, so profound, so unbearably potent with dreams.

It takes less time to make an Alice. Contemporary Alice, that is. They say it was different before the tourist boom. Old hands mourn, bitterly. It was nearly evening when we reached it, and the mountains were moving in close about hotels and motels and gem shops and rock shops, banks, garages, milk-bars, tourist agencies, boutiques, galleries and the Old Timers' Home. Is it Persian lilac that lines the main street? The scent in the evening air is enough to bowl you over. Fronded trees sparking delicately with little starry clusters, and between them a desecration of imbecile Op lighting, great lozenges of red and blue and green and yellow clownishly colouring the tourists stepping eager for bargains, souvenirs, and drinks before dinner. And through the tourists, the lilac-scented air, the hectic fun-fair illumination, the slow lurching drift and black shadow-weave of the disinherited, stripped of ancient dignity, degraded, subservient, aimlessly drunk on a Friday night.

A lady inheritor, sensible in drip-dry, shoulder-bag bulging—rocks? gems? berry necklaces? Mission grass-weaving? bad bark paintings? —postcards poised ready for the slot, pounces on a tall black trio teetering in the most curiously graceful progression. Cheap boomerangs, she wants. The real thing. Not the junk in the tourist shops. She is loud and articulate. Imperious. (I think of the last Afghan and the last camel train, also imperious, stepping out slow slow from the Alice and disappearing into the vast distance.) The black trio, thus accosted, are soft, slurred, incomprehensible and perhaps uncomprehending. They sway away and back again, surprisingly regrouped under the ghastly green of the street light, awaiting the lady's exasperated dismissal. Two barefooted women scuttle under

204

the Persian lilac and across the street to their men on the opposite corner. They are high in the haunches, long in the heels. Their legs are like thin crumpled brown ribbons flying, their hair pale straw. Drysdale has drawn them often and compassionately, by tin huts and shanties, patient with the heavy burden of life. Now they are patient on the street corner, movement arrested, patiently waiting as if waiting was an end in itself.

But the hotel bar is air-conditioned, clean, contemporary, anonymous. Around the small plastic-topped tables there are tourists in holiday gear and every degree of age and sunburn. The girls behind the bar—and this is to be true of most hotels, motels and restaurants in the Centre—are European or from the South. Girls on a working holiday. Transient population. But there is to be a cattle sale the next day, and among the clean white shirts ranked against the bar there are some of the men who brought the cattle in, so authentically themselves in jeans and battered drovers' hats, so weathered, leathered, creased and sun-cured, so thirsty, exuberant, excited and vocal that you can't quite believe in them, not even when one of them takes a guitar that is leaning against the bar and they all begin to sing. Cattle songs. Outback songs. Melancholy or ironic. They are probably film extras, togged up for another cheap outback drama. And the black one, confidently harmonizing, must be in make-up, because he cannot possibly be of the same race as the frieze moving on the other side of the plate-glass, although the frieze is also costumed in jeans and slouch hats, but out of step and co-ordination, somehow terribly vulnerable. Occasionally a figure detaches and pastes itself against the plate-glass, looking in.

'The Aryans,' one of my companions says. 'Looking at the Huns and wondering whatever happened.'

So this is the Alice. And the Alice is thriving and putting on sophistication, although a little uneasily, like finery to which it is not yet accustomed. Selfishly, I am glad of the comfort of the new motel where our working party makes base. Glad of the good bed, the air-conditioning, the hot water, the private shower, the swimming pool, the excellent food and wine and service in the restaurant. It is good enough to satisfy the most fastidious traveller. In the days ahead we are going to see many exciting places, talk with many unique people. There will be much discussion and instruction on the Question. The Problem. Let them die out. Assimilate them. Put them on reserves. Forget them. Wait. Keep out the do-gooders. And in all our comings and goings, reeling, all of us, with the revelation of wonders, I will be haunted by that daily frieze impasted on banks and tourist agencies and galleries and gem shops and rock shops. Patient. Waiting. Moving, if at all, from one side of the street to the other. The women and girls squatting in ripply black silk circles around groomed trees in a groomed park. Looking on.

I want to say, 'I'm sorry.' Apologize. Absolve myself. I want to tell them that I was not one of those maddened lice of explorers crawling to the discovery of their magic tribal place. I did not personally dispossess them of the ranges and the gorges and the waterholes and the caves where the Huns leave beer cans now, and crumpled paper tissues, and dubious identities chipped into the ancient rock. I did not personally disinherit them of the most sophisticated, ethereal concept of origin that ever a people dreamed. Their blood, for all I know, might be bluer than our heaven.

But here in the thriving Alice the guilt hurts intolerably. What are the dreaming people dreaming now?

The Rock

Between the ancient MacDonnell Ranges to the north and the even more ancient Musgraves to the south there spreads a great flat plain, apparently featureless and certainly without perspective. It is, in fact, more like a sea than a plain, which should not be surprising because very long ago it was.

It is not Moby Dick who heaves up over the horizon, however, but three extraordinary, isolated rocks, tors, mountains—there is nothing to compare them with to give you any sense of scale; they could be the gigantic eggs of the greatest auk that ever was. Away over to the left the flat-topped mesa of Mt Conner. In the centre the rounded hump of Ayers Rock. And further to the west, across miles of sand-ridges and scrub the completely improbable monoliths of Mt Olga, lifting their stately domes into the morning as fragile and insubstantial as a dream. In the distance the tors are misty lilac, floating: it is not until you are close that the red begins to burn and glow and you shrink to your own

206

insignificant human size. Ayers Rock, where you land on the strip if you are lucky enough to fly in as we did, is six miles in circumference and 1,100 feet high. It is a prolonged and momentous event in time about which one might well walk warily and with due humility, pondering on the brevity of one's own existence. It is a place for silence.

Perhaps it is some such oppression of the spirit in the face of majesty that incites inadequate, uneasy, or defiant human beings to acts of desecration. From the air you could not miss the heliographs of the empty beer cans. At the base you identify the oddly fringed foliage as torn paper tissues. Among the last lot of campers was one who dipped the soles of his shoes in wet paint in a madly pathetic attempt to register a despairing identity on that huge red indifferent surface. If he can be traced he will be asked politely to return to the Rock at his own expense and scrub out his footprints.

To police the monolith adequately against such vandalism would require, one imagines, a staff of permanent guards. The custodian of the reserve has one assistant.

I suppose it was inevitable that such a fantastic phenomenon of nature would have to become a Mecca for tourists. Half the world is presently engaged in rushing from the familiar to the unfamiliar— perhaps for instruction and enlightenment, but more likely for new colour slides, or something to do in the holidays, or because somebody else did it last year. Tourism is big business, and important to the Centre, which might well flourish exceedingly on nomadic traffic of such economic consequence.

And yet you could weep for the desecration of nobility, for the shoddiness of buildings thrown together too hurriedly and too cheaply to accommodate the floodtide of the eager and the curious, coachload after coachload determined to be gay, to have a good time, to get their money's worth. You could weep for the wire fences hung with campers' washing, the concrete latrine blocks, the Keep Out notices, the shanty-town atmosphere that prevails under the breath-taking scarps and buttresses which are spiked and chained now for easier climbing. The ants who crawl up the chains from dawn until dark say it is thrilling beyond belief, and the more thrilling for the notice that warns them of difficulty, danger, the possibility of injury, and even death. There are memorial plaques set in the rock to reinforce the validity of this warning.

Perhaps we are too inexperienced, too new at tourism yet. A little more thought and deliberation would surely have suggested that the reserve be left inviolate. Since nobody can come to the Rock without transport, motels and chalets and camping areas might well have been located some miles away, quite outside the reserve itself and designed to sit more harmoniously into the landscape than this aggressively ugly clutter that looks more like a refugee camp than anything else I can think of. The United Nations building would be tolerable, but anything with less authority should be so reticent as to play chameleon among the mulga and not even try to compete with the natural grandeurs. Such consideration of landscape costs money, I know, but I can't believe that the present disrespect of it is going to pay off eventually. It is too short-term and short-sighted.

For one thing I doubt whether overseas visitors can be entirely satisfied with the sort of service that was meted out grudgingly in the motel where our party put up for the night. If you are being adventurous you do not complain of discomfort or lack of civilized niceties. But this, after all, was not real adventure country. It was a thriving tourist outpost, and for myself I can see no reason why such a profitable outpost should be run on the disciplinary lines of a corrective institution. The staff was undoubtedly insufficient, and undoubtedly tired and abraded after a long, busy season. Undoubtedly, also, the arrival of our party was an unexpected nuisance to an establishment that is organized mainly for job lots and package deals. But surely it would be good policy to invest a little more money in extra staff and better working conditions? A contented staff would do much to change the resentful and grudging atmosphere into one of friendliness and co-operation. If it is really necessary for the generator to cut out at eleven o'clock at night is it entirely unreasonable to expect candles to be supplied? Suppose someone was sick in the night? And should one have to feel like Oliver Twist if one is hungry out of regulation hours? To be early or late was to invite not short shrift, but no shrift whatever. Sometimes I think Australians will put up with anything.

Perhaps they put up with it because they have come a long way and spent a lot of money and cannot bear to confess any disappointment. This theory was borne out by the air of frenzied gaiety that prevailed in the frontier-style pub half a mile away through the scrub. Rival coach parties shouted witticisms or wrote them on the weatherboard walls among the thousands and thousands of names and messages already recorded there. Even the pursuit of romance was being conducted with a sort of shrieking desperation, as if time might run out before any encounter could be really clarified: love on the run, dependent upon tour schedules. A fun-time place this, a hectic, transitory Dance-in, Drink-in, Shout-in, Laugh-in, Write-in. A Holiday Happening that must surely convince you that you are having a wonderful time.

And yet, in the aftermath of revelry and the cutting out of the generator the silence was profound, the majesty of the place awesome. If the culmination of desperate encounters took place in myth-haunted cave or on legend-haunted rock it would have been fitting. From the scufflings in the darkened encampment one gathered that this was not the case.

Our windows do not face the Rock—curiously enough only four in the whole motel do, which seems a queer oversight on the part of the designers—so we are up and dressed in half-light to wait for dawn to strike the soaring surfaces. Also to cringe to the cook for an early breakfast, because two of us are scheduled to climb one of the Olgas this morning, while the others involve themselves in some tricky and rather dangerous aerial photography above us.

Celestial lighting arrangements are perfect. At a given signal from a tree whose rustling foliage turns out to be green and gold budgerigars Prometheus Chained puts on incandescent glory. It is more than enough. Even to see such a thing through wire and washing. Nature's pure forms are after all triumphant over contemporary man's brutish lack of any form whatever.

And between Ayers Rock and the dreaming Olgas there is no habitation at all. After the Sunset Strips swathed into the vegetation for the convenience of evening photographers there are only the miles of red sand-dunes quilted with tufts of white grass and fragile formal posies of flowers, stunted mulga, grevillea branching yellow candles, rolling buckweed, jewelled finches and parakeets that escort us as playfully as dolphins. You would not do more than blink at a unicorn.

Is it too late already to hope that this will be left unspoiled by further tourist speculation? Or will the shoddy caravanserai creep out from behind Ayers Rock and advance across the flowered plain in the wake of the coaches that are limited to day trips now? If there is someone in authority who has foresight and even a rudimentary sense of aesthetics it is just possible, even now, to preserve at least part of this immemorial paradise, as a heritage for the generations to come. Perhaps they will be more sensitive to beauty than this one, more finely attuned to the nobility of elemental places, less uneasy, simpler in natural reverence.

You wouldn't, after all, leave beer cans or the evidence of natural functions in Chartres Cathedral, would you?

The Olgas

At the mouth of the gorge the ranger makes billy tea expertly, and we drink it with corned-beef sandwiches that are curling at the edges and taste like every childhood picnic one ever had. The temperature is in the low eighties, the breeze is gentle, above us the sheer smooth stately domes glitter a soft and brilliant red. I am still weak and foolish with relief that I am not after all expected to climb Mt Olga itself, jointless, seamless, polished from the silvery-green mulga at its base to the rounded summit reared 1,500 feet up. Deadpan outback humour is frighteningly convincing. But the ranger has relented and promised an easy scarp further on.

These must surely be the strangest mountains in the world. Probably fragments of the Musgraves to the south, torn by surf from the high rocky coast of the oldest land of all, Yilgarnia, and rounded through ages by rolling seas and fine sands, cemented together, polished smooth, and finally left exposed as a series of monoliths rising abruptly from the plain and slashed by chasms and gorges so deep and vertical and narrow that the sky is only a thin blue ribbon and the vegetation is lush with trapped moisture.

We have just been exploring one of these gorges where the silicious cemented conglomerate of boulders appears as the most intricate mosaic, finely honed and polished and looking slippery. All our faces are dyed bright salmon-pink with the reflection of so much dazzling red. We have the wrong sort of complexions for this unearthly light, and the wrong sort of bodies for this sort of terrain: we are soft and white and flabby and over-civilized and know it and are ashamed. If I could turn myself into a bronze Henry Moore figure I would and sit deep in the gorge for ever and ever, grown over with lianas and crowned with nesting birds. I am obviously not proofed against immortal longings. I suspect the others aren't either, because wordlessly we all fan out and each one walks alone, mysteriously, a tiny recession of Chirico figures moving deeper and deeper into the red slopes and verticals, listening to silence.

Neither do we talk about it much afterwards. We eat our sandwiches and drink our scalding tea, watch the territorial principle in action as a butcher-bird routs a crow from its individual tree, meticulously erase all traces of our alien presence in this grave and solemn place, and get the expedition under way before the coach lumbering up through the scrub in a cloud of red dust can disgorge its passengers and break the spell. Nothing less sturdy than a small tank could follow on the track we are taking, which leads us in a jolting, lurching, bone-rattling, muscle-wrenching half-circle over the sand-dunes and through the flowers—purple and white and yellow circular clumps two feet and three feet across, like no flowers you ever saw in your life before—skirting the bases of the glistening domes until we round them and pull up, shattered, under the scarp which we are to climb.

I think at first that this is another joke. Unseemly, because there is a slope to this buttress and it might be just possible for somebody young and fit and utterly fearless to actually scramble up the ridges and the polished red planes to the top. Not me, of course. I know film people are mostly insane, but not as insane as that. They are unloading the gear, checking and correcting each delicate piece for possible damage during the jolting. My shoulder-bag is being loaded with tapes and film and binoculars. The ranger cheerfully points out the easiest route of ascent, along the stream-bed, diagonally up and across the scrub to the watercourse streaked dark on the red at a dizzying angle. He will wait at the dead tree to guide us up the steeper planes.

Before we are out of the scrub my bare legs are lacerated with thorns and my sneakers are filled with bindies and I have given up smoking for good and all. By the time we are at the watercourse I realize that the conglomerate rock of this particular monolith hasn't been cemented properly: pebbles and boulders roll and slip alarmingly under agonized ankles: there is not an even surface anywhere and everything goes up. By the time I have reached the dead tree where the real climb begins I know I am a stranger in paradise, unfit, unworthy, with my immortal longings reduced to the overriding problem of keeping my lungs working: they seem to be sticking to my ribs and tearing at every breath. Only the sight of the men bowed and staggering across the mountain-face under the weight of cameras, tripods, sound equipment, lumpy duffle-bags of accessories keeps

211

me going. I am no longer a feminist: I am fiendishly glad to have been let off with the lightest load.

The ranger, older than any of us, is two planes higher, and going up with the lithe agility of a mountain goat. I wish I was a mountain goat. I dare not look up any more and I dare not look down. I look at my feet scrabbling for purchase. I listen to my breath screaming and whistling. I feel hysterical with pain and fear. I am a coward and a weakling and a sissy and I don't care. I want to sit down and blubber. I seem to think that thought for eternity, willing my jelly-legs to work, and then the breeze is cool on my face and the rock is level, and there is the ranger sitting on a cairn of stones in the middle of what looks like an Elizabethan herb garden, rolling a cigarette and grinning at me. The others lurch up over the rise one by one, faces suffused and eyes bulging. We all collapse in mad, gasping triumph.

'The only bloody Sherpa film unit in the world,' one says.

There are formal bunches of sweet-smelling spiky grass, posies of the most exquisitely delicate flowers, lavender in colour and flannel-soft to touch, green butterflies. The birds are flying below us and one is a shining unbelievable blue. We can see a hundred miles over the plain that is more like a sea than ever, its detail lost from this height and the vegetation swirled in weed patterns. Around us and still above us the pure bubble domes glisten. Kubla Khan never decreed anything at Xanadu more strange or more beautiful.

I don't think I want to write about it at all really. I would like to keep it to myself and never tell a soul. Afterwards, not then, I thought about what Kafka had written of paradise . . . that we were fashioned to live there, and paradise was destined to serve us. Our destiny has been altered, but that this has also happened with the destiny of paradise is not stated.

I see the altered destiny of the people who lived in this paradise in the Alice. I see the altered destiny of paradise in this coach far below us, pulling up at the bottom of the creek-bed. What has happened to paradise is being stated, loud and clear. We presumptuous people, making a film in this paradisaical herb garden, are part of the statement, no matter how carefully we erase our traces. Only the ranger belongs here, by right of love and knowledge. I hope, desperately, sadly, that he is able to preserve it.

The Gulf

Karumba is a name on the map of Australia, a dot on the mouth of the Norman River where it flows into the Gulf of Carpentaria and the hawks hang over the mangroves and the sandflies are murder. Thousands of jellyfish pulse on the tide, and the opaque, oily-looking water harbours huge coarse repellent fish, mud-crabs as big as large platters, sharks by the hundred, and still, they tell me, a few old and sagacious crocodiles.

It is sinister country. Evil to me since I react violently to landscape and am repelled utterly by this one that seems to be saturated with a sort of thick grey heat. The river here is broad, sluggish, yellow-grey in colour. The mangroves are green-grey, dense and heavy. And the blue-grey sky seems to have a tangible skin of heat on it. From the river the baking salt-pans and the sparse grey scrub recede into for ever. It is not, one would think, a desirable residential area. Still, I suppose frontier towns never did spring up because of residential qualifications. A frontier is pushed forward because of the commercial possibilities of the terrain—because of gold or minerals or gems or hides or seals or ships or apes or ebony or peacocks.

This frontier community of Karumba has mushroomed up in a few months because of prawns. Thousands of prawns, millions of prawns, the whole Gulf apparently teeming with prawns, banana prawns, tiger prawns, endeavour prawns, king prawns. A prawn bonanza whose extent isn't even known yet, although the C.S.I.R.O. is working up here methodically and patiently, weighing, measuring, examining, recording, tabulating, tracking down the breeding-grounds and the habits of every variety of prawn hauled in. Among the prawn-fishers who have been first in on the bonanza there is a certain scepticism tinging present jubilation. Prawning grounds have been fished out before. Exmouth Gulf in the west might be booming, but the east coast is giving only skimpy pickings, and Moreton Bay has been closed to all prawn-fishers. How long will this one last?

Presently there are only fourteen boats working out into the Gulf

213

from Karumba—Cindy, Kotuku, Audrey June, Rama, Toowoon Bay, Sea Marie, Santa Maria, Ulitarra, Sea Fever, Clan Nellie, Sea Tang, Vixen Star, Troubadour, Silhouette—boats ranging from thirty-six to sixty-eight feet, privately owned and operated by skippers who were willing and game to pioneer this enterprise, but all of them (except for Kotuku, which is known as the rebel boat) dependent upon the commercial plant which the firm of Craig Mostyn has set up on the riverbank to receive and process the hauls, to fuel, water and provision the boats, to supply the ice to preserve the catch at sea, and importantly, to provide the spotter plane that is used when the banana prawns run from March to July to pick up the mud boils and direct the boats in.

So the boats on the river and the plant on the bank of it are the heart of the matter. Reason enough for a frontier town. Although perhaps you could not call Karumba a town yet. There is the plant—utilitarian, ugly, looking a bit rushed-up and straining at the tin seams yet, although it is evident that extensions are under way. On either side of the plant, up the riverbank and down the riverbank, are the caravans where the fishermen's wives and children are living, at least those wives who were game enough or optimistic enough or gipsy-blooded enough to brave the Gulf to be with their men. Probably more will come later. Behind the plant is a new building to house the male company employees. The women who work in the plant (other than fishermen's wives) live temporarily in a long metal caravan divided into cabins. There is a bungalow for the manager, who also has his wife with him, and a very young baby.

But along the bank from all this hurriedly assembled caravan town straggling through scrub and sand, there are raked shell paths, borders of Japanese balsam, hibiscus, poinsettias, bougainvillea, tall feathery white cedars, docked bushes of Prince's crown, bird-of-paradise, young coconut palms, and though this vegetation looks parched it is extraordinary in the setting, and the more extraordinary in that it surrounds an oasis of elegance known as The Lodge. The Lodge is a complex that includes a big guest bungalow, cool and airy and polished, with a private shower and lavatory to every clean curtained room, and cherry-red counterpanes. Beside the guest bungalow is a chlorinated swimming pool, and on the other side of the swimming pool a long, high block on stilts that has living quarters, a big dining-room with cane and bamboo furniture, and a completely modern and rather sophisticated bar. There are storerooms behind, the generating plant, a bungalow for the licensee, and another for the domestic staff. It is so anachronistic that you could believe it to be a set run up for a film adaptation of a Somerset Maugham story. In fact The Lodge came first, long ago as a Qantas refuelling base, and through the war taken over as a base for the Catalinas and Sunderlands. After the war it was shut up for years and years, until Ansett took it over in 1959, and presumably restored it. The Craig Mostyn company bought it later.

Unless you count the pilot station and fauna reserve, or the Pawlowskis' crocodile farm away over the salt-pan by the airstrip, that is the extent of Karumba. Frontier new-style. Part shambles, part luxury. There are more than 150 people living here now. Next year, if the bonanza holds and the company can increase the water supply, there will be more. And the next year more still. In a few years there might even be a real town, kerbed and guttered around separate bungalows.

At the moment water is a nightmarish problem. There is only the original well to supply all the needs of the community and the even more urgent needs of the processing plant. Prawns have to be processed cold and frozen fast. The boats which are still unrefrigerated might need as much as seventy baskets of ice every trip. If the place is to expand to capacity there will need to be bores sunk, or a pipeline run from Normanton, the old port, forty miles away up the river.

In spite of the bonus of bar and swimming pool I suspect that life is tough enough on this frontier. The caravans have power supplied, and the wives have fitted them out as ingeniously and comfortably as possible, but they must be cramped quarters at best, and lonely living when the men are at sea. Also expensive living. As with any frontier town, everything—from frozen meat to razor-blades to soft drink for the kids—costs more here than it does anywhere else. And there is only the company store to buy from.

Company employees mess very well at the plant, but there is no canteen, no recreation hall, no newspapers, magazines, books, radio, or T.V., and nothing to do out of working hours and nowhere to go but up through the scrub and along the riverbank to The Lodge, where drinks are expensive too, but at least there, and you can sit for hours at the bar under the shells and the turtle carapaces and talk about prawns and prawns again and fishing-grounds and boats and engines and the latest gossip. Inevitably there is much gossip, but good-natured rather than malicious. A live-and-let-live attitude prevails.

215

This community, as a community, has only been in existence for a few months. In a place that has sprung up so quickly it is not surprising that amenities have failed to keep pace with commercial growth and consolidation. For instance there is no school for the children. There are no medical facilities. The school is not absolutely urgent yet since the married group is surprisingly young on the whole, and most of the kids haven't reached school age. The few that have are struggling, rebelliously, with intermittent correspondence lessons. But the medical position is worrying. The Flying Doctor comes in once a month, and if any health worry crops up in between there is Normanton forty-odd miles away.

In fact all the children look very healthy, rampagingly healthy actually, far too healthy and bouncing for good order and discipline in such boring surroundings: their young mothers look wan and tired sometimes coping with their devils, and they must worry quite a lot. The women and girls grading and packing the prawns in the processing plant complain of constant brine rash. Sandfly bites infect easily and turn into pussy sores. So does the slightest scratch. Many of the adults have sores bandaged or healing. And none of the women have been through a wet season yet. The heat is building up now, sticky and enervating in spite of the deceptive breeze off the river. The palms of your hands sweat, and the roots of your hair, and after you have been sitting for a while your clothes stick to your skin. When the wet comes the community will be cut off even from Normanton by flooded salt-pans, and only the plane will be able to get in.

The twice-weekly arrival of the old DC3 is the lifeline to civilization away across the salt-pans and the bleak cattle country and the abandoned gold-diggings and the Atherton Tableland to lush green Cairns on the east coast. One feels a great respect and affection for the old Dakotas that are still flying the wildest, toughest runs after so many years of service. And there is something gallant about the arrival of the DC3 here, bringing stores and mail and sometimes a stranger to enliven monotony. On Fridays the crew stays overnight, old friends now to everybody, and The Lodge is very gay and lively with news and gossip, and people sing spontaneously, as at an old-fashioned country social.

For there is, evidently, a very real feeling of community here. These are the pioneers, and they know it and have a sense of pride in accomplishment. Even when they complain it is without real rancour. The boats have had a marvellous season with the banana prawns—one

216

hauled 96,000 pounds, working only two or three days every fortnight when the double tides were running. Others hauled 40,000 pounds in the five months. At twenty-five cents a pound this is good money, even with deckhands to be paid, food and fuel to be discounted, and ice at thirty-six cents a basket. This first year of bonanza has only been restricted by the lack of storage capacity and refrigeration in boats accustomed to working on the east coast for skimpy hauls, and by the processing capacity of the plant. Presently the quarry is tiger prawns, which are being hauled in at the rate of 500 pounds to 600 pounds a night, and sold to the company at thirty-six cents a pound.

Most of the season's profits are being invested in more storage capacity, refrigeration to hold the catch longer, better gear, stronger masts and tackle, because many boats suffered such an embarrassment of riches that they could not haul in their catches without breaking their masts and gear, or store the prawns if they could.

So there is, in spite of boredom and monotony and heat and sand-flies, an air of high excitement about this place. The company's investment and the years of patient survey and exploration have paid off. So has the risk of the boats in coming up here. So far, that is. Now there is constant speculation. Will next season be as good? How many boats will head for the Gulf? Will there be other companies setting up competitive processing plants? Is this bonanza rich enough to be shared out among all the people who will want to be in on it? Next year. What will happen next year?

I expect next year will tell. But beside this inimical river, with the heat rising and the sandflies biting, and the hawks and the gulls swooping down on their bonanza of prawn-heads, and the weathered boats fitting out for sea or steaming triumphantly in-river with their storage tanks loaded, there is an atmosphere of challenge and adventure and high hope and endeavour that is about the most refreshing and exciting thing I have struck in Australia. In this most unlikely place a town called Karumba is away to a flying start. And Australia is a more exciting country than I ever dreamed.

The Island

The one certain thing about going north in Australia is that the further north you get the further north you want to go. And so I have fared north until I have fared right off the tip of the northward-pointing finger of Cape York and find myself, intrigued at the very least, on Thursday Island in the Torres Strait, a place which has been of some public interest lately because of certain medical revelations concerning the incidence of what is nicely called 'social disease'. It is a place, also, of which Somerset Maugham wrote a long time ago that there was nothing there but goats, and that the wind blew for six months of the year from one direction and then turned round and blew for six months from the opposite.

There are no goats any more, but the wind still blows. Presently from the south-east, a buffeting bouncing lively wind that clashes around in the coconut palms and tosses a waxy storm of cream and pink around the frangipani-trees, stirs even the dark heavy mangoes and figs to turbulence, and raises such a storm of dust in the unpaved streets that you are nearly blinded. Your hair streams backwards, your clothes belly out like sails, your skin is coated with a layer of fine dust and your mouth is permanently gritty, but at night it is blessedly cool under the billowing mosquito net and the palm shadows dance on your flimsy walls and the crepitant coconut fronds make a soft scraping rhythm to counterpoint the monotonous thrum thrum thrum of the power plant, which, with typical official cunning, has been built slap bang on the waterfront immediately in front of the main hotel. Obviously there is no scheme afoot to develop this as a tourist island. But you sleep well here and dream strange dreams.

It is not a lovely island. It is barren, dusty, the stony soil is completely uncultivated, the streets are, for the most part, unpaved, the beaches are scungy with oozy weed, rusting tin, and a million broken bottles, the habitations are ugly and utilitarian—even wood and roofing tin have to be brought up from the south. Everything has to be brought up from the south—meat and eggs and fresh fruit and vegetables and milk—what you eat and what you wear and what you drink and the very roof over your head. The only pastures are in the sea, and it is only the sea that is really beautiful, the sea and the near distances filled with the sensuous undulations of islands—Horn and Prince of Wales—which have an illusory enchantment. I say illusory because Horn is where you land on the airstrip, and at close quarters it is just as stony and barren and uninviting as Thursday Island itself.

But the flavour of Thursday is authentically tropical. If you have read enough Somerset Maugham and Graham Greene you will recognize it instantly—the heat, the dust, the rusting tin, the decaying jetties, the verandahed hotels, the rhetorical customs house, the mangy dogs, the anchored luggers, the visual impact of black flesh. The old hands stamped with the tired inescapable stamp of too many years and too much tropical knowledge, the bums washed up by freakish currents and beached here, the merchants—Chinese and Sinhalese and Philippine and European and every possible combination of race as well—officialdom pink and superior and aloof, twisting decorously with the hospital sisters at the three consecutive 'cabaret' nights, Thursday at the Grand, Friday at the Torres, Saturday at the Federal. At the Royal every night is cabaret, and every day too if it comes to that, black jellying joyful spontaneous cabaret to a juke-box blasting full-belt under flyblown posters of Esther Williams and Gene Kelly. The Royal is a gold-rush pub from Cooktown, freighted up here holus-bolus long ago and re-erected. Now it has reached the last stages of decay: the stairs have collapsed entirely, the top floor is reduced to a few gappy slats which reveal old intimacies of wardrobes and chests of drawers, and Heaven knows whether the bar and the couple of decrepit rooms which are all that is left of the ground floor can hold out under the exuberance of nightly gaiety until December, when the new Royal, presently only girders on the lot next door, is scheduled for completion.

The native population is now free to drink what and where and when it chooses, and mostly it chooses the wreck of the Royal and draught beer in great jugs and an absence of inhibition.

An old-timer who was good enough to give me a couple of hours of reminiscence regretted bitterly the passing of the protectorate, segregation, European supremacy, and the no-drinks-for-natives rule. What he was mourning, I think, was paternalism. He said that the native population was happier in the old days, and that their present freedom was only debauching them, and debauching the European population with them. He quoted rates of illegitimacy and venereal disease, mixed alliances, cross-breeding, and the somewhat forward behaviour of certain young women.

It is terribly difficult for a stranger to assess the complexities of the social structure of Thursday Island. I suppose it is presumptuous of me even to try.

To begin with Thursday Islanders aren't necessarily born on Thursday Island. They come, most of them, from other islands in the Strait—Murray, Darnley, Mabuiag, Badu, Saibai, Boigu, Dauan —to this trading post, administrative centre, and clearing house for labour. Here there is a hospital, schools for the children, hotels and shops and taxis, work in the town or on the pearling luggers, which still—in spite of all one has heard about the bottom having dropped out of the market—go out for commercial shell, although these days the main and profitable catch is live shell to feed the cultured-pearl farms on Friday Island and Horn and Possession and Good's, on Albany and Darnley and Boigu, at Poid on Moa, and the Escape River. Out of a native population of between 1,500 and 1,700, about 600 men are engaged directly in pearling.

From here too the enterprising or adventurous or ambitious islander can move south to swell the labour force on the mainland. The Torres Strait islanders are a big race, tall, and physically strong: they can earn good money labouring on roads and rails, in quarries and canefields. Education here is improving; there are schools up to the seventh grade on Darnley, Murray, York, Mabuiag, and Badu, and on Thursday Island itself a high school up to junior standard where children from the outer islands are brought in and housed in a hostel if their potential warrants it (only boys yet, which is a bit sad: the Australian attitude towards women carries through even in this fresh and exciting field of social experiment).

What is evident is that here the educated young have no avenues open to them in which they might profitably use their education. A few can be absorbed into the Department of Native Affairs, which still administers the Strait's islands, but the majority have to move south, often through Bamaga on the Cape, a settlement which has training facilities and operates as a launching pad to the south, economic and spiritual independence, and—one desperately hopes—eventual integration. It is a time of tribal movement: Thursday Island drains the outer islands of the young, the clever, the hopeful, the ambitious, and the south drains Thursday Island. One could, I suppose, foresee a time when the outer islands will become Twilight Homes for the aged, and, when the aged die, revert to nature and silence, which is a fairly spooky thing to contemplate.

In this movement of population inevitably—and I suppose unfortunately—much of custom and tradition is left behind as unnecessary baggage. On the outer islands there is still feasting and singing and dancing, but here on Thursday there is little evidence of any indigenous culture. No crafts are practised, except for the crafts of the sea, feasts of turtle meat and turtle eggs are not usual, and apart from All Souls' Cathedral ('. . . erected to the Glory of God and in memory of those lost in the wreck of the B.I. s.s. Quetta 3,484 tons, which about 9.14 p.m. on Friday 28th February 1890, struck an uncharted rock in the Adolphus Channel, whilst outward bound from Brisbane to London, and although in calm water & bright moonlight sank within three minutes with the loss of 133 lives out of a total of 293 on board'), where services are very High Church and hymns are sung in the native language to the accompaniment of a drum (and this is a breathtaking experience for a stranger), songs are likely to be pop, and dancing European.

And yet. And yet. This place tastes exotic, like strange warm fruit. The trades blow, the palms stream, the dust swirls in clouds and coats ugly houses, tropical trees, rolling children, and hurtling taxis filled with grinning black faces. The days of Assemblies, China boats, shell traders, pearl buyers, and the reign of Burns Philp, might be gone, but something lingers, a smell and a taste and an essence, half squalid and half romantic, something indolent, excessive, irresponsible, shameless and happy. One responds instinctively, and I suppose primitively.

Of course one should deplore drunkenness and promiscuity, illegitimate babies of uncertain fatherhood, and disease apparently spreading like the plague. But the drink and the disease are a white gift, and the illegitimate babies are beautiful and happy and adored. People laugh here, and wear flowers in their hair, and go fishing and get drunk and make babies and grow fat without concern or regret.

I cannot see that law or even incentive will alter this pattern in this generation, which, consciously or unconsciously, still pulses to old rhythms. Freedom is only a word until its meaning is deciphered; it needs time and the right key and constant usage.

But the children of this generation will understand it. Or some of them will. Their children's children will consider freedom, equality, independence to be a birthright. As it should be. Legally the Torres

221

Strait islanders are now Australian citizens, with all the privileges and all the responsibilities that devolve upon that state. Most other Australians don't even know they exist, and of course one wonders how long they will exist in their present state.

Civilization will take up, and responsibility, and material ambitions, taxes and plastic flowers and shoes on the feet and respectable alliances and temperate behaviour. The drum in All Souls' will be silent, the Department of Native Affairs a memory, and the new Royal will hold cabaret with due decorum and a four-piece orchestra.

I am glad I have tasted Thursday Island while the taste is still rank and wild. It will turn bland soon enough.

The Outer Limits

He told us, the manager of this cultured-pearl outfit, that the workboat left Engineers' Wharf at a quarter to seven, and we could go if we liked. We asked about food, but he said not to bother; he would contact Muroi, whoever Muroi was, and Muroi would give us lunch. So we only took some mangoes and a bottle of wine and our swimming things and presented ourselves, fairly clueless but as instructed, on the wharf at the proper time.

The workboat was already shuddering impatiently beyond a moored lugger where a beautiful serene old man in a purple lava-lava lounged, idling through a comic book. We had to drop from the pier where the women were already fishing to the lugger and then jump from the lugger to the workboat. Nobody offered to help us and not one of the natives on the workboat smiled, which shocked us momentarily. June said in a puzzled voice that they might be Badu natives, a more dour type. They were certainly in a hurry: we had scarcely skidded clumsily onto the deck before they had pushed off. Nothing indolent about this workgang: we sensed a stern authority operating from the island we were headed for, and were, I think, slightly and deliciously thrilled.

We had reached it by half-past seven, after threading the channels through the closer islands—ardent blue race of current and a black prince from a Roman triumph standing haughty in green board shorts and spindrift speckling him silver. But he was as anxious to get to work as the others. They all piled off the workboat into a launch, and we piled too, and scrambled out on a floating landing stage where pine-log rafts, supported on empty petrol drums, were moored. A pine and bamboo cat-walk, jiggling perilously on the lively sea, led right out into the jewelled channel to other rafts. There was a green sun-awning, a couple of sheds, piles of tarred wire baskets, a generating plant, a tractor, and a churned sandpath that led up the steep dunes to a long prefabricated steel hut with a row of doors painted cerise and yellow. The workgang scattered urgently, to machine shed, pitch barrel, or, with the pretty balance of tight-rope walkers, along the floating cat-walk.

We were ignored, and something irresolute, but thought that we ought to find somebody to present ourselves to. Eventually Muroi found us, squatting disconsolately on the beach and staring back to Thursday Island still visible, but not, alas, accessible.

He was a big Japanese, broad in the shoulders and broad in the face, and his hands were the most powerful looking I have ever seen. He wore white shorts and a fine loose white lawn shirt and he didn't smile either, and I think he had been watching us for some minutes before we saw him. But he gestured us to follow him up to the hut and led us into what was obviously his private office, and called the native cook in the adjacent kitchen to bring us coffee, and when he had given us the coffee and a big round green Granny Smith apple each, he bowed politely, indicated the awning at the landing stage, and left us to uneasy speculation. There were shelves filled with tattered Japanese books, piles of gramophone records, an old console radio, a blackboard with the cryptic chalked message 'Nucleii gloves', a set of golf clubs, a desk piled with papers, an abacus—everything neat enough, but old and worn and used. The room of a lonely man on a lonely outpost. We would have liked to have had an inquisitive riffle, but didn't quite dare.

When we went back down to the landing stage activity was intense. There were natives bent like black interrogation marks on the further raft raising and lowering baskets of shell. On the stage there were tanks of seawater with baskets of shell immersed in them. One native was selecting single shells according to some obscure law of preference and wedging each open with a wooden chock. Another, gloved, scraped each shell free of barnacles and growth and scrubbed it furiously.

Muroi himself was intent at a small table on which there was a foam rubber pad, containers of various chemicals, two jars of plastic beads of different sizes, and a row of surgical instruments. There was a wedged-open shell in a clamp at eye level, and inside the living flesh of this shell Muroi was performing an operation with those huge muscular hands of his, inserting a plastic bead deep into an incision and grafting live tissue over it again. The shell, unclamped, winced shut. I said, stupidly: 'Do they ever die?' Muroi, clamping the next victim, said with convincing brevity: 'Yes.'

But he didn't seem to mind how long or how closely we watched him, and he answered all our ignorant questions with unsmiling politeness. And his hands never stopped, probe, scalpel, surgical scissors, tweezers, so fast and so delicate and so rhythmic that if we had watched for years we would have been no closer to knowing how he did it. Once I asked him if there were any Australian technicians yet who could perform this operation, and for the first time his impassivity flickered with something like amusement. 'They try,' he said.

But however interesting all this was, we were superfluous there, and knew it—idle ignorant women interrupting urgent work with silly questions. Piqued and humbled, we took ourselves off to the furthest tip of the island to swim and explore. Sandhills and she-oaks and native figs, bunches of fat green pods bursting with black seeds, vegetation so weird and primeval that it was scarcely vegetation at all. We lost ourselves in burning sand gullies, ginger-footed on spiky dry carpets of oak needles, gathering seeds—for what?—such seeds as these would never germinate in civilized gardens. They would only burst darkly in the climate of a mangrove creek wading with witch claws, and a dead turtle putrid on the sand. We were far then from the blur of the Cape's tip just visible on the horizon between Horn and Prince of Wales, far from semi-civilization as represented by the distant small clutter of habitations on Thursday Island, far even from the mysterious complexities of pearl-culture and the mysterious complexities of alien Muroi performing unnatural operations to the end that throats and ears and fingers might be decked with sea-lustre.

We were on the outer limits of all our civilized continuities. We lived in weird green mansions, we bathed in virgin sea, and let the warm blue current take us, unresisting, and beach us on white sand. We were beyond the outer limits of everything, apparently, except the range of Muroi's binoculars, because in the middle of the day a launch came chugging up inside the line of pearl rafts, with instructions to collect us for lunch. But even waist deep in water we couldn't pull ourselves up to the deck, and had to walk back, soaked, sandy and discomfited.

'You rike bath?' Muroi asked so blandly that June and I dissolved into schoolgirl giggles, and marvellously Muroi became scrutable. We pantomimed our efforts to get into the launch, we clowned for him to keep him laughing, and back in the office he served us raw tuna steeped in green ginger, fluffy rice, sardines delicious in batter, raw cabbage, soy sauce, with a fried egg each and a piece of steak in case our tastes were rigidly Australian. He was hostly with the wine we had brought, and fathomable, a lonely man enjoying rare company. His wife and family were in Tokyo; he went back there every year. Yes, he was lonely. Five of his compatriots were on leave in Japan, and four others were working on other pearl farms in the Strait. He went in to Thursday Island every Saturday, but through the week he stayed here. He read, he listened to Japan on the radio, he played music, he putted on the sandhills. Our feminine egos reasserted. We discussed pearls as if we were ladies who habitually wore such adornments. We poured buckets of charm over him. And then the native cook cleared away and Muroi stubbed out his cigarette and enquired shatteringly if we took nappings.

We turned timid as snails. Dismay overtook us. Married ladies and mothers-of-three—what etiquette applied on the outer limits? We took nappings, each in a neat little cell with a bed and a hammock and touching personal things, postcards, and photographs of slant-eyed children, and the wind in the she-oaks sent us off like babies. And afterwards we swam below the hut, wading through the dugong grass, and knocked oysters off rocks, and found Muroi again late in the afternoon, supervising the beaching of a barge with quiet, persistent authority. It was so ancient, and so ritualistic, the black bodies straining on the ropes, glistening with sweat and the late sun, the chanted work-cries. Is this really Australia? And are we really here, June and I, soaked and saturated in this strangest of days, sun-addled, sitting with our feet scruffing through discarded pearls? Blister pearls that didn't grow properly. The shells that did not survive the operation.

The workboat left late. The barge had to be beached first, and beached to Muroi's satisfaction. He apologized for this, and held each of our hands warmly on parting. Work was over. He could smile again. In the end there is no communication between people. As our boat raced down the channel we watched him climb the path to the hut, a lonely white figure scuffing sand. At the top he turned and held one hand in salute. We wished we could shout him some words, some message, but there was none, and anyway he was out of earshot.

The black prince from the Roman triumph burst a dazzling smile on us, like a bonus, and our boat leapt against the current and raced for home.

The Hippy Warriors

In the evening of a most satisfactory day we are sitting, as has become our habit, in old cane basket chairs on a verandah, just around the corner where we can still see the front steps—and who comes in and goes out—but also keep the lounge under observation, and, through the lounge and across the passage, the bar, where we are not allowed, this being technically North Queensland and we being technically ladies.

The verandah is wide and wooden and there are plants growing in kerosene tins, including a weird white lily which has just plopped open, releasing a gust of indecently sweet scent that quite overpowers the more delicate smell of the dusty frangipani blossoms that are being blown in on us from a gnarled tree that grows beside the front palms —lashing and crashing about as usual, fragmenting a lurid sunset. We have just been told that there will be no plane into Thursday Island for several days, the pilots having flown their sixty-five hours already, so we are marooned irrevocably enough to relax about it.

Inside the lounge, which has been modernized to the extent of moulded plastic tables and chairs, black and orange and white, vinyl flooring to match, and paint, in a discreet riot of pastel shades, on the very old weatherboard walls, the juke-box is playing something about San Francisco and flowers in your hair, which doesn't seem all that inappropriate considering the number of hippies who are gathering for the evening Happening. Hippies in families and groups, happy hippies by the charcoal ton. What would be the yardage of flowered cotton required to so modestly encase mountainous Nelly?—Nelly laughing into beer froth with a hibiscus stuck in her woolly hair and a baby stuck on her apocalyptic bosom, clinging for dear life, as well it might. We might get a nurse of it later if we're lucky.

Big Florence, in a neat blue overall, is setting out more flowers in the lounge, but plastic ones, and reserved notices on the tables. The members of the band are setting out themselves and their instruments in the dining-room at the end, which has been cleared, and the orange curtain (plastic again but pretending to be bamboo) drawn back. Satin shirts. Electric guitars. Microphone. An elaborate and expensive set of drums emblazoned with the legend 'Y-Bens'. Florence is jiggling a bit with anticipation—how their bodies move, these girls, joyfully and instinctively, as though their muscles still remember something that has atrophied in our starched lot, or been squeezed out of us by centuries of rectitude and foundation garments.

The Y-Bens have called themselves after the original name of Thursday Island, Waiben, which means dry. What the original names of Sunday Monday Tuesday Wednesday and Friday islands were before dogged Bligh doggedly ticked them off day by day on his epic journey through the Strait to Timor, I don't know.

But names are interesting here. There are ordinary European ones, acquired second-hand I suppose from admired or feared or powerful white men, but the more suitable surname of Sailor is current. And so is Warrior. Sailors and warriors these people were before Bligh, and before Cook, before Torres's journals were ever discovered, and before Torres himself passed through the Strait in his search for the Great South Land. And missed it entirely.

This morning after breakfast we spent hours in the stony cemetery over the hill on the back road to Tamoi Town, deciphering old legends on old headstones guarded by crumbling angels. Younga David from Yam Island, Spear Sambo from Murray, Richard Fred Abednego, Poey Akiba, Sosefo, Assea Fonomoa from Rotumah Island, Aliasa Warrior, Dadu, Rosie Rau, Kuap Tiati, who was a Government teacher and Island councillor, Gagie Mosby from York, David Sebasio from Darnley. And Wigness. Just Wigness. Nothing else at all. And all these graves were eloquent in the dusty baking morning of a long proud tradition of sea people, warrior people, missionized, perhaps, but never quite tamed. (I thought of that savage drum beating in All Souls' Cathedral—onward, Christian soldiers indeed.)

Many of the graves had cups and saucers and plates laid out on them, in which offerings of food and drink had dried. There were some

227

enclosed by ropes from which paper streamers fluttered. Some had their headstones swathed in wrappings, waiting, I suppose, for some Grave Festival. And poking up among the Spear Sambos and Wignesses the austere stone fingers of the Japanese headstones, uniform shafts cabbalistically charactered, excepting for one, which read in English 'Ritsu Taguchi, Hiroshima, 1898'. Better perhaps for the blue salt sea to flood your lungs with death than the poison flood that lay in store for Ritsu Taguchi's home town.

But all that was far from then forethought of, the year of 1899 when William Vigers of Scone N.S.W. died on his way to India with horses. Did John Thomas Bebrouth, Master Mariner of Limehouse, 1853, leave any descendants? Love a girl as dark and gay as Florence, jiggling joyfully to the first tentative twanglings of the Y-Bens warming up? Who dictated the poignant words under the name of André Boitelle?—'mes memoires eternelle'. In that harsh, sun-baked, stone-strewn resting place one would not have been surprised to find, among all the half-obliterated names, one that said, simply, 'Lord Jim'.

Although it is more likely that Lord Jim is in the bar across the passage, talking pearls, customs duties, tides and shipping. Or taking his place at one of the plastic tables decked with plastic flowers and ordering a long cold drink for his partner, who is pretty and knows it. The European colony is out in force tonight, the men in crisp creased shorts and shirts, the women in shifts that are short and fashionable, and hairstyles that reflect ingenuity, since there are no hairdressers here. It is, for all the plastic flowers and the Y-Bens' marvellous percussion and the determined twisting of officialdom being gay, a curiously old-fashioned scene. Australian colonialism passing before Australia ever really knew about it, shadow and echo of British colonialism, not fake exactly, but not quite credible either, like an amateur theatrical company in costume, acting their heads off before the curtain comes down. Real professionalism is represented by a huge man in rumpled shorts and split sandshoes at ease in a basket chair, a British ex-Governor of an African state who came in on an untidy yacht today and is being patronizing in a hearty British way to a couple of imitation beachcombers. The curtain has come down already for him, but the professionalism stays, like a hallmark.

Here on the verandah the hippy warriors and sailors are loosening up. The beer jugs are emptying, the beer jugs are refilled. Couples essay the lounge and the waltz, which they perform with wonderful dignity and sometimes in shoes. Laughter rises, and voices take on a beautiful sing-song lilting intonation, using English words to the melody of native dialects. Four big men begin a chant in opposition to the Y-Bens, growling and stamping, and the women laugh until they shake all over, telling the men not to be such fools. The tin cans tacked on the verandah posts are overflowing with bottles, and the flower people are bringing more from the bar, for time is passing, and licensing hours, and supplies will be needed to continue the party on the beach later. And now the young girls, singly, or in pairs, take over the lounge and the last of the twist. They twist with every muscle. They twist until you cannot believe such twisting is possible. They twist with such laughter that everybody else must be laughing too at such fantastic parody. They twist the band out of music, and me out of breath, and the weekly cabaret out of further possibilities. Nothing can happen now but for the party to end. Which it does.

And we sit for hours on the empty verandah, blown over with frangipani flowers, thinking that San Francisco has a lot to learn, and laughing until we have laughed ourselves into gravity again and peace and wonder. Who, oh who, was Spear Sambo?

CONCLUSIONS

You've Got to Be Quick

A friend of ours had returned from a trip to Thursday Island with a tape of native hymns which a group had sung for him privately.

He felt, though, that it was nothing like complete, because they had really only just been warming up, and he wished very much that he had had more time, and also that he had been able to stay over the next Sunday to record in All Souls', the Quetta Memorial Cathedral, hymns being sung to the beat of the great drum. Having been fortunate enough to have attended a service at All Souls', I agreed with him wholeheartedly that somebody should record as much of that vibrant, pulsing sound as possible before it is too late.

We were talking about this when somebody else said: 'Well, if you want to do it you'd better be quick,' and I thought how often I had heard that phrase lately, and indeed how often I'd said it myself.

A couple of months ago I was like a boiling kettle, seething over with enthusiasm to film people I know about the visual possibilities of the old Royal Hotel on Thursday Island, the gold-rush pub shipped up from Cooktown and re-erected a century ago, and when I was there the favourite haunt of the islanders, who seemed to be more relaxed and gay and uninhibited in that atmosphere of utter desuetude than they were in the more conventionally respectable boozing establishments.

'It's marvellous,' I said then to the film people, 'but you've got to be quick.' They weren't quick enough for various reasons, and by this time the old Royal will have been pulled down to make way for the modern hotel that is to replace it, and I think it is a pity that there is no documentary record of its final riotous decay and dissolution, because it was really something. (There are probably painters and photographers scattered all over Queensland recording the last of the gold-rush pubs. I do hope so, and I hope they are quick enough, before the tiles and plastic take over completely.)

The rate of change has so accelerated, and is accelerating every day, that if you're not very quick indeed about whatever it is you want to do or see or record or preserve it is gone, and irrevocably gone, and nothing will ever bring it back again.

233

Going, going, almost gone already the curious or the charming or the exotic native custom, the interesting dialect, the tribal dance, the craft that is an instinct, the Drysdale street of a country town, the stone cottage in the orchard that somebody should buy and restore before it collapses, the perfect picnic place that nobody else knows about, the bush walk under threat of being turned into a municipal garbage dump and the lonely beach under threat of development into a housing estate, the memories of the old men who have seen and known things most of us have never dreamed of, the lore and the songs and the stories that have been handed down the generations but don't interest this one much, the noble tree that must be sacrificed to the new highway, the rows of terraces, the hitching post, the pocket of rain forest, the ancient bitten faces of the breed who are passing now, the painted rock gallery the tourist coaches don't stop at yet, the carving in the ledge at the bottom of the trail, the unspoiled island that might, next year, be covered with Mickey Mouse cabins, the little fishing port that will inevitably turn into a holiday encampment. The wildlife and the flowers. Going . . . going . . . oh, you've got to be quick.

It is not that one could, or would even want to if one could, stop time and change. Nobody, excepting perhaps antiquarians and the over-reverent, would want to live in a past that was fixed and immutable. Neither would one want to halt the education and the integration of the Torres Strait islanders just because their present ways are picturesque and charmingly raffish, or of the Aborigine because he might forget how to paint bark or not care about painting bark or even, eventually, not recognize bark if he saw it on a tree. Nor would one, deliberately, condemn the people of the outback to perpetual drought and toil and hardship without the convenience of any modern amenity or any transport other than horseback just because such a life makes for splendid character lines in weathered faces and laconic anecdotes. Or oppose the construction of a beautiful, functional piece of contemporary architecture to preserve an inferior building whose only merit is age.

It always puzzled me a little, when the tourist boom brought a new prosperity to Greece, that the professional Hellenophiles were so outraged and bewailed her lost poverty as if it had been her virtue. 'There were only dirt streets in this whole sector,' they would say, where now there was good kerbing and guttering. Or, 'The only way you could get to Bassae then was by mule, and if you were caught in the snow there was nowhere to sleep but in a shepherd's hut.' Or, 'The women were yoked to the plough, and all the kids had goat bells around their necks, and they only ate meat twice a year.' 'Oh, it was so simple and beautiful then,' they said. I thought it might be more comfortable though for the kids to be wearing shoes and going to school and eating up hearty, and more convenient to get to Bassae by a good road, and having slept in shepherd's huts on more than one occasion I had to admit that on the whole I preferred a good clean bed in a new hotel. I used to love the old sector of Athens with its dirt lanes and cracked steps and its taverns and old shuttered houses, and regretted too that it was rapidly becoming a tourist clip joint. And I preferred, and still prefer, the Parthenon without floodlighting. Also I was annoyed a number of times on shopping trips to go to a favourite shop and find nothing but a hole in the ground. But it only meant I hadn't been quick enough, and, on the whole, I thought the changes were good changes.

But here in Australia change is so urgent and so sweeping that in all the frenzy of haste to get on with it, quite often, it seems to me, things are changed that would much better have been left as they were, and things are swept away that we might profoundly regret and miss one day, virgin coast and bushland and wildlife, buildings of real beauty and real significance, bits of our own history and heritage that should properly be preserved.

We are not a people of noticeable foresight, nor have we yet developed much aesthetic appreciation, neither, until recently, have we shown a great interest in our own past or seen any reason why some of it should be preserved for the future.

But one hopes and believes that as a race we will develop aesthetic appreciation, and actually prefer bushland to municipal garbage dumps and untouched foreshores to shoddy developments, and that we will care eventually about how we came to be what we are and want to know something of the people who came before us and how they lived and what they said and what they did and the way they looked and what their customs were.

And if we're going to be all that, I have an idea we've got to be quick.

Come Off It, Kids!

Let us consider the young, the beautiful, healthy, intelligent, educated young, who attend universities, read books, write poetry, bring out little magazines and sell them on street corners dressed up in funny clothes, espouse causes, wear buttons and badges, produce satirical reviews, and cohabit without the benefit of law or clergy.

They toil not, neither do they spin, but live off their elders' bounty.

Mostly I like these kids enormously and am all for them living off their elders' bounty while they can, and wearing buttons and badges if they will, and espousing causes too, and being critical and iconoclastic and all the things young people should be. But oh Lord! I do wish sometimes that they weren't such prigs about themselves and their blessed convictions, so patronizing to their by this time rather weary Oldies, so supercilious of anyone who does not endorse with absolute enthusiasm their newly focused view on the world.

Leslie Fiedler says that between the ages of fifteen and twenty-one they are Germans, one and all. He doesn't explain it further than that, but I suspect that he means rigid and conformist, regimented, sad really and half-comic.

Recently we were asked to the opening night of a review—play—entertainment—exposition—statement—I don't know what to call it—produced by a group of bright young hopefuls at a very little theatre. Formal dress was required, which I thought pretty odd since jeans and sweat shirts would have seemed to have been more strictly appropriate, and I wondered at the time what the catch was. Finally we couldn't go, but I understand from those that did that the audience in their best long gowns, jewellery, and formal soup and fish, had to go through a sheep-race to get to their seats. Ha. Ha. Big joke.

Look kids, come off it. If we Oldies are a lot of sheep so, by golly, are you. You even rush around in mobs, mostly aimlessly, baa-ing and bleating your scornful slogans and current catch-cries as if you had invented something. Little sheep, you have invented nothing yet. You might do so in the future—and some of us Oldies are counting on you (perhaps with foolish optimism) to do so—but nothing has ever

236

been invented merely by destroying what exists. I agree that destruction is often necessary and wholesome, but you'd better have some idea of what you intend to build in replacement.

You are a spoiled and indulged bunch and I'm not blaming you for it because we did the spoiling and indulging and I would rather you used your blessings for all they are worth than piously counted them, but I would like to see you using your blessings towards some constructive purpose. I would like to see you come up with something really original, something you've nutted out all by yourselves, instead of so drearily conforming to whatever non-conformist pattern is currently in vogue.

Bonnie and Clyde outfits are certainly way-out, but I'll tell you something. When your Oldies were young they wore Bonnie and Clyde outfits not as a gimmick, but for real. Most of you are well up on Woody Guthrie songs, and some of you are Woody Guthrie disciples, but none of you knew the dust-bowl and the freight cars and the Depression the songs grew out of. Why don't you make up your own songs out of your own time? Last week I watched on television a smooth smiling sharply suited young man beaming and booping his way through Flanagan and Allen's 'Underneath the Arches', and I wondered what on earth that young man could possibly know about being homeless and jobless and hungry and what right he had to turn those words into a glib bright mockery of something that was terrible and tragic and brave and real. There are people sleeping underneath arches and on pavements and in gutters in other places in the world, but I expect they don't feel much like singing about it just now. I haven't heard any of you come up with an original protest song yet, and I wish you would, if only to give us Oldies a rest from Pete Seeger and Bob Dylan and that lot, who are, anyway, protesting in a different place and about a different set of conditions than those which apply here. I'm all for protest, and I love you dearly when you are in there fighting for a real cause, but I think you should save your fighting strength for the real issues and confrontations and not dissipate it by continual sniping at targets that are in no way inimical to you.

You might sometimes consider the proposition that Oldies are people too. So are Youngies who have not had your opportunities or are not so blessedly enlightened. So are conservative little old ladies, serving soldiers, Rotarians, monarchists, Bobby Limb fans, travelling salesmen, politicians, shopgirls, surfies, committee presidents, people who loathe Bob Dylan and have never heard of Wittgenstein, owners of motor lawnmowers and three-piece lounge suites, mums and dads, and members of the R.S.L. The Alf next door, big chin, jug-handle ears, beer belly, short-back-and-sides, Brylcreem, braces, athletic singlet and all, might even be deserving of your sympathy and goodwill.

He probably went to work at fourteen, dubbed in his fifteen bob a week to the family housekeeping, brought tea to his mum in bed on Sunday mornings, saved to buy a pushbike, took his girl to the pictures on Saturday night, went hiking at the week-ends, and when the time came went to war, believing sincerely that it was his duty and also his right and that by doing so he would contribute to a better world not only for his own children but for all children.

The war was the biggest adventure that ever happened to him, and if he clings to it nostalgically through Anzac Day and his local R.S.L. club why on earth shouldn't he? He was young too then, not as clever as you perhaps, and certainly not indulged as you are indulged or as he has indulged his own children as a sort of compensation to himself for what he missed out on, and he is entitled to be nostalgic for his youth and bravery and his own cause, just as he is entitled to ceramic ducks on his wall, a Namatjira print over the lounge, and the Saturday form guide. He is a fundamentally decent man and he doesn't really hurt you in any way at all. Quite probably, although you are bewildering to him, he secretly admires and envies you and places much hope for the future in you. It is unlikely that you will ever convert him, but why bother to humiliate him? You are not being funny, but only unkind.

I seem to be preaching and I didn't really mean to. It is only that I too admire and envy you and put my faith in you to accomplish something better than we Oldies managed, although we did the best we could with the tools to hand and I think you might sometimes remember that too. And I hate to see you doing less than your best.

You will have to do your very best, anyway, if you are going to get through the bitterly plausible mess of the world's current circumstances with anything like honour or decency or braveness or compassion or virtue.

Besides, the tax-man is coming soon, and children of your own to care for, and grocery bills, and all the dull pragmatism that is part of maturity and responsibility and that makes us seem conformist to you. Even sheeplike. Please try to be a little kinder to us, a little more tolerant of us. We do try, little sheep, to be kind to you.

As I Was A-Going to Muckbottom Fair

The Kinsey institute's 'long awaited report' on the sexual habits of the young (American young, but then I don't suppose they are all that different really) has thrown our lot into a fair tizz.

They are all falling about and hooting to be told so earnestly and in the most unimpeachable scientific terminology the glad news that the relationships between the sexes are actually of a pleasurable nature and rather than being revolutionary are in fact a continuation of long existing trends.

Well, fancy that! You mean the poor little revolutionaries manned the barricades for nothing? In fact they needn't have bothered waving flags or wearing buttons or so defiantly making assignations, one sex with the other, pairing off female with male and male with female, falling in love and out of it, setting up house, getting married even, panting and sighing and yearning and brooding and flying into passions and quarrelling and writing poetry and carrying on in similar revolutionary ways designed to confound all reactionary oldies who had never heard about any pleasurableness in the relationships between the sexes and would certainly have denied it vigorously if they had. Or even if they had suspected a *trend* in the direction of pleasure. Pleasure being synonymous with sin.

As a matter of fact I've always wondered about Victorian girls who were supposed, if they were properly brought up young ladies, to go to their marriage beds in a spirit of utter repugnance. What ever happened when they found out it was good-oh? Some of them must have. Did they have to go on pretending? Did none of them ever let on to some confidante over the tatting or hemstitching in the morning-room? And once they had exchanged the bridal wreath for 'the thorny crown of motherhood' (one of my favourite phrases from a Victorian novel) wouldn't you think they might have been generous enough to let their daughters in on such a delicious conspiracy?

Not one of us, even if we haven't read *The Naked Ape* (and I bet most of us have), needs a Kinsey institute report to tell us that we are a lecherous species. Beaumarchais said that man differs from the animal in eating without being hungry, drinking without being thirsty, and making love at all seasons. And these days, it seems, at all ages, and with increasing pleasure.

Premarital sex as a subject has been so chewed about and deliberated and pondered and pontificated over that I should really lay off it, excepting that I find the Kinsey institute report so funny in its utter pompousness. Consider how long it must have taken for a team of earnest researchers to interview between 1,000 and 1,200 young students all over America, how many reams of paper must have been used, must have been specially printed with lists of questions that took weeks or months or years to devise, how many ballpoint pens ran out in the process, how many memos, telegrams, phone calls, how many cards with how many punch holes were fed into how many computers clanking and grinding and growling and champing away, how many conferences were held in how many board-rooms, how many automobiles used how much petrol speeding across that vast eternity of a country from college to college, how many expense accounts were padded out over how many week-ends. One wonders, with John Donne, 'but, oh, to what end?'

I have been reading again, and again with the greatest pleasure, the historian Will Durant on the moral elements of civilization. He contends that the greatest task of morals is always sexual regulation, and the greatest problem of sexual regulation concerns premarital relations. Shall they be restricted, or shall they be free? That custom differs from one society to another does not mean that one society is more moral than another, but only that social order is preserved in ways that vary according to the sum of the prejudices of a community.

In the simplest societies premarital relations are generally free. Durant quotes North American Indians, the Soyots of Siberia, the Igorots of the Philippines, the natives of upper Burma, the Kaffirs and Bushmen of Africa, the tribes of the Niger and Uganda, of New Georgia, the Murray Islands, the Andaman Islands, Tahiti, Polynesia, Assam, etc. (As a matter of fact I think he must have had his tongue in his cheek about the Soyots and the Igorots. He probably made them up just for the fun of it, so he would be able to say that if you were a Soyot or an Igorot—imagine being such a thing!—you could go to with heart and spirit and nothing held against you.)

Chastity seems to have come as a late development. What the primitive maiden dreaded was not the loss of her virginity but a reputation for sterility. Before the laws of property influenced all

240

sexual conduct, virginity seems to have been held in contempt, as indicating unpopularity. Will Durant quotes the Kamchadal (I wonder if he made that up too) who found his bride to be virgin and 'roundly abused her mother for the negligent way in which she had brought up her daughter'.

It is obviously the institution of patriarchy and property that turned virginity from a fault into a virtue and from a virtue to a compulsion, a sense of obligation to chastity, because the virginity of a daughter brought profit to her father and a promise to her husband of marital fidelity that would not land him with surreptitious children to share his property.

Of course no men have ever thought of applying the same rule of chastity to themselves. In no society do any such restrictions apply to the male, nor do they in ours, or ever have. All controversy is centred around the young female, and whether the modern young female should or shouldn't, and if she does (whether she should or not) whether it is proper for her to enjoy it.

And that is what we all find so funny. Because in all the evidence of 'long-existing trends', like from primeval slime until now, with all the complex social patterns that have decreed this sort of behaviour and that sort of behaviour, and whether girls ought to be let loose or locked up or lent out or sold for gain or whatever, surely never a Kinsey institute report was needed to tell us that in the society we live in girls are liable to fall in love, prefer to give themselves first to the man they love, and find such an experience pleasurable.

There is a wicked Peter Sellars' parody called 'Muckbottom Fair' which I shall play now for my own amusement, with the Kinsey report in mind. And if you haven't heard 'Muckbottom Fair', it is all about an old English rustic recalling this event of his youth, with a toora-li-oora-li-oora-li-ay, and that the greatest delight of his life, he would say, was 'showing young maidens the way'. Ah well. . . .

On Coming to a Bad End

After reading, in a recent issue of a reputable American magazine, some hair-raising case-histories of young girls apparently hell-bent on moral anarchy, we were discussing the situation of young girls here, and how they might be affected by rapidly changing conventions, customs, and codes of behaviour. Since we all had daughters, and had been young girls ourselves not all that long ago, it was a discussion of absorbing interest.

When I was growing up it was said of a girl who was flighty, or flirtatious, or restless, or feckless, or gay, or more attractive than other girls, that she would undoubtedly 'come to a bad end'.

I know that it was said of me among others, and since the end (at least I hope) is not yet, I have no way of knowing whether the prediction was correct or not. There are all sorts of bad ends one could come to, like great loneliness, or a souring of the pleasure in living, or self-hatred, or hatred of others, or a bleak and bitter knowledge of uselessness. None of these, of course, was the bad end the gossips had in mind. Like a great many self-righteous people they equated morality solely with the reproductive functions. And certain it was in my home territory that, like the biblical sparrow, no local girl fell unheeded.

I've always thought it a difficult business to be a young female. I mean it was even then when at least we knew what was expected of us, and the social rules were fairly clearly defined. You did not transgress them with impunity, although in a natural and quite kindly country way, disapproval, scandal and stigma did not last for ever, and many a marriage celebrated in unseemly haste became in time a respected and respectable union: the rules had been obeyed and morality in the end satisfied.

But what are the rules for girls now? Who makes them? The Church? From all I've read the Church is divided between 'progressives' urging acceptance of a moral change that is taking place with or without their acceptance, and conservatives fighting heroically for a code of behaviour between the sexes that was doomed by the Pill. True, there are more young women being married in

242

white than ever before, but statistics seem to show that in a great many cases a blush of colour would be more strictly appropriate. I suspect that many lavish weddings are purely a social display.

Does society make the rules then? There are so many levels of society, even in this supposedly egalitarian country, and what is condoned on one level is punished on another. Chastity could be the deadliest of virtues among some groups of sophisticated young. It could be a necessary condition for survival in the jungles of the under-privileged, where the pitfalls of ignorance, superstition and brutish-ness are more numerous and more cruelly barbed than many complacent people suppose, and one missed step can spring the trap for good and all.

When does a girl become an actual delinquent? My dictionary says that a delinquent is 'one who fails to perform a duty or who commits a fault'. Duty to whom? Fault against whom? The law, properly, makes rules for the regulation of the conduct of young girls in the interest of their protection from abuse and exploitation. I don't believe the law uses the word 'delinquent' any more. 'Moral danger' would be closer. But the awful thing is that a girl in moral danger can be, and often is, committed to an institution. The particular case of a juvenile victim of biological exploitation that we were discussing is too horrifying to describe here, but I expect most of us have heard of horrifying cases in plenty. Girls who are victims of their own unfortunate lack of intelligence, of apathy, of greed, of boredom, of a hunger for stimulation in the monotony of contemporary urban living, of a blundering search for identity, of a lack of affection, of a compulsion to rebel, of an excess of trashy films, magazines, and all the enticements of cheap glamour, of an urge for thrills, for kicks, or just the approval of their peers.

It is not often that a girl from the more affluent, more educated strata of society is brought before the law, although she may have failed to perform her duty towards the law and committed faults against the law as often, more often, and with infinitely more contempt for it than the girl who is unprotected by family affection, concern, influence, and the more lenient (liberal?) conventions that operate among the sophisticated.

Young girls are committed to institutions for their own protection. But I wonder if the girls themselves, their peers, and society in general regard it as protection or as punishment. And what does such an experience do to a girl? How does it affect her in society afterwards?

I suspect that in spite of all the spate of discussion and debate on sex education and sex reform the tradition of the 'bad girl', most unhappily, lives on. And what was only a foolish beginning may well turn out to be a bad end after all, because she won't lose that stigma easily.

The moral code of any society must regulate the relations of the sexes, which are a perennial source of discord, violence, and possible degeneration. But our society seems to be floundering in a state of moral chaos. New customs have taken over before the old customs are outmoded. A film star or a bare-top dancer is rewarded with fame, wealth and world acclaim for what would have had her ostracized not so long ago. Excess could win a T.V. contract or a trip to an institution. And while discussion rages the rate of illegitimate births rises, disease spreads, the emancipated young make up their own rules, girls refuse to accept a double standard of morality, other girls get married in white and gentlemen in high places recommend that they do so 'unsullied'. Everything is variable and fluctuating. What is a girl to do?

More urgent, presently, what are we to do?—the adults, the educators, the law-makers, the parents of girls.

We have to remember, first, that our girls are caught up in a revolution, and this is confusing as well as exhilarating. Also, that every revolution has a casualty list.

If we are to help them fear won't do it, or outrage, or condemnation, or punitive measures, or turning our backs and pretending that nothing is happening. Or crossing our fingers or touching wood.

Education will help. Education and education and more education. Not just biological education, but social education too. If they can learn that freedom is the luxury of security, and that a secure person is a person protected by self-knowledge, self-discipline, aware of consequences and knowledgeable about causes, capable of decision and accepting responsibility for decision, then they will probably be able to make a new set of rules for themselves and abide by them. They won't be our rules, but then why should they be? It won't be our world.

But if we don't help them now with all the understanding we have then we are the delinquents, and we will deserve a very bad end indeed.

Pitching Woo

One of the prettiest girls I know is a red-head, Venetian red, with that particular translucent white skin that sometimes, but not always, goes with it, and cornflower eyes. She is a gentle, good-tempered, uncomplicated creature, but as gay and gregarious as a girl of her age should be, and without being avid for pleasure she loves dancing and parties and clothes and company. She has worked interstate for the adventure and experience, and presently rooms in a small flat with another girl of her own age. She is responsible and independent and deliciously attractive.

So when she told me that she had never once been taken out to dinner I was flabbergasted. And the more flabbergasted that she didn't seem to think such criminal neglect on the part of the male sex extraordinary in any way at all. With her peers and playmates apparently this is the normal behaviour pattern. There is a group, and the group frequents a discotheque, but the girls arrive independently, pay for their own drinks, and leave independently too, unless someone with a car is going their way, or several of the group decide to make a party at somebody's flat or house. Couples pair off rather casually, some have even been known to progress as far as becoming engaged. And if I understood correctly her amused little dissertation on current tribal customs it would be possible within this behaviour pattern for a girl to achieve the state of matrimony without actually having been courted at all.

Mercy! No flowers, no candles, no personal table, personal corner, personal waiter paternally misty-eyed (the 'our place, remember darling?' of tender reminiscence on anniversaries years later), no park benches in the rain, no midnight vigils under an enchanted window, no agonies and ecstasies of quarrel and reconciliation, no despair over a mute telephone, no tokens, signs, passwords, favours, secrets? No foolish things? No banners, bugles, trumpets, tuckets, drums? No pale loitering? The pavements, one gathers, stay firmly fixed beneath this generation's feet, and mooning is for the birds, only not these birds.

Should one mourn the passing of the pitching of woo? Maybe this present level-headed camaraderie is really more sensible, the pay-for-yourself idea more realistic. Perhaps such a system is more in accord with a move towards sexual equality, and wooing as anachronistic to this lot as Victorian delicacies of courtship were to us.

Gone for ever now, excepting as nostalgic shades whirling around Bobby Limb, are a whole generation of navy-blue suits, the wooers who wore brilliantine to their wooing, and bought boxes of chocolates in the interval at the Saturday might pictures and gardenia sprays with maidenhair fern to grace their ladies' chiffon or morocain for the evenings of intoxicating fox-trotting. Gone the Sunday drive in the country, tea with the family, and afterwards the dark verandah where the fuschias shielded the wicker lounge with the cretonne cushions.

Gone the ritual gradation of presents, the manicure set, the brush-comb-and-mirror, the cut-crystal powder bowl, the toiletries scented with old English lavender, the blue satin bedroom mules racy with ostrich feathers, the penultimate commitment of the eighteen-jewel wristwatch and the tacit understanding that the ring came next.

Gone too the ardent wartime wooers, made reckless by a well-cut uniform, a full wallet, a brief leave, and the heroic aura of imminent peril. I'll be down to get you in a taxi honey, with a purple orchid for your pompadour and a silver chain for your ankle and six pairs of stockings I picked up from an American, and we're going to paint the town red, paint it pink, paint it yellow, paint it spotted and striped honey, we're going to dance all night and have champagne for breakfast and I'll keep the handkerchief with your lipstick on it under my paybook and over my heart until I come home to you you you.

What a perfectly splendid time that was for the pitching of woo, and what a wonderful variety of pitchers there was to choose from. Even the most timid men acquired style and dexterity with so much fervent practice and so much competition, and girls never had it so good. We collected eternal vows like beads for a wampum belt, and although most of these proved in the course of time to have been ephemeral, we had, as they say, our memories.

Personally I've always thought that poets have an edge on other chaps when it comes to real pitching. To begin with they do so enjoy it, which is essential to the game. I was discussing this with a poet one day and he confided to me (not at all boastfully) that tears had seldom failed him and poetry never, especially if there was blotted evidence of the tears on the poem, which ideally, he said, should be composed in the small hours of the morning and delivered, with one simple flower—like a daisy or a single jasmine blossom—under the beloved's door at dawn. He had had great success with vigils too. He said that you didn't actually have to stay up all night . . . it worked just as well if you took up your position on her doorstep just before her normal getting-up time. As long as you looked haggard and unshaven and she found you there sighing beside the milk bottles. He told me a lot of pitches, in fact, which left me rather thoughtful.

Of course a wooer doesn't have to actually write poetry to use it. The sonnets are eternally serviceable, and Marvell and Herrick and Lovelace and the rest churned out enough really first-rate woo to be re-usable for hundreds of years. So did John Donne. But I wonder, just in passing, whether Dowson would work still. Does any young man with hollow cheeks and haunted eyes swear still that he has been faithful in his fashion? No, perhaps not. Or is it middle-age that gives me the retrospective giggles?

Foreign languages are of some advantage to pitchers too. Even now I know girls who succumbed to the soft incomprehensibility of broken foreign phrases where the most plausible pleading in impeccable English had never even swayed them: sometimes, perhaps, it is better all round not to understand too well. And Continentals, like poets, play the game so well and so enjoy playing it that they can make poverty work better for them than big-time wine buying, and a bunch of field flowers do duty for two dozen perfect red roses.

Well, glory be! I suppose if you've never had it you don't miss it, and these young things will find their mates eventually without all the complicated rituals and heartaches and headaches and feastings and fastings that were so entrancing and absorbing, but, crikey, I'm glad I was young in the days when men pitched woo.

Preserver With a Book

The only things I ever learned at school that proved to be of the slightest value to me in later life were reading and writing, so perhaps I am not really qualified to discuss the subject of education at all.

Then again, that statement in itself may be a pertinent point, since it is nearly thirty years since I decided to tackle the world ready or no rather than submit for another moment to the monumental boredom and frustration of amassing dreary facts towards no foreseeable purpose: one might reasonably assume that in thirty years schools and schooling have progressed towards enlightenment.

Yet everything I read and hear and observe about the state of education in this proud, progressive, prosperous society bothers me more than a little. Grants slashed, staffs cut, overcrowded classrooms, temporary accommodation, seething playgrounds, antiquated equipment, lack of facilities, lack of space, lack of funds, lack of schools, lack of teachers even, or teachers who are poorly trained, partly trained, or actually unqualified to teach at all. And anybody who is seriously concerned with education seems to be begging around like blind Belisarius, with both pride and dedication rather out-at-elbows. Rather seamy.

The historian Will Durant said that man differs from the beast only by education. 'Which may be defined,' he said, 'as the technique of transmitting civilisation . . . as the very instrument through which we are turned from animals into men.'

The one thing certain about civilization is that nobody is born in possession of it. It has to be newly acquired by every generation. And as it is not inborn neither is it imperishable. The racial heritage of knowledge and culture, of language and morals, of technology and arts has to be handed down from generation to generation. What has been acquired must be systematically reacquired, and if some cataclysm broke the continuity of transmission for a generation or two or three, civilization would cease to exist. Science fiction is filled with such dire imaginings, but history is filled with the actual records of extinction, and the sands and the deserts and the waste places of the world are studded with the actual evidence of glory and grandeur that indubitably was and indubitably crumbled, stone to stone and earth to the earth from which it was proudly made.

One would think then, boasting as we do (and we do) of the achievement of our own particular civilization, that we would give a little more thought to the people who will preserve it if it is to be preserved. That is to say, the teachers. Surely these should be of special caste in the community, specially selected, specially dedicated, and once dedicated specially honoured.

A few days ago I heard with fascination of a teacher at an infants' school in one of the smarter suburbs who assured a mother presenting her child for the first time (and a bright, eager child, avid to learn and to make and to do) that the little one would be perfectly happy because all they did in the first two years was to sit and conform. The teacher assured the mother that the children loved conforming.

One also remembers, with a shudder of absolute horror (and whatever happened to the follow-up on this particular story?), of the reports of a brain-washing experiment on a group of children, who were allegedly inculcated with the belief that an inimical people lived on an island to the north of Australia, a people to be feared and abhorred because of their sinister intent. The mind, as they say, boggles.

On the other hand, my own small boy, who goes to school at one of the more overcrowded and financially harassed suburban primaries in this city, comes racing home day after day wild with the day's discoveries of latitude and longitude, of the relation of the earth to the planets, of shape, movement, force, pattern, of the triangularity of three and the squareness of four, of the flexibility of the English language, and of the infinite wisdom, knowledge and kindness of that minor deity who is presently his teacher.

One's immediate thought, conditioned by this community, is one of puzzlement that such an obviously first-rate teacher should be wasting his talents in a hopelessly overcrowded and completely un-status primary school in an un-status suburb. Why on earth hadn't he done better for himself? One suppresses the thought with a twinge of shame and sends up a small prayer of thankfulness that there *is* such a grade teacher in that particular primary school. But still. . . .

The general social attitude to teachers under the rank of headmaster (and even including most headmasters) is one of polite indifference, as to failures in the status game. Teachers do not, as a rule, own two cars or a swimming pool or six suits or Italian shoes or a bar leading on to the patio or dine out regularly at the smarter restaurants or be seen at first nights or keep charge accounts for their wives at the best stores. And these things are the symbols of success. There is also a pervading suspicion, if people bother to think about teachers at all, that teachers only became teachers because they weren't good enough to become anything else. (And I must admit that sometimes, listening to the droning platitudes and clichés and admonitions and exhortations of school speech nights, I have sometimes thought so too.)

That teaching is regarded as a second-best profession is evident from the attitudes of the young, who are inclined to say, deprecatingly, and with a small shrug when all other more exciting avenues appear to be closed to them: 'Oh well, I can always be a teacher.'

And as long as teaching remains a second-best profession how can we, as a society, recruit for the preservation of our own continuities the minds of imagination and vision and wisdom and kindness and tolerance that are necessary to fire young minds with a desire for understanding beyond the pages of the prescribed text-books? The marvel of it is that such teachers do exist, even within the shabby framework of this shabby system that offers them neither honour nor reward nor even the space and the tools and the time necessary for them to function efficiently, let alone memorably.

Even if it is presumptuous of me, lacking as I do anything but the rudiments of formal education, to suggest such a thing, I will suggest anyway that unless we make it our urgent business to procure the space and the tools and the time for education, and to elevate the educators to a position of status and honour in our community, all the millions and billions we spend on the business of destruction, all the time and the training we devote to it, will not preserve a heritage for our children. The preservers do not carry guns, but books.

The Cocky Walkers

'The Cocky Walkers' is the title of a poem that was written by an English poet called Mervyn Peake, and it is one that I used to like very well, although I don't remember it by heart any more excepting for a line that describes this group of boys as 'treading the reedy springboard of green days' (or maybe it's 'years': I forget).

Thinking and writing and talking lately about street packs has led me back to 'The Cocky Walkers', and the perils and hazards of growing up for anybody, and the murk and the pinnacles and the black despair and the flashes of glory. And added to this my mail has included a letter from a mother deeply troubled with self-doubt at her own instinct to encourage her son, just entering university, to pursue studies which have, in this country, no commercial value whatever.

As if the world's room isn't wide enough for a dreamer. 'He has always been a loner,' she writes. As if we are all not. And another letter accusing me of leaning over backwards in defence of the young, and I suppose I do, because that bewildering journey from childhood to adulthood is one I remember in sharp and sometimes frightening detail and wonder, even now, and now appalled, whether it was terrifying innocence or terrifying knowledge, or some chancy balance of both, that brought me at last to the beginnings of self-recognition, which is the beginning of being an adult.

I have been fortunate enough to have lived in a community, artificial perhaps, where people's ages were of no particular importance in social and intellectual contact—one's friends were eighteen or eighty—and I am still fortunate enough to be much in the company of young people. Once you have fallen into the habit of forgetfulness about rigid age divisions you can't fall back again into the conventional social patterns of separate compartments for separate ages, and no communication channels between. So that sometimes I hear things and see things that pull me up with the sharpest sting of recognition, and I think, incredulously: 'Yes, yes. That's the way it was. Exactly like that.'

The thing about growing up is that it is quite unprecedented. Everybody has to do it alone, for the first time in the world. There are some clues, and a few ambiguous signposts, but no Ariadne's thread to guide you safely through this labyrinth. Not all the moral precepts nor snippets of second-hand experience handed you down by your impatient or complacent elders from the Arctic wastes of middle-age will tell you, finally, who you are. Which is really the only thing you need to know.

Growing up is being a genius, is being insane, is being vile and muddied with impurity, is standing on inaccessible crags, wallowing in swamps, groping in mists. And being a cocky walker, which is, after all, only practising at balance, like being cynical, and irreverent, and iconoclastic. Such attitudes cover uncertainty, and frequent dismay, which, as far as you know when you are growing up, might be your permanent condition. What is necessary for you treading that reedy springboard is not purpose, but equilibrium.

So one hides his dismay under conventional clothes, library-frame glasses, and pedantic opinions. One effects Italian shirts and suede jackets and a stylishly vintage sports car. One is gentle and puzzled and presently depressed by examination results, himself, and the whole damn world. One doubts the existence of the world at all and has created his own, in which he bumbles about brainily, immune to all practicalities. One is so uncertain of his own importance that he dwells on it incessantly. One clothes his youth in a Tudor beard and outrageous clothes, one wears a long bob, one has lately changed to a style more Roman. One is newly in love and one newly out of it, happenings that are momentous, absorbing, unprecedented. One girl is pregnant, and that is unprecedented too: she is outraged and disbelieving, because that is something that happens only to other girls. Another girl has left home and set up house with a lover: her audacity is generally admired, and much talked about, as if she had invented an original situation.

Actually they are all inventing everything all the time, ideas, attitudes, opinions, relationships, experience. Things do not so much happen to them as they happen to things: they are monumentally selfish and self-centred and self-absorbed.

Out of all their blunderings and collisions and inventions and happenings and balancing tricks and flashes of intuition they will eventually build up a knowledge of themselves and their own capabilities and talents and limitations and where they stand, humanly, in relation to the rest of the human race. Or most of them will. Some people never become adult at all and go on for the rest of their lives trying to catch reflections of themselves in other people's eyes and attitudes and opinions. Some people have to make themselves up painfully out of bits and pieces copied and borrowed from others and botched together into a semblance of wholeness. Some people will always inhabit themselves uneasily and importune others to reassure them of their own validity as human beings.

I often think, watching my own young people groping and blundering for self-realization, that if it is a bewildering journey for these, who are privileged in intelligence, education, health, native wit, talent, and opportunity, how much harder it must be for those who begin the journey impoverished of these desirable traveller's aids. Those who have to carry with them stupidity or disease or a bleak and early knowledge of brutality and meanness and deprivation and dirt and disorder. The world must, to them, be idiocy and chaos, and to have been born into it an irremediable disaster. That so many of them turn vicious is not so surprising as that so many of them, so handicapped, fight their way through and become whole human beings.

So, yes, I lean over backwards to defend them, and yes, I like to see them walking cockily, whistling in the dark, trying for equilibrium, floundering in uncertainty, and standing on pinnacles trailing clouds of glory.

They are the future. They're the only immortality I know about. I think they are worth more than disapproval. Even some quite serious consideration.

Banners, Causes and Convictions

Going through files the other day in an attempt to sort out a messy accumulation of bits of paper, I came across a whole bundle of letters that my husband had written to me two years ago when he was newly back in Australia and I was still in Greece.

One letter, commenting on Australian youth, said that he thought the young comely, but mentally flabby. I suppose, he wrote, that everything is really too easy. They lack the stimulation of causes.

This was like the echo of discussions we had had ten years before, when we had been trying to come to some sort of understanding of the young Americans who were invading Europe then. Strange, we found them, with a curiously unformed chrysalis quality inside their lavish cocoons of education. The only cause they believed in was the utter futility of all causes, and they expounded this theme monotonously in their flat, sad, voices. Kerouac and Ginsberg were their prophets. Inaction was their creed. When they were not turned on with pot they seemed soft, somehow, and defenceless. The angst of their young European contemporaries was of a different order: it had the veracity of real cynicism, of observed—and sometimes experienced—anguish.

I found such ennui, such a reduction of the human qualities of hope and desire and passion, as mystifying as their jargon. What extraordinarily long and esoteric words they used to express . . . what? Not failure, because they had never tried. Not even perplexity. They were incurious, and it always seemed to me to be odd that they travelled about so much: there seemed to be no real reason why they should be in one place rather than another.

One of them, I remember, was a near fatality that summer at the cave where we used to swim. After he had been fished out and resuscitated and dried off someone asked him what had been his last thought before he lost consciousness. With a perfect earnestness he said that he had thought of all that education wasted.

I am sure that they found our enthusiasms naive, our indignations a useless squandering of mental energy, our more cherished beliefs and convictions childlike.

'You get so worked up about things,' they said.

I suppose that until complacency sets in a generation brought up in a Depression and then plunged into a war is bound to fall into the habit of getting worked up about things.

As a child I remember the fervour of politics that affected whole family relationships, shattered lifelong friendships, split up young lovers and ostracized schoolchildren. Voices rose high and vehement on street corners where men in flannel undershirts gathered in the evenings, watched from verandahs or behind curtains by tight-faced wives who were tired of the dole.

And at the time of the Spanish Civil War my father used to pace around the house at night, restless, bitter, impotent of action. It was all so far away, he was no longer young, there was nothing he could do. He was a liberal humanist, his passion for justice was intense, his rages against persecution and oppression were monumental, his condemnations absolute and unalterable. We were conscious through all our childhood of vast forces working for good and evil and that such forces directly concerned us: at the time of Munich my father wept.

My husband says that in those years he had two young journalist friends in Melbourne, who paid their passage money in reichmarks on a German ship and sailed off to Spain to fight, the one for the Government and the other for Franco. They shared a cabin all the way over and argued the right of their different causes until they separated to fight for them. One of them was killed quite soon so it is impossible to know now whether their friendship would have survived.

The young Americans we knew (or failed to know, rather) a decade ago in Europe were as ignorant of the Spanish Civil War as if it had happened on an evening star. So soon does time blur great events.

Thinking about all this I have been interested to read a number of recent articles in American magazines and periodicals that report in some detail on the activities of the present crop of American youth. Their causes, at this moment in time, are legion. In a country convulsed by violence and communal eruptions, where hatred and terror can explode even from the formless and the inexplicable, platitudes no longer satisfy, or even soothe. It is necessary to choose sides. The social rebels are active and vocal, and the kids are setting up new icons of their own choosing. Protest singers are rewarded, as one article points out, by a grateful America with riches in return for being their whipping boy.

Is something like this happening here? Certainly attitudes have changed considerably since my husband wrote me that letter only two years ago.

The list of Action Committees grows. The slogans multiply and surely beget their opposing slogans. More and more people are positively for or positively against bureaucratic policies. Students meet and march. Banners are snatched and torn like battle trophies. Political rallies are stormy and even physically violent. Mothers of sons march for one cause and outraged architects for another while another group vigorously demands racial equality. Dissension spreads. Hostility also. Vigils, protests, sit-ins, teach-ins and even freedom rides are becoming usual. Debates are passionate with opposing convictions, and television cameras record some fairly startling scenes as meetings are broken up officially.

Post-war apathy of the complacent affluent society has exploded into drama suddenly. Emotions run high, if not riot.

I believe this to be a far healthier state of affairs than that curious formlessness and lack of belief or definition that was so apparent even eighteen months or a year ago. Lack of interest. Lack of purpose in other than immediate material gains. Non-involvement.

One thing is certain. No state of affairs was ever bettered by putting up with it, no wrongs ever righted by passively accepting them. A cause, a purpose, a goal, a creed, an idea, a cherished attachment is the stuff all human evolution is made of. Without some belief most passionately held we would expire for want of vitality.

The great reptiles, that most stable society, died out because they could not adapt themselves to changed circumstances. The lotus-eaters dreamed their way into oblivion. I think we, who are still young as societies go, ought to put out more flags.